# Infantry Small Arms of the 21st Century

# Infantry Small Arms of the 21st Century

Leigh Neville

Pen & Sword
**MILITARY**

First published in Great Britain in 2019 by
**PEN & SWORD MILITARY**
An imprint of
Pen & Sword Books Ltd
47 Church Street
Barnsley
South Yorkshire
S70 2AS

ISBN 978-1-47389-613-0

Typeset by Concept, Huddersfield, West Yorkshire, HD4 5JL
Printed and bound in India by Replika Press Pvt. Ltd

Pen & Sword Books Ltd incorporates the imprints of Pen & Sword Archaeology, Atlas,
Aviation, Battleground, Discovery, Family History, History, Maritime, Military, Naval,
Politics, Railways, Select, Social History, Transport, True Crime, and Claymore Press,
Frontline Books, Leo Cooper, Praetorian Press, Remember When, Seaforth Publishing
and Wharncliffe.

For a complete list of Pen & Sword titles please contact
PEN & SWORD BOOKS LIMITED
47 Church Street, Barnsley, South Yorkshire, S70 2AS, England
E-mail: enquiries@pen-and-sword.co.uk
Website: www.pen-and-sword.co.uk

Dedicated to
the late Kevin R. 'Hognose' O'Brien,
'the Weapons Man', SFC US Army,
1958–2017

# Contents

# Acknowledgements

Before we get to the 'meat and potatoes', the author must thank a number of people without which this book would have not been possible. Thank you to Doug Beattie, Phil Boshier, Bobby Casey, Ron Dahlgren, Miles Vining, Nathan Vinson, and a couple more folks who prefer to remain anonymous – all combat veterans of Afghanistan and Iraq with strong views on military small arms and who were willing to share their experiences with me.

Miles Vining, along with being a USMC combat vet of several tours in Helmand Province, writes for both www.thefirearmsblog.com, one of the internet's best firearms news and reviews sites, and his own excellent www.silahreport.com with its focus on small arms in MENA and Central Asia – both sites are heartily recommended. Miles also assisted greatly with this project in many ways and deserves a special thanks.

Thanks to the incredible input of Eric Graves, a former US Army and USAF SOF veteran and former Blackwater contractor and founder of industry bible www.soldiersystems.net which is again recommended as a daily visit for all interested readers who want to keep up to speed on small arms matters, including the often-convoluted procurement processes. Likewise to Matthew Moss (www.historicalfirearms.info and www.armourersbench.com), a British small arms historian who has been an incredible source of obscure information and photographs and a useful sounding board during the preparation of this book.

Whilst mentioning websites, the author would like to point readers to that of the late Kevin 'Hognose' O'Brien, a US Army Special Forces veteran and diligent small arms researcher. His website (www.weaponsman.com) remains online following his untimely passing in 2017. Although the author only communicated with Kevin a handful of times, the influence of his thinking around the practical realities of small arms use in combat were and remain very influential. 'Hognose' is very sadly missed.

William ('Wilf') F. Owen, a former British Army soldier and one of the world's leading operational research gurus very kindly took time to discuss and debate a number of theories with me – his insights have made this book immeasurably better. Similarly, Thomas Ehrhart, US Army battalion commander and author of the ground-breaking monograph *Increasing Small Arms Lethality in Afghanistan: Taking Back the Infantry Half-Kilometer* also contributed much to my thinking on current small arms challenges and I thank him for graciously responding to all manner of queries.

My personal thanks also go to photographer extraordinaire Vitaly Kuzmin, a number of whose photos illustrate this book. Thanks too for the use of imagery from Accuracy International (thank you Alice Bond), Andy Falcone at H&K, Max

Popenker at Kalashnikov Concern, Kelly Stumpf at Colt Canada and Nathan Wyatt at Knights Armament Corporation.

Finally, my deepest thanks as always to my wife Jodi Fraser-Neville, my fellow author John Walter and my editor at Pen & Sword, Henry Wilson, who graciously accepted a number of failed deadlines on the long road to publication. Matt Jones and Irene Moore from the editorial team also deserve my thanks for their outstanding efforts on this and my last book for Pen & Sword.

# INTRODUCTION

This book follows in the wake of the author's *Guns of the Special Forces* that was thankfully rather universally praised after its publication in 2015. Instead of Special Operations Forces (SOF), this new work focuses primarily on the small arms in use by the militaries of the world and specifically by the infantry soldier in the first two decades of the twenty-first century.

Weapons covered range from pistols to medium and general-purpose machine guns – the small arms that are most commonly found in the hands of soldiers across the globe. Some mention of SOF is inevitable as they exert a considerable influence on small arms procurement decisions, but first and foremost we are talking about the weapons of the infantryman.

There is a necessary and acknowledged bias toward the Western nations and their experiences in Iraq and Afghanistan due to the wealth of English language research material available and access to interviews with a large pool of veterans of these conflicts. Efforts have been made to include as many non-Western militaries as possible and it is hoped the book will provide a useful overview or snapshot of what small arms are in use around the world.

Please note the interchangeable use of the terms 'squad' and 'section'. Commonwealth and former Commonwealth armies tend to refer to their infantry platoons as being formed of three sections, each of two fire teams. In American and US trained armies, the term squad is more common.

The author has also taken into consideration two recurring feedback points concerning the earlier volume, the first being the inclusion of some rudimentary comparison charts to allow the quick examination of weapons of a similar type. The second request was for even more photographs – with some calling for an image of every single weapon mentioned in the text. This second point is sadly more problematical as it affects both the physical size and distribution and thus the eventual retail price of the book. The author would love to include an accompanying picture for every weapon discussed, but the practicalities weigh heavily against us – unfortunately this is not *Jane's Infantry Weapons*, but nor does it attract the same retail price of one of the *Jane's* volumes which run into the thousands! We have however increased the number of images as much as possible and hope that these selections assist the reader.

Before we go much further, it is firstly worth putting infantry small arms in some kind of context in the scheme of the world's armies. The biggest killer in modern warfare is airpower and artillery. Small arms make up a very, very small percentage of enemy deaths and woundings. Even in asymmetric conflicts like Afghanistan or Syria, the vast majority of enemy are killed by air-delivered bombs and rockets, or indirect fire from mortars, artillery and multiple-launch

Italian soldiers conducting a dismounted patrol in Afghanistan 2010. From the left, they carry a

rocket systems. Put simply, explosives do the killing. Noted defence researcher and former British Army infantry officer Dr Jim Storr puts things in perspective: '*Small arms fire kills and incapacitates very few people in a typical infantry battle.*'

A third of US fatalities during the Vietnam War were caused by small arms. Today, from the wars in Iraq and Afghanistan, that number covers a little under 5 per cent. This is due to a number of factors – the vast improvements in combat body armour, the incredible advances in the standard of medical care provided both in the field and on the evacuation helicopter, and that Western nations can reliably transport a wounded soldier to a trauma centre within the golden hour after his wounding. (However, in future so-called peer-to-peer or near-peer conflicts, against Russia for instance, this latter ability cannot be taken for granted.)

It also has something to do with enemy tactics. Insurgents know that they will lose a stand-up fight against Western infantry and thus have come to rely upon a weapon that accounted for some 75 per cent of fatalities during combat operations in Iraq, Afghanistan and increasingly Syria and Yemen: the IED or Improvised Explosive Device. The IED is perhaps the ultimate asymmetric weapon. It can lie undetected, requiring no sustenance or shelter until triggered by an unfortunate soldier or civilian. Its life expectancy is as long as the battery pack powering it.

A Russian Naval Infantryman pictured in 2003 with his issue 5.45 × 39mm AK-74M.
(*US Navy, PH1 Chadwick Vann*)

Even when engaged by insurgent small arms in something more akin to a conventional firefight, the disparity is obvious. Typically, insurgents have received little or no training, they have generally very poor weapon maintenance regimes, their ammunition is likewise poorly maintained and often of questionable origin and, in Afghanistan at least, there is a high level of congenital eye disease which makes accurate shooting even at relatively short ranges difficult.

As we will delve into in a moment, in most small arms contacts the Afghan insurgent relies upon his status weapons, the PKM medium machine gun and the RPG7 anti-tank grenade launcher (often incorrectly termed the rocket-propelled grenade). Both of these weapons are the insurgent's principal casualty-causing platforms and are respected by Western troops.

The United States Marine Corps' Intelligence Activity sponsored a study into Afghan insurgent tactics during the late 2000s which noted:

Most ambushes began with a volley of RPGs, followed by small arms fire. In most attacks, the insurgents broke contact before air support arrived (though in a minority of cases, they fought through airstrikes). Casualties, if any, were usually inflicted during the first few minutes of fighting. In most incidents, each insurgent knew his role and escape route; all details were worked out ahead of time to reduce the need to communicate before or during the fighting.

The signal to open fire was usually an RPG fired by the leader of the group. As the Taliban came under increasing pressure in 2007 and 2008, they turned increasingly to IEDs. When using IEDs in an ambush, the Taliban triggered the device, then launched a volley of RPGs, and withdrew under the cover of small arms fire.

Indeed, the Marine study of a wide range of engagements between 2006 and 2008 pointed to the fact that insurgents tended to conduct ambushes and direct attacks within common infantry small arms range, some 200 to 300 metres. There is a distinction in the study that notes IED use increased dramatically after 2008 as the insurgents realised they would inevitably lose any close range engagements.

Interestingly the British Army observed the following about the insurgent employment of the RPG:

- The RPG is used widely by the insurgent and every direct fire engagement can be expected to contain a volley of RPGs at some stage. There is a plentiful supply.
- An experienced operator is able to judge the distance at which the grenade self-destructs (approx. 900m from the firing point) producing an air burst munition which is very effective against troops in cover without overhead protection.
- Persistent use of known FPs [firing points]. Assessment that INS [insurgents] return to FPs due to knowledge of ranges and effective impact points from previous incidents

A French infantryman in Afghanistan 2008 carrying an 5.56 × 45mm FAMAS with FAB Defense vertical forward grip incorporating a weapon light and unknown magnified optic, likely a private purchase item (usual issue is the Scrome J4). *(ISAF, Cpl John Rafoss)*

- Various types of warhead have been used by the insurgent but rarely matched to the type of target that they are engaging.

In 2006 and 2007, the insurgents employed more traditional tactics but were roundly beaten, even when vastly outnumbering Western forces – look to the British experience in Helmand Province where platoon houses were surrounded and under near continual attack. Along with better training and equipment, the Western forces also possessed air support which would prove decisive in ending many such engagements. Mortars, artillery and guided missiles were also available and were often employed when the insurgents could not be defeated through manoeuvre of infantry forces alone. They realised that the IED offered them was the perfect weapon without risking large numbers of fighters.

The comment about congenital eye disease is also worth examining for a moment. The myth of the Mujahideen marksman is largely that – a myth. General health standards in Afghanistan (and also in other conflict zones like Somalia and Syria) mean that a sizeable proportion of the population, and thus of the insurgents, suffer from poor eyesight due to untreated disease.

A US Marine interviewed by journalist and USMC veteran C.J. Chivers in an article entitled *The Weakness of Taliban Marksmanship* explained what he experienced on his 2009 tour of Helmand in southern Afghanistan:

> [Bravo Company] has participated in over 200 patrols and been in countless engagements over the course of six months with actual boots on the ground. We have been in over a dozen actual Troop-In-Contact (TICs) warranting Close Air Support (CAS) and priority of assets because of the severity of the contact or pending contact. The only weapons systems the insurgents were effective with were machine guns, and only at suppressing our movement. We only had one instance where Marines reported single shots (possibly a 'sniper' or insurgent with a long-range rifle) being effective as suppression. [Bravo Company] had no Marines struck by machine-gun or small-arms rounds, some really close calls but no hits.

This is not an uncommon experience. The same has been reported by Australian, British, Canadian and Danish troops serving with the International Security Assistance Force (ISAF) in Afghanistan. The insurgents will often miss even at staggeringly close ranges. Some of this is down to lack of training – note even when trained by Western forces, Afghan security forces seem to still have a cultural barrier to using the sights on their weapons, preferring the 'spray and pray' method as some wag once put it – and some is undoubtedly down to eye disease.

In Iraq, with a better health care system under Saddam Hussein, insurgents still missed their targets more often than they hit, but observers also noted numbers of marksmen who would stalk Coalition Forces and successfully engage targets from a distance of several hundred metres (although again most such contacts, even against presumably seasoned gunmen, were at the 100 metres or less mark).

There were also many more foreign jihadists, some with training or combat experience, in Iraq than in Afghanistan where the most typical 'foreign fighter'

Marine machine gunners from 2nd Battalion, 5th Marines man a pair of 7.62 × 51mm M240Gs equipped with the × 6 Trijicon ACOG Machine Gun Optic (MGO), the closest of which also mounts an RMR mini red dot; Afghanistan 2012. (*USMC, Lance Cpl. Ismael E. Ortega*)

hails from just across the border in Pakistan. A proportion of the Iraqi insurgency, at least in the early days, was also composed of former Iraqi military and security services personnel who had received military training and sometimes were veterans of the decade-long Iran-Iraq War.

\* \* \*

So, what really happens in a firefight? Interviewing a large number of combat veterans over the last decade from the militaries of the United States, Canada, the United Kingdom and Australia, the one common factor to draw from these accounts is that everyone's experience is different, often markedly so. Terrain, the enemy strength and disposition, the weapons used and the training and experience levels of the troops and their enemy all play their part.

A few broad statements can be made, however. Firstly, forget whatever you've seen from Hollywood or *Call of Duty*. In films and console games, the enemy is almost always depicted as easily visible and can be engaged directly by small arms. In reality it is very, very difficult to spot exactly where the enemy are. Most fire is thus speculative. This is not to say that Coalition troops in Afghanistan, for instance, blaze away in every direction. They more than most are aware of collateral damage and the impact of civilian casualties. Instead they will fire at likely enemy positions or firing points once they have a handle on the direction and distance of the enemy fire. Even judging the general direction of enemy fire can be difficult. Once a likely firing point is identified, troops will engage the position with speculative fire with the aim of suppressing the enemy.

Combat optics, particularly magnified ones, are a terrific boon to identifying firing points, but they need to be widely issued and troops trained in their use. Other emerging technologies, like clip-on thermal imagers which work in conjunction with combat optics, are also improving the chances of identification but are only just beginning to see more common use with infantry soldiers.

There is the associated challenge of 'PIDing' which is the 'positive identification' of a person as a combatant – a necessary requirement under most forms of rules of engagement (ROE) which govern when a soldier can engage a target. This is further complicated when apparent non-combatants are acting as spotters for the enemy, or ferrying ammunition to gunmen. A good optic is essential to ensure the target is actually an insurgent and not an unlucky farmer caught in the middle.

In Iraq too, soldiers were faced with a ghost-like adversary: '*You can't even see them, but you see where everything is coming from. I'd see a muzzle flash ... pretty much just a muzzle flash. I've never seen anything other than that,*' reported one US Marine who served in Iraq. Another agreed: '*I have not seen the face or even the figure of an Iraqi or an Afghan firing at me. All I have seen is a muzzle peeking around a building and have shots impact on the ground in front of me, or to see an RPG detonate in front of my vehicle. They will not fight you face-to-face.*'

US Marine Sgt. Jason Burch displays his ACOG equipped 5.56 × 45mm M16A4 that has lost part of its front sight from an enemy bullet. (*USMC, Marine Cpl Rich Mattingly*)

US Army soldiers in Parwan Province, eastern Afghanistan 2011. The soldier to the left carries a 5.56 × 45mm M4A1 with underslung M203, whilst the soldier to the right carries a 5.56 × 45mm M249 SAW PIP fitted with a vertical forward grip and collapsible stock. (*US Army, PFC Zackary Root*)

Firefights are wildly chaotic. They are not the choreographed affairs seen at the movies. Targets will appear where they are least expected, weapons will malfunction at the worst possible moment, ammunition will run low … and all whilst terrified young soldiers try to identify where the enemy is launching RPGs from.

*   *   *

So, what can we learn in terms of infantry small arms from two decades of war in Iraq and Afghanistan?

- The key challenge as noted above is identifying the enemy. One British officer noted: '*The Taliban are not presenting easy targets.*' Insurgents by their very nature typically understand and appreciate the local geographic environment far more than even the best trained 'foreign' soldier. Insurgents in Iraq could use the urban jungle for concealment, in Afghanistan the insurgents are adept at using natural concealment, in irrigation ditches for example, before withdrawing unseen to an already plotted secondary firing point. The key here is that the enemy are often hard to see.
- Enemy can and do engage at ranges that are beyond the capabilities of most common 5.56 × 45mm calibre weapons carried by NATO troops. The enemy fire from their PKMs, RPGs and Dragunov SVDs at extended ranges is, however, very rarely effective. For the reasons outlined above, the insurgent is not a great marksman nor soldier.

- The range of engagements will still most likely be in the 200–300 metre mark, as it was for much of the Second World War and which informed much of the thinking around infantry small arms development including the design of the first true assault rifle, but it could be as close as 10 metres or rarely as far away as 700–800 metres.

- For the reason above, the relatively recent adoption of DMRs or designated marksmen rifles make much sense. These are generally chambered for the heavier 7.62 × 51mm round and are accompanied with magnified optics. In essence, they give a 'sniper-lite' capability to every squad or section. The Russians seem to have understood this decades before anyone else with the issue of SVD sniper rifles to every platoon.

- Snipers are more important than ever. Again, snipers have the optics (and specialist training) to identify enemy firing positions and PID targets. They also have an extremely lethal but precise weapons platform to engage them with little to no risk of collateral damage or danger to non-combatants. They are justly feared by insurgents.

- Short barrel light machine guns (LMGs) have been found wanting in certain environments like parts of Afghanistan. Whilst hugely appreciated in more close quarter urban fights in Iraq, the 5.56 × 45mm LMG simply does not have the range or accuracy to engage or suppress targets beyond 200–300 meters (it's again interesting to note that the Russians never really gave up their 7.62 × 54mm PKMs even after the adoption of the RPK and RPK-74 LMGs). We will discuss this at length in a later chapter, but the effectiveness of such LMGs have been called into question along with what their actual role in the infantry platoon really is.

- Suppressive fire wins firefights. This is nothing new but the importance of medium machine guns and grenade launchers, along with accurate rifle fire, has been reaffirmed. Suppression allows either an infantry element to flank and close with the enemy or to fix them in place, allowing mortars and artillery or air support to decisively finish the encounter. What exactly constitutes effective suppression fire is something we will look at in a moment.

- The combat load of the individual soldier is now at ridiculous levels. Infantry are overburdened with an ever-increasing catalogue of essential items – body armour with plates, night vision, batteries, water, radio, electronic counter-measures … This has led to both casualties from heat exhaustion and in combat as soldiers are slowed to a waddle (the Taliban even labelling them 'donkeys', with one British officer commenting *'our infantry find it almost impossible to close with the enemy because the bad guys are twice as mobile'*.

- .50 outclasses everything. Despite numerous advances in weapons and ammunition development, the elderly .50 Browning employed as a heavy machine gun is still king of the hill. One soldier summed it up succinctly: *'5.56mm the Taliban ignore; 7.62mm worries them; .50-calibre scares them.'*

Platoon Leader 1st Lt. Brandon Harper, US Army, scans for insurgents, Iraq 2008. He carries a 5.56 × 45mm M4 equipped with a Trijicon ACOG, Surefire weapon light and KAC vertical grip. (*US Army, Spc John Crosby*)

- Pistols are important. Particularly for vehicle crews and weapons teams including snipers; having a close range self-defence option against the threat of suicide bombers and the like is essential and a lesson that has been relearned. We will look again in detail at this in the following chapter.

\* \* \*

Most of these points will be covered later in the book but let's briefly look at a few key ones which relate to all infantry small arms. Firstly, suppression and what it really means.

Jim Storr defined it as follows:

> Suppression is the effect of small arms and other weapons systems which temporarily prevent the enemy firing its weapons or moving in the open. In simple terms, it makes them keep their heads down. It is critically important. In the offence it allows the attacker to move forward, to find gaps and weak points, and exploit them. In the defence it prevents the enemy moving forward and firing, and thereby sets him up for counter-attacks. In both cases it pins the enemy down for incapacitation (or destruction) by other weapons.

Suppression is key to winning any firefight but is still a concept that defies a neat algorithm to explain its effect, or how to induce that effect. Operational research like that conducted by the pseudonymous Leo Murray in his brilliant book (which is very much recommended to all readers), *Brains & Bullets: How Psychology Wins Wars*, argues that the fighting effectiveness of an enemy unit can be halved by well applied suppressive fire, particularly that which includes both direct and indirect fire such as from grenade launchers. What constitutes 'well applied', however, is still open to debate.

Historically, armies trained their soldiers to apply the maximum amount of firepower in the hope of suppressing the enemy. What now seems to be apparent after decades long wars in Iraq and Afghanistan is that the proximity and thus the accuracy of the fire directed at the enemy is as important, if not more so, than the volume. Volume is still hugely critical in the initial seconds, to 'win the initiative', gain fire superiority and put the enemy literally on the back foot. A factor often not commented upon is the positive psychological effect this also has on the firer – it empowers him or her and helps to steady the nerves. Once the enemy has gone to ground, accuracy takes over as the key to maintaining suppression. One British officer tellingly mentioned to the author that the section LMG, the 5.56 × 45m L110A2 Minimi, was providing *'morale boosting firepower'*.

A real-world example from the Welsh Guards' 2009 tour of Helmand is worth mentioning to give the reader some idea of just how many rounds are expended in an infantry firefight. Journalist Toby Harnden relates that in one 40-minute contact with numerous Taliban in multiple firing points, a fifteen-man patrol

Welsh Guards engage insurgents in Afghanistan 2009. Closest to the camera is the 5.56 × 45mm L85A2 (SA80A2) with SUSAT optic, the centre gunner fires a 5.56 × 45mm Minimi LMG (L110A2) again with SUSAT sight, whilst partly obscured in the background is a 7.62 × 51mm L7A2 GPMG gunner. (*Open Government License v3.0*)

expended more than 10,000 rounds; the Minimi LMG had fired all 800 rounds that the gunner himself carried. Consider this when we discuss combat loads later in this chapter.

A nearby Forward Operating Base provided suppressive fire and expended over 20,000 rounds of 7.62 × 51mm from its four general purpose machine guns (the GPMGs eventually suffered stoppages as the barrels overheated) and close to 400 × 40mm rounds from an automatic grenade launcher. This amount of firing is not unusual in a prolonged firefight (many are over however within minutes as the opposition fire a few rounds or an RPG and take to the hills).

DARPA or the Defense Advanced Research Projects Agency in the United States conducted a major 1972 study, including data from the Vietnam War, which found that the 'major factors producing suppression' were:

- The loudness of the passing rounds
- The proximity of the passing rounds
- The number of passing rounds
- The signature of the impacts of passing rounds

Jim Storr agreed:

> In general, small arms fire has to pass within roughly a metre from the outline of the target to be effective. A small number of rounds passing through that area in a few seconds (perhaps 3 to 5 rounds in as many seconds) will suppress the target, or re-suppress him if required; whilst just one round every three seconds will keep him suppressed.

Noted defence authority, former British Army officer William F. Owen explained to the author:

> Suppression is an action that causes the enemy to cease activity through fear of harm. It exists as either active suppression – doing something, or passive suppression – threatening to do something so [even] observation can deliver suppression IF it cues a weapons effect.
>
> You can actually measure suppression, so we have good data on what causes it. A bullet generates a pressure wave which can be measured. This means you can develop a model which can be used for doctrine development/training. The UK model most often cited is something like, 'someone is suppressed if a bullet passed within a meter of their head every three seconds'.
>
> Actually, the bigger the pressure wave, the better the suppression, so 12.7mm [.50] has a bigger suppression footprint than 5.56mm etc. High Explosive [also] deliver suppression via 'Flash, Bang and Fragments'. Fragments generate pressure waves, as do explosions themselves.
>
> Which weapons suppress best? A sniper rifle will suppress as well as a GPMG. It just depends on context. Putting one round every 3–5 seconds through a window will most likely stop anyone returning fire from that window.

US Army SAW gunner during a contact with insurgents in Kunar Province, Afghanistan 2009, firing his 5.56 × 45mm M249 Paratrooper fitted with Elcan M145 optic. (*ISAF*)

The United States Marine Corps is slowly adopting this new paradigm of precision over volume. In 2009, as we will detail later in the book, the USMC purchased a number of German 5.56 × 45mm Heckler and Koch 416A5 rifles equipped with optics and bipods which they christened the M27 Infantry Automatic Rifle or IAR as a supplementary issue to the M249 Squad Automatic Weapon (the SAW, the US version of the Belgian Minimi light machine gun).

The M27 did not fully replace the M249, some are kept in reserve for urban warfare for instance. Within each infantry company, there are currently six M249s held by the Weapons Platoon and twenty-seven M27s issued out to the squads. The reasoning was deftly explained by Retired Chief Warrant Officer 5 Jeffrey Eby who was integrally involved in the testing of the M27 platform: '*Experiments by Marine Corps Operational Test and Evaluation Activity proved that the M27 significantly outperformed the M249 in suppression, used significantly less ammunition and had less downtime during reloads when total down time was measured through a full combat load of ammunition.*'

He added: '*The loss of the psychological effect of a high volume of inaccurate fire provided by the M249 will NOT be an issue, as any combat veteran who has heard gunfire can attest to, as after the first "dive to cover" occasion has been conducted, the sound of inaccurate fire passing somewhere nearby no longer impresses the veteran to the point of taking cover.*'

What Eby mentions here seems to be key. Inaccurate fire, no matter what the volume, does not seem to suppress. What suppresses the enemy appears to be consistent fire that is placed within close proximity of his position. Murray notes again that from studies carried out during the Second World War and echoing both Storr and Owen: *'One round passing within 3 meters every six seconds would appreciably degrade return fire ... two rounds every three seconds would prevent any return fire at all.'* It is the accuracy of the fire that seems to maintain the suppression.

Major Charles Clark III, Infantry Weapons Capabilities Integration Officer at USMC Headquarters, was blunt in explaining this change in thinking for the Corps: *'Fire superiority is based on both accuracy and volume of fire. The greater your accuracy, the less volume of fire you need.'*

Calibre is also important, but not as much as accuracy. Field studies in Afghanistan have found that larger calibre rounds will do a better job at suppressing – remember the oft quoted *'5.56mm the Taliban ignore; 7.62mm worries them; .50-calibre scares them'*. It appears, as claimed in that original 1972 DARPA study, to be the visual cue of rounds impacting nearby and the audio cue of the rounds cracking past overhead that help deter the enemy. Larger calibres make a louder sonic crack, as Owen explained, thus increasing the likelihood of suppression occurring and being maintained.

Does this always work in practice? No, of course not. One Marine Corps study of Afghan insurgent tactics noted that: *'In some instances, they continued firing accurately and methodically despite sniper rounds landing within inches all around them. Their fire was disciplined and accurate. RPGs landed in clusters, within a beaten zone*

An Australian sniper pair shooting the .50BMG Barrett M82A1 (M107 in US service).
*(Commonwealth of Australia, Sgt. Mick Davis)*

Bundeswehr soldiers armed with 5.56 × 45mm G36A2 and 7.62 × 51mm G3A3ZF designated marksman rifle (at gate), Afghanistan 2012. (*IMZ/Bildarchiv, Andrea Bienert*)

*of 6–12 inches.'* Experienced fighters with good leadership will always stand a greater chance of fighting through suppressive fires.

The British Army is following a similar path to the Marines. In 2018 it was announced that the Minimi LMG would be withdrawn from service. It will not be replaced with another LMG. Instead, the 7.62 × 51mm L7A2, the iconic GPMG or general purpose machine gun, will be available to infantry sections and the issue rate of the 7.62 × 51mm L129A1 designated marksman rifle will be increased. Although this decision seems to be the right one, it has been understandably controversial and is examined in detail in a later chapter.

*   *   *

Now let's consider the prickly issue of overmatch. It is a difficult concept to study objectively as many who claim that so-called overmatch is a key challenge facing militaries in Afghanistan do not cite their sources, or rely on government studies which are inevitably classified or otherwise unavailable for study. Overmatch in this instance means that the enemy has better weapons than you, particularly in terms of range.

In his last book, *Guns of the Special Forces*, the author argued that there was some merit to the argument, particularly based on the influential monograph *Increasing Small Arms Lethality in Afghanistan: Taking Back the Infantry Half-Kilometer* written by then US Army Major Thomas Ehrhart. Today he has modified his views based on the performance of enhanced 5.56 × 45mm bullets and greater operational research into the dynamics of the firefight, particularly in Afghanistan, including visually identifying the enemy and the actual performance of soldiers under fire (and including actually seeking out and interviewing Ehrhart to find out his feelings now, a decade or so after his original report).

Some suggest that what pundits should be claiming is that on occasion, Coalition Forces were out-ranged by insurgent weapons. Combat veterans from the Iraq and Afghan wars whom the author has spoken to ardently seem to disagree with the very idea of overmatch. They were sometimes 'out-ranged' but 'overmatched'? This is however nothing new. In every conflict since the advent of black powder, soldiers have been faced with enemy weapons that have out-ranged those they carried. Surely in terms of rifles, the enemy AK-47 and similar are already 'overmatched' by all principal Coalition assault rifles such as the L85A2 and the M4A1. Does the assault rifle have to 'overmatch' enemy machine guns and sniper rifles too, a task they were never designed for?

Well regarded firearms authority Nathaniel Fitch commented that such expectations of infantrymen are far from realistic:

> The focus on a hypothetical but much-hyped long range engagement centering around each individual infantryman achieving 'overmatch' *versus* enemy 7.62 × 54mm medium/general purpose machine guns, while not a complete fantasy, doesn't seem to reflect the realities of modern combined arms

Bundeswehr soldiers conduct pre-deployment training in preparation for Afghanistan, 2012. All carry the issue 5.56 × 45mm G36A2 with vertical foregrip and LLM01 laser and weapon light. (*US Army, Spc. Tristan Bolden*)

warfare, and seems to point towards the US Army seeking a procurement solution to what may well be an organizational problem.

This is extremely worrying to someone like myself who is familiar with the skill set of the common individual, and who is very aware of the difficulty of long-range shooting under even ideal conditions. Expecting every soldier to take advantage of weapons designed to 'overmatch' enemy weapons out to these extreme distances is an attitude that would take a considerable weight of empirical evidence to prove as valid and realistic.

The standard assault rifle of the insurgent, whether they be in Afghanistan, Syria or Yemen, is the AK-47 family. Many observers have claimed that the AK-47 outperforms comparable NATO rifles due to its calibre, the intermediate 7.62 × 39mm M43. Whilst the round itself is an excellent compromise design, when fired from most common examples of the AK family it lacks both accuracy and range.

Although the 7.62 × 39mm maintains its velocity for further than most 5.56 × 45mm rounds, the NATO round suffers from approximately half of the vertical dispersion or ballistic drop of the 7.62 × 39mm, meaning that the shooter has to account for this drop by modifying his or her aim. For close range engagements of 100–150 metres this is of little concern, but once the engagement envelope widens, the Soviet round shows significant drop versus the flatter shooting 5.56 × 45mm. For example, at 400 metres, the 7.62 × 39mm experiences approximately 2 feet of bullet drop.

The vast majority of AK users have no understanding of this, and it undoubtedly contributes to their questionable accuracy, especially when the AK's noticeable recoil – particularly versus the relatively soft recoil of the 5.56 × 45mm – is added into the equation. Most insurgents seem to fire their AKs on fully automatic, again adding to the chances of a miss. The author has fired several AK variants on fully automatic and can attest that muzzle climb is significant even in short bursts of two to three rounds.

So in real terms the M4A1 and the L85A2 (and the G36A2 and other similar NATO 5.56 × 45mm weapons) already overmatch the standard weapon of current adversaries. With the widespread adoption of 5.56 × 45mm and more commonly 7.62 × 51mm designated marksman rifles, this overmatch is significantly increased. Ehrhart, whose study *Increasing Small Arms Lethality in Afghanistan: Taking Back the Infantry Half-Kilometer* is cited by many who argue that Coalition Forces suffer from overmatch put his views in perspective, and context, when he graciously agreed to a discussion with the author:

At the time of my paper, we were severely restricted in the use of CAS [close air support] or artillery. The enemy was engaging us from extended distances, hoping to get lucky. Ideally, we always want to get the most into the fight, to include mortars, artillery, CAS, and attack helicopters. Take those away and we are limited to our own organic capability.

The discussion on 'overmatch' is really concerning a particular threat with ceramic armor protection that could only be defeated by current 7.62 AP ammunition. This threat is not likely, nor consistent. Most threats will only

An Australian sniper provides overwatch with his 7.62 × 51mm SR-25, Uruzgan Province, Afghanistan 2007. (*Commonwealth of Australia*)

include limited numbers that can engage from distance; mostly SVD type weapons and PKMs. RPGs self-detonate before one kilometer, and your typical dude isn't that accurate past 200 meters. Typically, one or two of each system per platoon size element. It can be addressed by adding a couple larger caliber precision rifle systems at the platoon level to include adequate training.

Historical data from the Second World War showed that the vast majority of conventional infantry combat occurred within 300 metres. With the expectation of many future battles occurring within mega-cities, this seems unlikely to change. Indeed, the British have conducted internal studies from their deployments to the Balkans, Iraq and Afghanistan, finding that over 80 per cent of firefights occur within 200 metres. In the 200 metre and under battle, the infantryman's assault rifle and grenade launchers are the tools most employed.

William Owen agreed: '*It is section weapons and HE projectors that win firefights, not IWs* [individual weapons like the L85A2]. *Where the performance of IWs is critical is at short range.*' The British Army in their campaign study of Operation Herrick in Afghanistan likewise stated: '*Close range precision is still required and this was delivered by the 5.56mm rifle.*'

This does not mean that longer range engagements did not and will not occur. The same campaign study noted, '*as the campaign developed, engagement ranges increased. This was due to insurgent tactics and the range and firepower of their weapon systems.*' This matches our earlier discussion on the impact of the IED and the insurgents' reluctance to engage in pitched firefights that they historically inevitably lost. They were and are a highly adaptive enemy and were simply 'playing to their strengths'.

For longer range engagements, other weapons systems come into play. Infantry patrols are rarely isolated from the rest of their platoon or company. A serving British soldier who saw extensive combat in Helmand in 2009 told the author:

> I was quite lucky to have a GPMG [in my section] because it's nice firepower and you're able to pin back the Taliban and it's obviously a better capability. Once you've pinned them back far enough the snipers or Javelin come into play and you're able to eliminate the enemy threat. Sometimes they get quite close, so it is good to have a personal weapon or shotgun.
>
> Plus, you've got mortars, fast air and artillery, you've got everything so you can't complain really. We're totally a better fighting force than them but people I think back home underestimate the Taliban because I've been in quite a lot of contacts and only on the past two ops I've actually really seen the Taliban. I've been shot at but I never actually saw the Taliban until about a month ago.

There's a lot to 'unpack' here, as they say. Firstly, he acknowledges the indisputable capability of the 7.62 × 51mm belt-fed machine gun. It's a well-liked and respected platform and is universally popular. Next however he notes that the GPMG – or the 'General' or 'Gimpy' as it is widely known amongst UK forces – is really used to fix the enemy to allow other weapons systems, namely sniper rifles and Javelin-guided anti-tank missiles, to carry out the actual destruction.

Next there is the awareness that the fire team, section or platoon is not fighting in isolation. He mentions the vast array of kinetic support available. Finally, he is only too keenly aware that his opponent exhibits good fieldcraft, making a difficult job (spotting the enemy) exponentially more difficult. At no time did he mention the fear of being 'out-ranged' or 'overmatched' by the enemy. In fact, a review of the literally dozens of first-person memoirs from service members who have served in Helmand are also curiously devoid of mention of overmatch. This is also true in comments made during interviews with a dozen recent, former and current service members from the British Army and a number of US Marines who have served in Helmand. Contacts are noted at extended range, sometimes up to 800 metres or even further, but these are the exception rather than the rule and are terrain dependent. Soldiers will note that they have been suppressed, normally by PKM or RPG fire (and in one notable case by a Taliban automatic grenade launcher – likely an old Russian AGS-17 – but they never felt they were overmatched).

The USMC recorded:

> The terrain dictated very close-in fighting. Unlike north-eastern Afghanistan, where engagement ranges tended to exceed 400 meters, in Helmand (based on interviews) they tended to fall under 200 meters. AH-64 Apache attack helicopters often fired at targets within 150 meters of British troops (danger-close).

These enemy are dealt with like most others not contacted at close range – by machine gun, sniper, mortar, air support or artillery. There is little of the expected

A British Army sniper, Afghanistan 2008. He is equipped with the .338 Lapua Magnum L115A3. His 9 × 19mm SIG Sauer P226 is just visible attached to his body armour.

(*Open Government License v3.0, Sgt. Anthony Boocock*)

A Mexican Army Cuerpo de Fuerzas Especiales soldier firing his issued 5.56 × 45mm FN F2000 bullpup fitted with EOTech optic. (*US Army, Cpl Joanna Bradshaw*)

dismissal of the 5.56 × 56mm individual weapons or LMGs, although the short effective range of the Minimi LMG is often commented upon. Importantly however, the soldiers themselves do not appear to have felt they were overmatched.

The author has identified only one expression of frustration at the range capabilities of the soldiers' 5.56 × 45mm weapons, lamenting the lack of '*a few SLRs*' as '*the GPMGs hammered away, duelling with an enemy machine gun some 600m away on the high ground*'. The contact is eventually settled in favour of the British as 81mm mortar rounds land amongst the insurgent position. The same author noted that whilst the Minimi LMG was generally reliable and popular, he identified the short Para length barrel as compromising accuracy at range, a claim we will examine again in a later chapter.

Lieutenant Colonel Detlef Rausch, Director of the Infantry Future Development at the German Infantry School, provides another example in his study of small arms effectiveness by Bundeswehr units in Afghanistan:

Reports from theatre say that the target effectiveness of 5.56mm standard rounds at ranges exceeding 300m is insufficient. Troops in theatre use the 7.62mm MG3 machine gun to engage enemy targets at ranges greater than 300m. Furthermore, some designated marksmen at squad level have been equipped with 7.62mm G3 rifles with telescopic sights for the engagement of individual targets. In the medium term, the German infantry needs follow-on weapons to replace the MG3 and the G3 rifle.

It must be emphasised here that the performance of the 5.56 × 45mm at 300 metres should be no surprise. The calibre was designed to engage targets only to 300 metres based on operational research studies that we have previously noted. Indeed, an Australian Army study commenting in 1971 after several years of the M16 being in service with Australian infantry in Vietnam, noted:

> The M16 is thought to be extremely lethal at short range. The extra velocity probably causes more serious wounds. But as range increases, velocity of the 55-grain bullets drops more rapidly than for the M14 and even the Russian 'intermediate' power round. Beyond about 250 yards the bullets of the enemy begin to have considerably more energy.

Now this officer was commenting on the original 55-grain M193 5.56 × 45mm. A vast gulf of performance exists today between the M193 and the latest enhanced 5.56 × 45mm rounds like the M855A1. More to the point, can the average infantryman hit a barely glimpsed target at ranges beyond 300 metres, in the haze and extreme stress of combat? Recall that according to a number of experienced operational research analysts, a soldier's combat performance is roughly 75 per cent less effective than on a rifle range in controlled conditions.

Well informed commentators have noted that training plays a huge part in what soldiers can realistically hit. Ammunition budgets are often limited and some infantrymen may only receive a handful of range sessions each year. Many of these are on static known range targets which, while improving basic shooting skills, do nothing to represent moving, vaguely seen enemy at varying ranges. If leaders want to improve infantry lethality, training (and optics) are the key, far more so than any reactionary move to an interim calibre or to 7.62 × 51mm.

Ehrhart added:

> One aspect I wasn't able to get to based on the limited space available in my original paper was the various training programs to increase marksmanship and capability. Here is a favourite quote [H.W. McBride, *A Rifleman went to War*]; 'Probably no other single thing in the soldiering game is so little understood as rifle shooting. The general impression seems to be that all that is necessary is to give a man a rifle and some cartridges and that, in some miraculous way, that man immediately becomes a perfectly good and competent rifleman, able to knock over any number of the enemy at most any range.'

Ehrhart contends that training can appreciably add greater range to the individual infantryman armed with a 5.56 × 45mm platform:

> With minimum training, new soldiers can quickly be trained to engage targets to 500 meters. With advanced training, soldiers can rapidly engage targets from contact distance to 500 meters in urban, wooded, or open terrain. Training should include a combination of static and moving ranges at short, mid, and long distance.

In a conventional war against a peer or near peer enemy, the vast majority of firefights will still occur within the magic 300 metres for the simple fact that: (a) the attacker, unless in a meeting engagement, wants to maximise their chances of producing casualties, so they wait until the target is well within range of the majority of his weapons; and (b) engaging from distance (such as the oft stated example of Taliban insurgents firing from 800 metres) invites almost immediate destruction by airpower or indirect fire.

Particularly in a conventional war scenario, rather than in the counter-insurgency wars that have dominated the past two decades, there will be far, far less emphasis on Collateral Damage Estimates and *'Courageous Restraint'* (the tactic of limiting the use of kinetic fires to reduce the chance of inadvertent death or wounding of civilians or the destruction of infrastructure which is counter-productive in a COIN scenario).

William F. Owen added:

> Overmatch just means you have a better weapons set than the enemy. The bit that gets missed – and this applies to suppression as well – is weapons optics and sensors. An M27 IAR with a thermal scope is many times more useful than one without. The low hanging fruit in infantry capability is not new or better weapons but better optics, sensors and communications.

The problem is indeed largely one of locating the target. Better optics and training on how to use those optics will pay huge dividends. Look at the reception of the USMC M27 and the British L129A1, both are comparable weapons, although in different roles, but comments from end users are markedly similar. Both allow the marksman to spot targets beyond the capabilities of the issue Elcan or the 4-power magnification ACOG and to engage them with accurate precision fire.

A related topic often raised when the overmatch concept is argued is the alleged ineffectiveness of the standard NATO 5.56 × 45mm bullet. We will return to this topic in detail in later chapters, particularly in our discussions around assault rifle and light machine gun calibres, but it is worth briefly covering the salient points here. Criticism of the 5.56mm is a largely American phenomenon, something which it does not seem will ever abate. Like the perennial .45ACP versus 9mm arguments that populate innumerable internet forums and gun magazines, even after the FBI concluded that trauma surgeons have a difficult time ascertaining the calibre of a wound inflicted by a handgun of any calibre from .38 Special upwards, the 5.56 × 45mm 'debate' looks set to continue.

The 5.56 × 45mm has gained a somewhat unfair reputation as a poor 'stopper'. This stemmed initially from the experiences in Vietnam where the first M16s issued suffered catastrophic failures due to the type of powder used and over-inflated claims of the requirement to clean the weapon. Poorly manufactured magazines also added to the failures. The propellant powder was eventually changed and a suitable cleaning regime was instituted, but the rifle was already cursed and never really recovered (something which somewhat mirrors the British Army experience with the L85A1 years later).

The issue round at the time, the 55 grain M193, was suitably effective when it struck tissue but had no real ability to penetrate through even light barriers such as jungle foliage. The M193 was replaced by the NATO standard SS109 or M855 in US service in the early 1980s. The M855 was both heavier at 62 grains and was designed with a steel core penetrator which reduced velocity but improved armour penetration and what is termed 'barrier blindness' – the ability of a bullet to pass through intermediate obstacles in the path to the target (for example, car doors or internal walls).

Conventional 5.56mm ammunition (non-expanding) needs to yaw to be effective. Otherwise the bullet will simply punch through the target unless it strikes bone or a major organ, a result sometimes known as 'ice-picking'. Military 5.56 × 45mm has traditionally been of a full-metal-jacket design to meet the Hague Convention's restrictions on expanding ammunition which is prohibited in conventional warfare. A by-product of the yawing of the 5.56mm is a legal way of maximising the destructive potential of the round without resorting to non-Hague compliant fragmenting ammunition.

Both the M855 and SS109 round was designed with one particular enemy in mind – Soviet soldiers wearing body armour. When employed against insurgents for example, who typically do not wear body armour, the round would sometimes penetrate straight through the individual because of two factors: the steel core penetrator and the increased stability of the round. It would often fail to yaw as it was designed to penetrate. Accounts of failures of the M855 'Green Tip'

An Estonian infantryman during NATO exercises in 2014. He carries the B&T upgraded 5.56 × 45mm Galil ARM with Aimpoint and weapon light. (*US Army, Sgt. John Carkeet IV*)

are examined in a later chapter but the US military eventually adopted an improved M855A1 in 2010 which seems to have gone a long way to solving both issues.

Dr Dan Pronk, a former Australian SASR combat medic, notes that '*the optimum projectile to shoot someone with is one that has a decent mass; is very, very fast; and is guaranteed to come to rest in your target so as to dissipate as much energy as possible into it, and hence do maximal damage.*'

From treating dozens of gunshot wounds in Afghanistan, Pronk came to the following conclusion:

> Despite being a jacketed round, because it's smaller, lighter and faster than an AK-47 projectile, the 5.56mm tends to yaw faster once it hits tissue. The shearing forces on the bullet once it is travelling at 90 degrees through the tissue often tears the bullet into pieces, thus creating multiple smaller projectiles and increasing the chances of all of the bullet parts remaining in the target, and hence dissipating more energy.
>
> The AK-47 round, being slightly heavier and slower than the M4 round, has a tendency to remain intact as it strikes tissue, and while it will penetrate deeper, it tends to remain intact and not yaw until it has penetrated much deeper than the M4.

US Army Major Glenn Dean, whom we again encounter in a later chapter thanks to his involvement in the pioneering development of the M855A1 Enhanced Performance Round, gave what is perhaps the most succinct, and realistic, description of what is required from military small arms in a 2008 study:

> The major problem occurs at the very beginning: What is effectiveness? As it turns out, that simple question requires a very complex answer. For the soldier in combat, effectiveness equals death: the desire to have every round fired result in the death of the opposing combatant, the so-called 'one-shot drop'.
>
> However, death – or lethality – is not always necessary to achieve a military objective; an enemy combatant who is no longer willing or able to perform a meaningful military task may be as good as dead under most circumstances. Some equate effectiveness with 'stopping power', a nebulous term that can mean anything from physically knocking the target down to causing the target to immediately stop any threatening action. Others may measure effectiveness as foot-pounds of energy delivered to the target – by calculating the mass and impact velocity of the round – without considering what amount of energy is expended in the target or what specific damage occurs to the target.
>
> In the end, 'foot pounds of energy' is misleading, 'stopping power' is a myth, and the 'one-shot drop' is a rare possibility dependent more on the statistics of hit placement than weapon and ammunition selection. Effectiveness ultimately equates to the potential of the weapons system to eliminate its target as a militarily relevant threat.

He further explains how 'effectiveness' translates in the real terms of the effect on the human body:

> Upon impacting the target, the bullet penetrates tissue and begins to slow. Some distance into the target, the tissue acting on the bullet also causes the bullet to rotate erratically or yaw; the location and amount of yaw depend upon speed of the bullet at impact, angle of impact, and density of the tissue. If the bullet is moving fast enough, it may also begin to break up, with pieces spreading away from the main path of the bullet to damage other tissue.
>
> If the target is thick enough, all of these fragments may come to rest in the target, or they may exit the target. Meanwhile, the impacted tissue rebounds away from the path of the bullet, creating what is known as a 'temporary cavity'. Some of the tissue is smashed or torn by the bullet itself, or its fragments; some expands too far and tears.
>
> The 'temporary cavity' eventually rebounds, leaving behind the torn tissue in the wound track – the 'permanent cavity'. It is this permanent cavity that is most significant, as it represents the damaged tissue that can impair and eventually kill the target, provided, of course, that the damaged tissue is actually some place on the body that is critical.

We will return again to the question of incapacitation and the capabilities of the $5.56 \times 45$mm when we discuss assault rifles.

Another issue identified by long combat experience in Afghanistan and Iraq is combat weight. It has an outsized effect on small arms, particularly in terms

British soldiers from 2nd Battalion, The Rifles, Helmand Province, Afghanistan 2010. Note the tremendous loads carried by the infantrymen. *(ISAF, Cpl. Timothy L. Solano)*

of the weight of the weapon and ammunition carried. William Owen sagely cautioned the author: '*Organisation, training, budget and even mechanisation have all impacted weapons issues. Most of all understand that physical mass (weight) of weapon, ammunition, optics, ancillaries and even batteries is a massive driver.*'

\* \* \*

So, what does a combat soldier carry? According to the UK's Infantry Battle School, infantrymen deployed to Afghanistan carried the following combat loads: section commanders routinely weighed in at 55 kilograms, the grenadier at 42.5 kilograms and the GPMG gunner at an astounding 72 kilograms. The poor soul tasked with carrying the man-portable Electronic Counter Measures (ECM) kit topped the scales at 63 kilograms (the ECM is a backpack unit that effectively jams certain types of IED initiators and provides an electronic umbrella of protection over the patrol). Even infantrymen who operated from vehicles carried some 33 kilograms of personal equipment.

What makes up these horrendous loads? Body armour with plates, helmet, radio, personal weapon and ammunition, sidearm, grenades, ammunition for support weapons like mortar bombs or link for machine guns, night vision equipment, batteries, water (one report noted that in Helmand's Green Zone each soldier needed to carry and drink up to 12 litres to avoid heat exhaustion on a typical four hour patrol), minimal rations and field first aid kit.

This weight will only increase as new, and often operationally valuable, technology is added. A case in point is the emergence of platoon level or even section level drones or UAVs. These provide such a vital capability that they cannot be ignored so must be added to the packing list. So too with improved mine detectors with ground penetrating radars. Or thermal imagers. And of course the batteries for all of these gizmos.

Along with inducing fatigue and causing potentially career-ending injuries, this weight means that the infantryman cannot effectively manoeuvre against the enemy because he or she is simply carrying too much to do so. Not so the enemy. In Iraq and Afghanistan (and much of Syria), the average enemy combatant is carrying little more than an AK, a couple of extra magazines, a cell phone or walkie-talkie and maybe, if they're lucky, a bottle of water and something to eat. Far less than 50 kilograms. Whilst largely limiting the manoeuvre of friendly forces, the weight discrepancy has played into the hands of the insurgents who, travelling light, can quickly cover the distance to their next firing point or close in to hug friendly forces and thus limit the effectiveness of supporting indirect fire or air support.

The simple answer is, of course, to reduce the weight carried by the infantryman. But at what cost? An article in the *British Army Review* puts it bluntly:

Spotting the soldier load problem is easy; doing something about it will be very hard. No commander will ever risk the false ire of the press, the ill-informed judgment of coroners or the genuine grief of relatives by dumping body armour, firepower or gadgets. There aren't many soldiers or marines who would voluntarily dump kit and risk their own lives for some vague idea about the collective good.

The same *British Army Review* (no. 150) published a fictionalised account of a typical Helmand patrol which is worth quoting at length as it starkly illustrates much of the reality on the ground where over-burdened men and women try to take the fight to the enemy (and is a very enjoyable read that should be more widely shared):

The patrol moves on into the half cultivated, compound-dominated ground to the west of the hamlet. It's not yet 10.00am but the temperature is in the mid-thirties. Despite the steady pace the patrol starts losing body water and salts faster than they can be replaced. They're fit people but by the time they swing onto the last leg toward the patrol base they've been plodding up and down in the heat for four hours.

They've been at a high alert state for longer than their bodies can sustain it. Mental vigilance has dropped off and their reactions have slowed. Knees, necks and shoulders ache, eyes are gritty, vision is that little bit blurred. Dehydration, fatigue and the stress of being on the alert have already biased their choices to the simple but risky; they've started to bunch up and the mine clearing drills have become a bit sloppy. And then they're bumped.

200 metres to the west (the patrol's right) are four well-rested, well-watered, wiry little men. They have opened fire from the shady spot they've been lying in for the last half hour. The fire is 'ineffective' in cold war terms but our hot war patrol is pinned for a minute. Having already used up much of their high-alert reserve capacity it is difficult for the patrol to work out where the fire is coming from in this Afghan Bocage.

Corporals shout, radios crackle, fire is returned. After a few false starts and much shouting, the patrol's fire has been directed at the right bit of cover. In this environment locating the enemy is often as much luck as judgement but today the patrol has just enough of both. The patrol's fire builds until it looks like our guys are winning the firefight and can think about getting up close to the enemy. But the enemy have other ideas.

Those four nasty whippet-men are already moving off to a secondary position. Well rested and carrying less than 20kgs apiece, they can scramble through cover at quite a lick. A lucky UGL shot might cause some damage but their covered route means all the patrol's direct fire is just noise.

With a bit more shouting the patrol commander manages to drop the rate of fire to a level he calculates will keep the enemy occupied but not waste rounds. Then, after a quick chat in a ditch, he opts for a classic Brecon move. Another rapid fire surge from the machine guns (directed at the original firing point) is used to cover a move by a four-man fire-team led by the patrol commander. Taking a risk by using open ground that has not been Vallon-cleared, the fire-team tries to outflank the enemy and heads off southwest at a clumsy trot.

After 70 metres they've nearly reached the next bit of cover when they're engaged by another couple of well-rested men. 100 metres to the fire-team's north, in the shade of a compound wall, these two men are taking shots at the fire-team with an old but effective sniper rifle. The fire-team don't notice this fire for a while – at full trot they are already gasping and the noise of their own bodies half masks the crack and thump. Luck is on their side again; nobody is hit. But by the time they reach the cover of a knocked-down wall, the original enemy have reached their secondary position.

This cautionary tale continues with the lead fire-team effectively suppressed from several directions leading to both the call-out of a vehicle mounted Quick Reaction Force and a number of 'show of force' passes by a Coalition aircraft. By this time of course, all of the enemy have faded away. Neither side incurred casualties but neither did they claim anything resembling a conclusive victory. The whole of the article, *Donkeys led by Lions*, is available via a Google search and is recommended reading to understand exactly how combat loads, and the tactics of the enemy, effect small arms selection and performance.

Remember also Jim Storr's research into combat effectiveness: '*It appears that a soldier's ability to hit a given target is typically reduced by a factor of ten or so when he is moved from a static rifle range to a field firing area where he has to select cover, move, shoot and so on. It is reduced by a further factor of ten or so if there is an enemy firing back at him. It is reduced by another factor of ten if the enemy has machine guns ...*' Add in a combat load of anywhere between 42 and 72 kilograms, and one wonders how infantrymen ever get the job done.

The British Army, under the suitably titled Project Payne, is considering ways to 'increase precision' amongst its infantry small arms whilst reducing the load carried from the typical 40- to 60-kilogram loads in Afghanistan, to a far more manageable 25 kilograms. Part of this requirement will be met by the wider spread adoption of a platoon level all-terrain vehicle and weight reductions in improved body armour. The weight of small arms is also being considered.

A recent US Army Research Laboratory Study has looked at combat loads and in particular the weight of body armour and came to similar conclusions: '*Increased soldier load not only slows movement and increases fatigue, but also has been experimentally demonstrated to decrease situational awareness and shooting response times.*' According to their research, between 2004 and 2007 in Afghanistan, twice as many medical evacuations of soldiers were caused by '*spinal, connective tissue, or musculoskeletal injuries*' as combat.

The report concluded that commanders should '*clearly delegate authority to company-level commanders to modify the level of protection as needed, based on the specific threat and mission. Wearing heavy body armor may not be operationally practical on a long-range multi-day patrol in mountainous terrain, such as in Afghanistan.*' As noted in the *British Army Review* article however, how many leaders will actually be comfortable telling their soldiers to reduce their protective equipment?

\* \* \*

As an adjunct whilst discussing external factors that affect infantry small arms and small arms performance, it is worth also briefly mentioning the popular idea of soldiers being resistant to killing the enemy. A former American Army officer Dave Grossman has produced several books based to some degree on the writings of S.L.A. Marshall who claimed to have conducted a large number of interviews with American servicemen during the Second World War. He controversially concluded that less than a quarter of US soldiers – actually somewhere between 15 and 20 per cent – were firing their weapons in a contact with the enemy.

Marshall claimed that this non-firing was due to an in-built 'fear of aggression' common to all humans, that, *'an inner and usually unrealized resistance toward killing a fellow man that he will not of his own volition take life if it is possible to turn away from that responsibility'*. Although Marshall's methodology has been largely discredited, there is still some truth in his findings. Soldiers were, and are, doing what the American military sometimes terms 'posturing' or what William F. Owen calls *'displacement activities'*.

Owen told the author that Marshall was *'half right based on being 100% wrong'*. What he was seeing in his results was not that soldiers were not necessarily not firing because of some aversion to killing, as advanced by the likes of Grossman, but that the infantrymen, being human beings despite the occasional doubt, were experiencing natural and wholly normal fear and were doing anything they could to appear to be contributing to the fight whilst reducing their personal risk. Owen cautioned: *'Most firing (is) a displacement activity not connected with actually killing the enemy.'*

Operational researcher Leo Murray explains displacement activities for the infantryman as: *'Jobs like assisting crew-served weapons, carrying ammunition, repairing equipment, fetching water, manning radios or helping casualties can all slip into being displacement activities; simple jobs that a man can do instead of the really hard job he is supposed to be doing.'* The really hard job is the job of placing effective fire on the enemy.

Some studies have characterised the human response to combat somewhat over simplistically as *'fight, flee, or freeze'*, which doesn't take into account the idea of these displacement activities nor situations where freeze can move to fight. Combat is undoubtedly amongst the most frightening things a human can experience. Not surprisingly, few memoirs mention incidents where infantrymen freeze or flee. One that does is *Attack State Red* by Colonel Richard Kemp, an Iraq, Northern Ireland and Bosnia veteran, who co-wrote the book with journalist Chris Hughes.

The soldier in question, had deployed as a member of the Royal Anglian's Battlegroup to Afghanistan in 2007, and had been nearly catatonic with fear earlier in the battle, but was now providing security for the passage of a critically wounded infantryman when he was surprised by *'a tall thick-set bearded man wearing a black turban . . . and holding an AK-47 assault rifle'*. The British soldier *'had never shot anyone before or even seen anyone shot. This was a nightmare. His heart* thumped into his chest. He knew what he had to do. But could he? Could he? No time to think.'

He fires, *'spitting out a 5.56mm bullet that hit the man square in the chest. He went straight down, and [the soldier] fired twenty more rounds at him in rapid succession'*. His shooting stopped the infiltration of the insurgent onto the flank of the platoon. This is a fine example of what good training, and the interpersonal bonds formed by the members of the platoon, can do to reduce and eventually negate the fear impulse. The soldier was still undoubtedly petrified, but he fell back on his training and his psychological need to protect his mates.

*   *   *

Let us now talk briefly about the organisation of modern infantry and how small arms plays into that organisation. It also plays heavily into the selection of infantry small arms and their combat effectiveness. Before we discuss the formation of the infantry, we do need to identify that different armies use different terms.

In particular, most former Commonwealth nations such as the UK, Canada and Australia use the term 'section' to describe the basic building block of the infantry rather than 'squad' which is typically an American term or used by armies that have been trained or associated with the United States. We will use both terms interchangeably. Whatever the exact term used, all armies now split into two or more equally sized fire teams.

Major V. Sattler, CD, and Captain M. O'Leary, CD, writing in the Canadian Army's professional journal in 2010 spelled out the advantage of the infantry section subdivided into two elements, commonly known as fire teams: *'The infantry's ten-soldier section, organized as support and assault elements, permitted the section commander to deploy a fire support element to cover the movement of his assault group. Such an arrangement allowed the section to conduct its own manoeuvre/movement supported by fire to gain a position of advantage.'*

In many armies this ten-man group was reduced through ever-present manpower and budgetary pressures to eight or nine. In the US Army for instance, a squad is formed (on paper at least and we'll get to that in a moment) of two fire teams of four soldiers each, commanded by a squad leader. In the British and Australian armies, that squad leader is rolled into the fire teams resulting in an eight-man section. Typically, each of these fire teams were equipped with a mix of small arms: two soldiers would carry assault rifles, one would carry a rifle mounting a grenade launcher, and one would carry a light machine gun (LMG) or similar automatic weapon, principally designed to suppress the enemy. The idea behind such a weapons mix was that the fire team could provide its own organic suppressive fire using the LMG and UGL, whilst the rifle-armed soldiers could administer aimed fire on point targets or conduct close assaults into enemy positions, previously suppressed by the other half of the fire team. Modern infantry sections can direct an impressive amount of firepower compared to their Second World War counterparts.

The late military historian Paddy Griffiths commented in 1991 on the change to fire teams from larger sections:

> Infantry is likely to become more specialised and fight in smaller groups, albeit packing more firepower than ever ... A task which would once have required a platoon of 30–40 men may now be carried out by a section of 8 to 12 men, each divided into two or three 'fireteams'. An example of such a development in today's British Army is the 10-man Warrior-mounted infantry section, which boasts 10 fully automatic weapons, compared with the three machine guns held in 1945 by a British platoon (or two in a 1914 infantry battalion) and six in a 1945 German platoon.

Such groupings also allowed a significant amount of tactical flexibility as LMGs could be grouped to provide a base of fire for assaults on enemy positions. The original structure, when Britain went to an eight-man section split into two fire teams, was based on the SA80 family adoption with the L86A1 LSW (light support weapon) providing the base of fire that had been the role of the GPMG and all other soldiers armed with L85A1 rifles. Interestingly, a 1990 report from the US, *The Infantry Rifle Squad: Size Is Not the Only Problem*, argued that in testing having two automatic weapons like the LSW *'does not axiomatically mean more effective firepower'*.

British soldiers, Helmand Province, Afghanistan 2007. The lead man carries a SUSAT-equipped 5.56 × 45mm L85A2, the grenadier carries the UGL or L85A2 with underslung L123A2 grenade launcher, whilst the last carries the 5.56 × 45mm L110A2 Minimi Para LMG.
(*US Army, Corporal John Scott Rafoss*)

The report concluded that without direct supervision of both weapons, '*much of the ammunition is not effectively directed*' and recommended that one LMG and one grenade launcher be assigned per squad. '[*This*] *would provide the most effective firepower to allow the* [*infantry squad's*] *riflemen to assault an enemy's position or to keep an attacking enemy at bay.*'

The British Army infantry section comprises eight men at the time of writing. This section is further divided into two equally sized sub-units known as fire teams. One fire team is commanded by a corporal, the other by a lance corporal and are similarly armed and equipped, although some differences may be seen with one team carrying a marksman rifle, for instance, whilst the other carries a GPMG. Three of these sections make up a platoon when a small command element is added. This typically is composed of the platoon commander, most often a junior lieutenant; his signaller or radio operator; the platoon sergeant who is second in command of the platoon and responsible for resupply and medical evacuation in the field; a medic and a rifleman to operate the 60mm commando mortar attached to each platoon (which appears to be being currently withdrawn from service).

When deployed in Afghanistan, a typical British Army infantry platoon will also be buoyed by the likes of interpreters, mortar fire controllers, JTACs (Joint Tactical Air Controllers who manage the ever-crucial air support), snipers, engineers and EOD (Explosive Ordnance Disposal) operators. At other times, particularly when under-strength due to casualties, leave and similar attrition, the platoon may be much leaner with only three to four fire teams available. These may operate as formations known as a 'multiple' of one enlarged section (the term originating in Northern Ireland where it denoted an *ad hoc* patrol structure of fire teams that were known as 'bricks').

The 'multiple' concept came into its own again in Afghanistan where a reasonably full-strength platoon would be split into two 'multiples' of three fire teams each, with one commanded by the platoon leader and the other by the platoon sergeant. This compromise was felt to provide sufficient mutual support to allow bounding movement (a process wherein one fire team moves whilst under covering fire or overwatch by a second fire team. The role is reversed to provide a continual movement to contact with 'one foot on the ground' and also enough intrinsic firepower to deal with most contingencies.) It also meant that if a casualty was incurred, one 'multiple' could deal with extracting the unfortunate soldier whilst the other provided covering fire against enemy firing points.

In terms of weapons carried, the infantry fire team will have two L85A2 assault rifles (otherwise known as the SA80A2), one L110 series LMG (the Minimi which is currently being withdrawn from service), and one L85A2 with an underslung 40mm L123A2 single-shot grenade launcher fitted. In Afghanistan, all will carry pistols as secondary back-up weapons. One of the L85A2s has been frequently swapped out for the GPMG when available and, after 2010, the L129A1 designated marksman rifle began to be issued at a rate of one per section.

The French followed a similar tack to that recommended in the US report by splitting their squads into a close-range manoeuvre element and a supporting element. However ungainly this looks on paper, it seems to work well for them in both Afghanistan and Mali. The two elements are known as the 300-metre and 600-metre teams. One is designed to fight the closer range battle, including assaulting objectives, and thus is equipped with assault rifles and disposable anti-tank rockets, whilst the 600-metre team is armed with a 5.56 × 45mm Minimi LMG, rifle grenades and, more recently, an underslung grenade launcher. Marksmen and machine gunners can be attached as needed from a platoon support group.

The USMC has traditionally operated in large squads of three four-man fire teams and a squad leader for thirteen men in total. There are indications that they may either increase this to fifteen with the addition of new billets for designated UGV/UAV (unmanned ground vehicle/unmanned aerial vehicle) operators or reduce the squad size to twelve for three evenly manned fire teams. In terms of weapons, all but the leaders would be equipped with the M27 with one per fire team fitted with a bipod and acting as the automatic rifleman. One M320 standalone grenade launcher would be issued to each team. The three fire teams would be designated as assault (and equipped with a Carl Gustav 84mm recoilless rifle when necessary), support and security, led by a three-man command element.

Currently all Marine riflemen are armed with the M4A1. An M27 is assigned to each fire team as is an M203 or M320 grenade launcher, although the M27 is beginning to fully replace the M4A1 for all riflemen. One rifleman acts as the designated marksman and is supplied with the 7.62 × 51mm M110, a semi-automatic rifle equipped with a magnified optic that is due to be replaced by another M27 variant. Note the lack of LMGs/SAWs and 7.62 × 51mm machine guns which are held at company level by a separate weapons platoon.

There are others, such as the Finnish Army, who include two 7.62 × 54mm PKM medium machine guns in each of their nine-man sections. Intriguingly the Finns do not issue grenade launchers as the rounds are negated by the terrain (forests that impede indirect fire and often heavy snow that literally dampens their effectiveness). Other armies have also maintained an integral medium machine gun. The Irish Army for instance has always deployed a 7.62 × 51mm MAG58 in each infantry section. Interestingly they do not issue an LMG.

Once the infantry section was ensconced within an armoured personnel carrier (APC like the venerable M113 series), or the more modern infantry fighting vehicle (IFV such as the FV510 Warrior, M2A3 Bradley or the Russian BMP-2), the strength of the unit diminished as soldiers were required to crew the vehicle and protect it from attack or booby trapping whilst the remainder of the infantry were dismounted. A current Canadian Army ten-man section, for instance, features only seven dismountable infantry supported by three serving as vehicle crew in their LAV III armoured vehicles.

This impact on fighting strength was recognised by some armies which decided to crew vehicles organically rather than use the traditional mechanised infantry approach. MRAPs (Mine Resistant Ambush Protected vehicles, best exemplified by the British Mastiff or American MaxxPro) and PMVs (Protected

Mobility Vehicles like the Australian Bushmaster) in Afghanistan were crewed by soldiers specifically trained and deployed to conduct that function and thus did not reduce the numbers of infantry soldiers available.

Mechanised infantry sections have also shrunk due to the design of some of their rides. Perhaps inconceivably, the likes of the British Warrior is not capable of transporting a full infantry section. There is also the question of what a dismounted infantry squad or section can carry as compared to its mechanised counterpart in either wheeled or tracked vehicles. Mechanised infantry have the very real advantage of a safe repository for ammunition resupply (in the normally armoured vehicle that has transported them to the battlespace) whilst his dismounted brethren must rely upon, at best, the platoon sergeant arriving at the opportune time with sufficient stocks on a quad bike (all-terrain-vehicle) or similar.

As alluded to earlier, the reader is reminded to keep in mind that all such organisational structures are subject to change once units are deployed to a conflict zone. Tactical considerations such as the role envisioned for the unit (units may strip soldiers from squads to form fire support groups, for example), manpower (even units that arrive in-theatre with a full complement of soldiers are soon reduced by wounded, non-combat injuries, sickness, leave, training courses and promotions) and even the difficulties of shipping replacements for combat

Dutch soldiers in Uruzgan Province, Afghanistan 2008. The soldier to the left carries a Minimi Para with Elcan optic, whilst the soldier to the right carries the Dutch variant of the 5.56 × 45mm Colt Canada C7 with Elcan M145 optic and AG36 grenade launcher. (*mindef.nl, Richard Frigge*)

Scout Sniper Marines in Helmand Province, Afghanistan 2014. They are operating a well-worn .50BMG Barrett M107. Note the 'dope card' (data on previous engagements) taped to the stock. (*USMC, Sgt. Joseph Scanlan*)

losses (such as in environments where there is a lack of helicopters, or there is a significant or persistent anti-aircraft threat) all play their part in ensuring that few infantry platoons remain fully manned for long.

In these cases, it's common to see a greater proportion of support weapons being carried in favour of the standard assault rifle. Soldiers have always tried to maximise their available firepower, from American 82nd Airborne soldiers scrounging BARs to supplement their .30 cal air-cooled machine guns in France in 1944, to British Paras almost forty years later carrying double the issued rate of GPMGs in the Falklands (with one battalion also getting their hands on as many L4 Bren light machine guns as they could to further enhance their firepower).

From organisational structure, to reducing the soldier's physical load, to the ballistic performance of certain rounds against both the human body and armour plate, all of these considerations and more will be examined at various points in further detail throughout the book. At this point, the reader should simply be aware that catch-all terms and buzzwords such as 'increasing lethality' or 'maintaining overmatch' engender far more than calibre or range. Many disparate elements combine to affect an infantryman's success on the battlefield with his or her small arms. Hopefully we can shed some further light on these as we examine each broad class of infantry small arm in turn.

# CHAPTER ONE

# COMBAT PISTOLS

## Overview

Simply put, service pistols are at the absolute bottom of the food-chain in terms of military small arms procurement. For the most part, they are a weapon that will never be fired in anger. It's rare too that sufficient time is devoted to training soldiers in their use. Most will go through their entire military careers often having only accomplished a basic course for familiarity during their initial training and perhaps the odd refresher, particularly prior to deploying on operations.

Apart from special operations forces, the pistol is generally considered as a weapon of convenience and a last resort. Crew-served weapons gunners are often issued a pistol rather than a carbine or rifle to give them a close-range defensive capability whilst adding minimal additional weight to already crippling combat loads. In fact, one American Iraq veteran told the author that within his infantry unit: *'The only personnel issued a sidearm in an infantry line squad in my experience were the M240B gunners which were issued an M9.'*

For many years, pistols were also considered a status symbol for officers, although their indisputable effect of attracting enemy sniper fire put paid to such notions in modern warfare. In the militaries of developing nations however the pistol is still seen as a privilege of rank and an obvious signifier of the importance of the individual who wields it. There are also interesting associated cultural dimensions to pistol employment. Pistols, for instance, held an intriguing place in the Iraqi state under Saddam Hussein's dictatorship – citizens were often cowed by their very appearance as they knew executions would likely follow, whereas the much more common AK-47 caused no such fear. After Hussein's downfall in 2003, Coalition Forces found that unruly mobs would retreat in the face of pistols being displayed, whilst the presence of heavier weapons was routinely ignored.

Although in the big picture they are very much the least important of all military weapons systems, they elicit considerable debate and passion amongst firearms enthusiasts. Arguments about calibres and types rage across the internet and in the gun press. It's difficult to ascertain why such passions are aroused by such a seldom employed weapon although Hollywood has played its part.

It must be reiterated though that pistols make for very poor killers. They fire small bullets, are accurate only to comparatively very short ranges (combat distances for the average user is probably 10 metres) and have exceedingly short barrels by their very nature. Barrel length effects velocity, meaning pistol calibre rounds do not create the secondary or temporary wound channel that rifle calibres do, thus limiting their terminal effectiveness. Put simply, pistols are not the weapon of choice if you're expecting to run into bad people.

A blood spattered 9 × 19mm SIG Sauer P226 used by British Gurkhas in Helmand Province, Afghanistan, 2011. The blood is not from insurgents but from sacrificial goats slaughtered for Dashain, a Nepalese religious festival. The blood is sprinkled on the weapons for good luck.
*(ISAF, MC1 Kurt P. Wesseling III)*

Today, pistols are principally carried by armoured vehicle and aircrew as a personal weapon should they be forced to dismount under fire, for instance if their vehicle is immobilised. Despite carrying pistols, most vehicle crews will also have a number of shortened carbines on board, be they M4s, AKS-74Us or the L22A2 (being the shortened version of the L85A2/A3 assault rifle carried by most British infantrymen), which will provide far better stand-off range and terminal ballistics than any handgun.

In the narrow laneways and alleys in the Green Zone of Afghanistan's Helmand Province, pistols also proved their worth for vehicle crews who were forced to engage targets at virtually point-blank range. UK standard operating procedures in Afghanistan explicitly called for Mastiff and Jackal vehicle crews to be ready to use their pistols to defend their vehicles: *'Vehicle crews should continue to carry a pistol that provides a degree of protection close in to the vehicle. This is especially true when operating in and around Karez tunnels where a single fighter armed with an RPG can emerge at very close range and engage.'*

In Iraq, pistols also proved very useful for drivers, particularly in open top vehicles like the Land Rover WMIK (Weapons Mounted Installation Kit) or the much-derided Snatch. British veteran Jake Wood wrote: *'I remembered the streets in Iraq when I had been a driver, when every HAC [Honourable Artillery Company] driver had an issued pistol strapped to their chest as their only realistic means of self-defence while in that seat.'* Many American and Coalition troops in Afghanistan would wear a pistol holstered on their body armour whilst conducting mounted operations in vehicles. It is the only weapon that can be reliably fired one-handed from the close confines of a vehicle. With suicide bombers a constant threat, issuing drivers in Iraq with pistols was common sense.

As noted, pilots and aircrew typically carry a pistol to provide some meagre protection against capture, particularly after the recent barbaric treatment of captured Jordanian and Syrian pilots by Islamic State and related insurgent groups. In the case of a Russian aviator shot down in Syria in early 2018, the pilot used his Cold War vintage fully-automatic 9 × 18mm Stechkin APS machine pistol in a desperate and one-sided last stand against encircling insurgents.

In terms of the pistol as a weapon of last resort for the infantryman, it has been issued as a kind of insurance policy to a number of armies deploying to Iraq and Afghanistan in recent years. Prior to this, pistols were a rarity within the infantry, apart from the aforementioned use by officers and even then most carried rifles. The Australians and British began the trend with a mandate for all deployed serving members to be carrying at least a pistol at all times, even within the confines of notionally secure areas. The Americans even decreed that all personnel should carry their service rifle at all times, including within base areas to guard against so-called 'insider' or 'green on blue' attacks by turncoat Afghan or Iraqi personnel.

In Helmand Province, southern Afghanistan, the British Army realised that their infantry needed a pistol for use whilst clearing compounds. Experiences in 2006 and 2007 during the vicious 'break-in battles' saw the need for marksmen and snipers in particular to be issued a sidearm to defend themselves at close range as their L98A1 and L115A3 bolt action sniper rifles were simply too slow and unwieldy to deploy whilst moving down alleyways and through buildings. A pair of snipers from the Royal Anglians' Viking Battlegroup experienced exactly this type of encounter during their 2007 tour – both were forced to employ their pistols to deadly effect when insurgents surprised them at extremely close range inside compounds.

Pistols were also used when investigating tunnels and rat-runs employed by the insurgents where even the relatively compact L85A2 rifle would be difficult to employ. Combat engineers and EOD [Explosive Ordnance Disposal] personnel would often be deployed to clear tunnel entrances armed only with a flashlight, mine detector and pistol in a flashback to the Vietnam-era 'tunnel rats'. Searching the Afghan Karez (semi-underground irrigation channels) proved the pistol's worth. One account from the Queen's Dragoon Guards notes: *'Armed with a pistol, torch and Vallon he set out through the overgrown and sewage strewn tunnel. After only a couple of minutes he came across a hessian sack filled with ammo, drugs and explosives.'*

One Australian combat engineer found himself face to face in a terrifying encounter with an Afghan insurgent armed with an AK-47 as he explored just such a tunnel in 2013. Armed only with his 9 × 19mm Heckler and Koch USP fitted with a weapon light, both opened fire simultaneously at point-blank range.

Newly issued British Army 9 × 19mm Glock 17 in issue drop holster.
(*Open Government License v3.0, Andrew Linnett*)

The Australian was hit in the leg, however his compatriots quickly killed the insurgent as he attempted to flee.

Even non-combatants may be forced to employ the pistol in certain extreme scenarios in today's asymmetric wars. Veteran journalist Christina Lamb experienced exactly such circumstances during an embed with 3 Para in Helmand in 2006 for the British newspaper, *The Sunday Times*: '*"Have you ever used a pistol?" yelled Sergeant-Major Mick Bolton amid the Kalashnikov fire and bursts from a machinegun as we ran across a baked-mud field and dived for cover. "If it comes down to it, everyone's going to have to fight."*'

Although most armies today issue relatively modern pistol designs, this is a recent phenomenon. Perhaps surprisingly, most armies maintained stocks of Second World War issue pistols as their general-issue sidearms up until the 1990s, and in many cases far beyond. The British still carried the 9 × 19mm L9A1 Browning Hi-Power into the twenty-first century, as did the Israelis, Australians, Indians, Peruvians, Canadians and nearly one hundred other nations around the world. Even the Argentines carried the Browning in their 1982 conflict with the British over the Falkland Islands. The Germans too used a slightly modified variant of their famous wartime 9 × 19mm Walther P38 (known as the P1) up until the 1990s.

A number of nations had, however, developed post-war designs to replace their Second World War vintage sidearms. France was one with the MAB M1950 (or MAC50) in 9 × 19mm, a 9-round magazine design influenced by the Hi-Power. Some elements of the French military also adopted the MAB PA-15, again in 9 × 19mm but with a larger 15-round magazine and closer to modern perceptions of a service pistol. Russia was another, introducing the 9 × 18mm Makarov PM (Pistolet Makarova) in 1951 to replace the venerable wartime Tokarev TT33.

Spain had adopted a Colt M1911 derivative, the 9 × 19mm Star Pistola Modelo B Super, based on an earlier design in the unusual 9mm Largo chambering and featuring an 8-round magazine. It was later replaced within the Spanish Army by the high capacity 9 × 19mm Llama M82 in 1980 and the 9 × 19mm Star M30 in 1990 for the Navy and paramilitary police. All of the Spanish designs were domestically designed and produced.

In truth, however, there was little evolution in the field of military pistols post-war. As can be seen, most of the designs adopted were based on the tried and true Browning action and innovated only through increasing magazine capacities; what forced manufacturers to finally look at real innovation was the German police pistol trials of the mid-1970s. These issued the first new specifications for a truly modern combat pistol, requiring safety, accuracy and reliability above all else. Heckler and Koch, Walther, SIG Sauer and Mauser all entered a number of models into these trials.

The Mauser HSP design was the only one to be withdrawn. Variants of the H&K P7M8 (known as the PSP at the time and revolutionary in its 'squeeze cocker' design – the weapon would only engage the firing pin when grasped in the correct manner, releasing the pressure on the 'squeeze cocker' disengaged the firing pin), the Walther P5 and the SIG Sauer P225 passed the trials and were

The Australian issue 9 × 19mm Browning Hi-Power – the Self-Loading Pistol, 9mm Mk3 – in recoil. (*Commonwealth of Australia, POIS Rick Prideaux*)

issued to regional German police forces. These were the first true modern combat pistols designed from the ground up to incorporate the lessons learnt from the numerous Second World War and post-war designs. One other design, and one that would revolutionise the military combat pistol, was only a few years down the road.

The Austrian military was searching for a new service pistol to replace their Walther P38s and convened a set of tests in 1980 for the Pistole 80, their requirement for a reliable high capacity 9 × 19mm design. Amongst the weapons put forward for trial were the P7M13 (a modified version of the P7M8 with a 13-round capacity), the SIG Sauer P220 and P225, the Beretta 92S and the Steyr GB. One outlier, Gaston Glock, a man more used to manufacturing plastic curtain rods than pistols but with some experience in military procurement, also applied with his design, the Glock 17 (allegedly named after the pistol being the seventeenth patent the Glock company had submitted, rather than the number of rounds in the magazine).

Gaston Glock's design, type classified by the Austrian military as the P80, won the trials and was adopted in 1983. Denmark soon followed in adopting the Glock the following year. Norway and Sweden were the next two European nations to adopt the Austrian pistol. The Glock 17 was revolutionary in that it was made primarily from polymer. It was not alone in this form of construction – the Steyr GB was similarly futuristic in its construction and before that, the early 1970s Heckler and Koch VP70 design had been similarly largely plastic. Where the

A Swedish soldier employing his issue 9 × 19mm Glock 17 in a training exercise from the turret of his armoured vehicle. (*US Army, Gertrud Zach*)

Glock had the advantage was in its simple reliability and minimum of moving parts. There was no external manual safety on the Glock – instead it used a patented 'safe action' trigger safety. Glock explains in its marketing:

> The trigger safety is incorporated into the trigger in the form of a lever and when in the forward position, blocks the trigger from moving rearward. To fire the pistol, the trigger safety and the trigger itself, must be deliberately depressed at the same time. If the trigger safety is not depressed, the trigger will not move rearwards and allow the pistol to fire.

This lack of a traditional external safety would actually limit the Glock's adoption for many years as traditionalists viewed the weapon as unsafe for military use. Today, however, it is by far the most common combat pistol issued across the globe.

\* \* \*

Whilst the Pistole 80 was a rare example of small arms procurement done right, ineptitude, politics and inter-service bickering would mar the next large-scale military pistol procurement. The US military were one of the first non-European nations to attempt to replace their own ageing sidearm, the classic .45ACP Colt M1911A1, with a more modern design in 1985. The process of identifying and testing a replacement is worth exploring in some detail. It illustrates the complexities, both technological and political, in small arms procurement for a large, first-world military. Not surprisingly, similar tribulations emerged decades later during the next attempt by the US military to replace their sidearm. But first, let's look back to the 1970s and how a US Air Force (USAF) request for an improved .38 Special cartridge led eventually to a new 9 × 19mm service pistol.

It all began innocently enough in 1977 when the US Air Force requested a budget appropriation to develop an improved .38 Special load for its Smith & Wesson Model 15 revolvers carried by aircrew. Why did pilots carry .38 revolvers rather than semi-automatic pistols? Revolvers could be more easily operated one-handed (no need to work the slide to chamber a round) and USAF wartime studies had identified that aircrew often injured an arm or hand during crashes or ejections, so the revolver made a lot of sense.

During budget meetings for the improved .38 round, the House Defense Appropriations Sub-Committee wondered, not unreasonably but without con-sidering the specific needs of the aircrews, whether all of the services should be issuing the same basic pistol to maximise the benefits of simplified logistics and associated costs. The sub-committee discovered that some twenty-five different sidearms were in service within the US military and were appalled. The chair of the sub-committee commented at the time: 'The current proliferation of hand-guns and handgun ammunition in Armed Forces inventory is intolerable.' Instead of releasing funding for the developmental work on the improved .38 Special load, the sub-committee directed that a selection programme be implemented to identify and procure a new standard sidearm for all of the US military to replace the .45ACP Colt M1911A1 with a weapon in the NATO standard calibre of 9 × 19mm Parabellum.

The task was given to the then newly established Joint Service Small Arms Program (JSSAP) Committee but would be carried out under JSSAP auspices by the USAF's Armament Laboratory (AFAL). The AFAL issued a list of require-ments for the new pistol; it had to be 9 × 19mm Parabellum for NATO compat-ibility with a magazine capacity of at least 13 rounds, be fitted with an external, thumb-operated, safety catch and slide lock (that would lock the slide open on an empty magazine) and an 8-in-5,000 Mean Rounds Between Failures (MRBF) rate (simply the number of rounds fired between stoppages or 'jams'). One can see that the Hi-Power was perhaps the baseline for these requirements.

Examples of the issue M1911A1 and the Model 15 revolver acted as controls. From the first stage of the competition, focusing on accuracy and reliability, the Beretta M92S-1 (a modernised M1951 Brigadier), the Browning DA (Double Action) and FA (Fast Action), modernised versions of the venerable Hi-Power; the Colt SSP (Stainless Steel Pistol), an improved 1911 chambered for the 9 × 19mm; the Smith & Wesson 459 and the Spanish Star M28 all passed the 'down-select'. From these contenders, three potentials emerged to complete the endurance testing phase – the Beretta, Smith & Wesson and Fabrique Nationale Browning designs – and that is where the programme ground to an inglorious halt.

The Air Force trials attracted extensive criticism, mainly from the US Army, at least some of which was valid, but much seemed to have been designed to influ-ence the competition and maintain the status quo of the issue M1911A1. The trials ammunition, for instance, was of poor quality which contributed to the failures of a number of otherwise reliable pistols like the Heckler & Koch P9S (a suppressed version of which was moving into service with the US Navy SEALs at the time) and the Star Model 28 (which was later adopted by elements of the Spanish military in 1989 in a product-improved version known as the Model 30). Both were otherwise excellent pistols which were hamstrung by poor ammunition.

The US Army was also critical of the testing procedures which saw their issue M1911A1 eliminated early and called for the tests to be redone. Central to their argument was that old M1911A1 magazines had been employed which resulted in a less than stellar MRBF rate. Magazines have always been the 'Achilles Heel' of the Colt design (and many others) and old, well-worn magazines virtually guaranteed failure. The Army seemed to view this as something of an Air Force plot to eliminate their beloved .45.

A second round of trials was begun in 1981, again under the Joint Services Small Arms Programme but this time administered by the Army, although the winner would become the new joint service pistol for all four services. The Army trials team developed a staggering list of eighty-five individual requirements that the new pistol would have to pass to gain acceptance – again one now wonders whether this was deliberately designed to fail each applicant as early as possible.

Wary of the process, only four manufacturers put forward test weapons for the trials after the initial AFAL debacle – Beretta and Smith & Wesson with the M92S-1 and 459 respectively, Heckler and Koch with the P7M13, and a new

A US Army NCO works the slide of his issue 9 × 19mm M9 Beretta to chamber a round. The M9 is being replaced by the M17 (P320). (*US Army, Sgt. Jonathan M. Cobert*)

contender, SIG Sauer with its P226 which had been developed from their success-ful P225 specifically for the Army trials, featuring a new 15-round capacity versus the 8-round capacity of the P225.

All of this was to no avail. Predictably, the Army programme announced in the following year that all of the pistols submitted for trial had failed. Of the stagger-ing seventy-two 'mandatory' requirements and thirteen 'desirable' requirements specified by the Army trials team, not one of the pistols met or exceeded more than a dozen. The result only fuelled rumours that the tests had been destined for failure from the beginning with the Army doing its utmost to keep its American produced M1911A1s in service. Whether any political lobbying from interested parties, including manufacturers, shaped the results is unknown but was certainly suspected in some quarters.

The official statement read:

> The Army, in its role as Defense Department executive agent for 9mm hand-gun procurement, has cancelled the procurement. It was not possible to make an award because the submitted weapon samples substantially failed to meet the essential requirements contained in the procurement solicitation. The Department of Defense intends to re-examine its requirements for a new handgun.

An incredulous Congress and its Government Accounting Office (GAO) ordered the Army to again redo the tests. Somewhat amusingly, to 'encourage' the Army to quickly comply, Congress put a stop on all purchases of .45ACP ammunition and parts until such time as the new trials were scheduled. These new tests would be known as the XM9 Service Pistol Trials. In 1983, they began. The Colt SSP, the Beretta Model 92SB-F (an improved version of the successful M92S-1), the S&W 459, the SIG Sauer P226, the Fabrique Nationale DA and the H&K P7M13 were re-entered into the competition by their respective manufacturers. Several new entrants also joined the trials – the Walther P88 and the polymer framed Steyr GB.

In this third chapter of the overwrought saga, the Beretta and SIG Sauer designs were the only ones to emerge having apparently passed all essential criteria. Beretta won the contract on price by offering a lower unit cost than SIG Sauer. In point of fact, however, SIG Sauer had offered the lowest price initially only to be undercut by Beretta. Along with price, Beretta had already established a US manufacturing facility, a key requirement for fulfilment of the contract. The Italian firm subsequently won the contract for what would become known as the M9 with their Model 92SB-F and 315,930 pistols were ordered. This resulted in official protests by SIG Sauer, H&K and a lawsuit against the government by Smith & Wesson. Both of the protests were dismissed but the Smith & Wesson legal action resulted in a Congressional mandate that, whilst the initial tranche of the Beretta M9 order would stand, any future procurements of combat pistols, including further stocks of the M9, would be required to undergo a further set of new trials before proceeding.

Yet another set of competitive tests was authorised in 1988 ahead of an M9 order for an additional 57,000 pistols. Christened the XM10 Service Pistol Trials, most manufacturers declined to enter. Only the Beretta, an improved S&W 459 and a sole new entrant, the Ruger P85, joined the competition. Both the S&W and Ruger designs failed during testing and the Beretta was awarded the new contract.

The M9 has soldiered on through multiple wars although often dogged by complaints about its magazines (the Army purchased cheaper non-original manufacturer magazines that commonly failed). It was not a well-liked weapon, but it appears to have been reliable enough for its role. After decade long deployments in Iraq and Afghanistan, many US military small arms were becoming worn out (most visibly their stock of M249 squad automatic weapons as we will discuss later, but also the M9 pistols) and this led to the issue of a new set of trial criteria to identify a replacement.

The US Army conducted a failed procurement programme to replace the issue 9mm M9 with what was termed the Modular Handgun System or MHS. The MHS programme itself began in 2008 again with a US Air Force requirement for a new joint service pistol for all four services. The programme was on the back-burner until it began to be championed by the Army in 2014 with a set of requirements issued to manufacturers in 2015. The eventual weapon that would be selected from the competitive tender would be termed the XM17 with the X precursor dropped once the pistol entered general service (X is US military terminology denoting an 'experimental' or trial weapon).

By early 2016, twelve manufacturers had expressed an interest in joining the MHS trials. These apparently included the striker-fired Beretta APX developed expressly for the MHS solicitation; the polymer-framed Czech CZ P-09; Fabrique Nationale's FiveseveN Mk 2 in its propriety $5.7 \times 28$mm (which from the outset must have been considered an outlier due to its calibre); the Smith & Wesson M&P (Military & Police) which has proven popular within US law enforcement but has not to-date been adopted by any military; Glock's $9 \times 19$mm MHS and .40 S&W Glock 23M, and the SIG Sauer P320. Intriguingly, no calibre specification was mandated and thus $9 \times 19$mm, .40 S&W and $5.7 \times 28$mm designs were entered.

Beside the APX, both the P320 and the Glock MHS (based on a Glock 19 variant known as the Glock 19X which featured a 19-sized slide and barrel and Glock 17-sized frame) were developed specifically to meet the requirements of the programme. The down-select eventually identified just two contenders, the Glock and SIG designs.

The delays in procuring a new sidearm became increasingly public when US Army Chief of Staff General Mark Milley, who was obviously frustrated by the procurement process, famously exclaimed in April 2016: '*You give me $17 million on a credit card, and I'll call Cabela's* [a US sporting goods chain] *tonight, and I'll outfit every soldier, sailor, airman and Marine with a pistol for $17 million. And I'll get a discount on a bulk buy.*' He placed the procurement in stark perspective,

The 9 × 19mm Glock 19X developed for and entered into the Modular Handgun System trials won by SIG Sauer. *(USMC, by Lance Cpl Colton Brownlee)*

*'… We are not talking about nuclear subs or going to the moon here. We are talking about a pistol.'*

The official US Army announcement eventually stated:

> The US Army awarded the Modular Handgun System (MHS) contract on January 19, 2017 to SIG Sauer, Inc. The caliber of the weapon is 9mm, and the XM17 MHS handgun is a variant of the SIG Sauer model P320. It is 'Coyote Brown' in color and has interchangeable hand grips and is ambidextrous allowing the user to tailor the ergonomics to best fit their hands and optimize their performance. The contract allows the Army and other services to procure SIG Sauer's proposed XM1152 Full Metal Jacket, XM1153 Special Purpose ammunition and training rounds; their proposed full size and compact variants of the MHS; and ancillary components. The contract ceiling is $580M which is sufficient to procure Army requirements, other service requirements, and potential Foreign Military Sales requirements.

Glock launched a complaint to the GAO, arguing: *'By not completing the testing on both proposals on a competitive basis, the Army never determined which pistol would better meet the warfighter's needs.'* This related to the testing of the reliability of the compact variant requested in the initial submission, a process the Army apparently ignored along with alleged discrepancies in the number of expected 'awards' (the opportunity for multiple procurement tranches), although it's difficult to envision a situation where both the SIG and Glock contenders would be

9 × 19mm M17 MHS (P320) fitted with weapon light/laser in full recoil.
(*US Army, Sgt. Christopher Gallagher*)

awarded a contract. The full seventeen-page GAO report is available on the internet for those who suffer trouble sleeping, but the end result was that the Glock complaint was dismissed. The appointment of SIG was also no doubt aided by price – at $169 million, some $103 million cheaper than Glock; the SIG entry was *'overall the best value to the government'*.

The USMC has now signed on to also adopt the M17 with a planned purchase of 35,000 pistols beginning in late 2018. These will replace the mixed fleet of M9s, Glock 19s and .45ACP platforms employed by various units within the Marine Corps. Only MARSOC (Marine Special Operations Command), the Marines' special operators, will keep their Glocks, at least for now. They had argued that the Glock was better suited to their needs than either the M9 or the M45 MEUSOC and had been allowed to procure the Austrian weapon to match its use by other US military special operations forces.

\* \* \*

Whilst the US acquisition of the P320 is the largest such purchase in recent times, other militaries are slowly replacing their issue weapons with more modern designs. The British, for instance, adopted a modified Glock 17 whilst the Canadians are looking to replace their Brownings in the next few years. Smaller nations like New Zealand have completed pistol replacement programmes with far less of the drama of the American programmes mainly due to the relative size of their militaries. New Zealand was also one of the few nations to replace their

Brownings early with a more modern design, the SIG Sauer P226, in 1992 before adopting the Glock as its issue service pistol in 2015.

Many European nations soldier on with Glock, H&K or SIG Sauer designs, whilst in Central and South America the Glock is emerging as the weapon of choice to replace a bewildering variety of sidearms. In Asia and the Middle East too, the Glock largely reigns supreme although Česká Zbrojovka's (CZ) recent announcement of the establishment of a factory presence in Egypt and significant orders from the Egyptian security forces, may upset the balance. CZ are making inroads in Africa too, challenging Glock's dominance. Globally however, the three major players will continue for the foreseeable future to be Glock, SIG Sauer and Heckler and Koch.

The Russians and Chinese cannot be forgotten, even though their current issue pistols are not widely exported. The numbers of service members under arms that both countries can muster dwarfs Western militaries and thus are amongst the largest users of pistols. Intriguingly, as we will discuss in a moment, both saw combat body armour as the key challenge to overcome with their latest issue pistols. One, Russia, accomplished their objective to penetrate Level III body armour and ballistic helmets by developing a bullet that operates at high velocity with a steel core. The Chinese People's Liberation Army or PLA followed Western developments in the field of Personal Defense Weapons and introduced a new small calibre round, also featuring a steel core, but propelled at extremely high velocities. Although their pistols may not be viewed as state of the art, they are solid attempts to meet what their respective nations' militaries believe is required in a modern combat pistol.

## Calibres and Ammunition

The 9 × 19mm, first developed in Germany in 1902, is the most popular calibre in the field of modern military combat pistols. Although the focus of complaints over the years, tellingly often from sources bemoaning the loss of the .45ACP, it has proven a reliable and effective pistol calibre. As we will discuss again in later chapters with regard to the also often maligned 5.56 × 45mm rifle round, it is

| | Calibre | Magazine | Weight Unloaded | Length |
|---|---|---|---|---|
| Glock 17 | 9 × 19mm | 17 | 0.705kg | 202mm |
| Glock 19X | 9 × 19mm | 17 | 0.704kg | 189mm |
| SIG Sauer P226 | 9 × 19mm | 15 | 0.964kg | 196mm |
| SIG Sauer P320 (M17) | 9 × 19mm | 17 | 0.833kg | 203mm |
| Heckler and Koch USP | 9 × 19mm | 15 | 0.748kg | 194mm |
| Browning Hi-Power | 9 × 19mm | 13 | 1.000kg | 197mm |
| Grach 6P35 (MP-443) | 9 × 19mm | 17 | 1.000kg | 198mm |
| Makarov PM | 9 × 18mm | 8 | 0.684kg | 161mm |
| QSZ-92 | 5.8 × 21mm | 20 | 0.760kg | 190mm |

exceedingly difficult to actually identify incidents where the 9 × 19mm has failed to incapacitate an adversary, at least in the world of military small arms.

There have been any number of reports of failures to stop from US law enforcement but even these tend to be caused by poor bullet placement (i.e. not striking the target in the centre of body mass or head) or bullet design rather than any inherent issue with the calibre itself. The 9 × 19mm ball, often known as full metal jacketed (FMJ) ammunition, will simply not perform as well as a bullet designed to expand and/or break apart, creating a large permanent wound cavity in the target. Some earlier 9 × 19mm hollowpoint designs also failed to perform as advertised (with many pointing to the infamous 1986 FBI shootout in Miami where at least one well-placed 9 × 19mm Winchester Silvertip hollowpoint failed to perform adequately), leading to questions about the suitability of the 9 × 19mm even for police work.

In the 1990s this led to the development and widespread adoption of a new calibre by US police, the .40 S&W. The .40 S&W was hailed as providing more 'stopping power' than the 9 × 19mm, whilst still allowing for a double-stack magazine that outstripped most rival .45ACP designs in terms of capacity. The new calibre found widespread acceptance within US law enforcement, but failed to impact on the military pistol market that was tied to 9 × 19mm, largely due to NATO commonality requirements. (The US Coast Guard did adopt the .40 S&W SIG Sauer P229, although they are planning to transition to the M17.)

The .40 S&W was popular although some users battled with the increased recoil. The pressures generated by the round also caused wear and tear on many 9 × 19mm pistol designs that had been rechambered to take advantage of the success of the calibre. It was briefly used by at least one US Army special mission unit in combat in Iraq and Afghanistan, but the unit in question eventually reverted to 9 × 19mm Glocks as the .40 S&W was found to be too punishing on the frames of their weapons.

The 9 × 19mm was also far gentler in terms of felt recoil and permitted faster follow-up shots. The ammunition itself was also generally cheaper and far more common to source, meaning that more could be allotted for training purposes. The popularity of the .40 S&W began to trail off during the late 2000s as results from the FBI's exhaustive pistol calibre study became more widely known and the Bureau themselves reverted to 9 × 19mm. The FBI's study concluded that with modern hollowpoint designs there were negligible differences between the wound profiles of the 9 × 19mm, the .40 S&W and the .45ACP. It also documented that users firing 9 × 19mm calibre pistols were far more likely to actually hit their intended target due to the reduced recoil of the round.

The greatest change in 9 × 19mm lethality has been the development of a number of superb hollowpoint designs. Unfortunately, until relatively recently these were banned from military use by the Hague Convention, at least outside of specialist counter-terrorist scenarios. With the US MHS programme however came a new type of ammunition – the XM1153 Special Purpose round, a hollowpoint by any other name. That these hollowpoints have been approved by US military lawyers would suggest that they have found a way around the Hague

A Canadian soldier firing a Danish 9 × 19mm SIG P210 (M/49). The P210 is being replaced by the SIG Sauer P320. (*US Army, Staff Sgt. Michael Behlin*)

Convention's provisions on the ban of expanding rounds by signatory nations. The US, for instance, is not a signatory to Article IV which expressly forbids the use of expanding rounds and lawyers have likely made the case that hollow-points are in fact more humane in that they reduce the risk of overpenetration and are more immediately incapacitating than the 9 × 19mm ball.

There are also ways to accomplish the hollowpoint effect without the bullet itself being a hollowpoint, neatly bypassing Hague concerns. One example is the rubber-tipped Expanding Full Metal Jacket that was designed by Federal and now available in a range of calibres including a 110-grain 9 × 19mm loading (they also make a +P loading in a heavier 124-grain design). As it has no exposed 'plug' it also helps with feeding problems sometimes associated with hollowpoint rounds, particularly in older pistols and SMGs. The problem with such ammu-nition for military users is generally cost – although SOF units can often afford sufficient quantities to train with these rounds, purchasing for the infantry becomes problematic.

As noted the adoption of the M17 (P320) also saw a new bullet emerge – the Winchester-produced 147 grain XM1153 Special Purpose. The 'Special Purpose' title conceals the fact that the XM1153 is a hollowpoint and the US military admits as much: '*The JHP* [Jacketed Hollow Point] *cartridge is required for use in situations where limited over-penetration of targets is necessary to reduce collateral damage.*' One programme manager noted: '*We have a law of war determination that stated that this type of ammunition is usable.*' Another went so far as to say that the XM1153 was

Soldiers from the US 101st Airborne Division, the first unit to receive the 9 × 19mm M17 MHS (P320), test fire the weapons. (*US Army, Sgt. Samantha Stoffregen*)

now the US Army's 'go to war' ammunition. Unfortunately, we are not privy to the legal discussions behind this decision.

The US military's Special Operations Command (SOCOM) are also adopting a hollowpoint round as standard for in-service 9 × 19mm Glocks. The Speer Gold Dot G2 147 grain jacketed hollowpoint is a popular and effective law enforcement round and is also eminently suitable to use with suppressed pistols. How the XM1153 Special Purpose round will impact upon this procurement is unknown.

In spite of all of this, will we see a wider adoption of hollowpoint or similar expanding 9 × 19mm bullet designs amongst the world's militaries? This is unlikely purely due to the vast stocks of 9 × 19mm ball ammunition which are held by most countries. Very little of it is fired in training outside of special operations units and it's not uncommon to be issued ammunition dating back to the 1980s or beyond. Again, outside of SOF, the purchase of hollowpoint ammunition is also hardly a priority for such a little used weapon type. Add in the fear of legalities concerning their use under the Hague Conventions, despite recent US 'law of war determinations' regarding the XM1153, and it's easy to see why hollowpoints will remain a rarity, at least outside of the US military and SOF circles.

Again, it must be emphasised that shot placement is literally everything when it comes to lethality and no more so than with pistols which are at best a poor choice of weapon if one expects an armed confrontation. As stated earlier, the military pistol will be used in combat only when that particular soldier is having a very bad day; either his or her principal weapon has been disabled, empty or is too long to wield effectively in close confines; he or she has been surprised whilst driving a vehicle or manning a mounted weapon; or they have been seriously wounded and the pistol is their last resort.

*   *   *

As we have mentioned, Russian designs have long focused on providing an armour-piercing capability from their pistols, even though this reduces lethality as the round punches through the target rather than expanding or breaking apart to increase the dimensions of the wound channel. Indeed, the standard Russian 9mm rounds, the 9 × 19mm 7N21 and 7N31, both contain a steel core able to penetrate Level III Kevlar soft body armour and 8mm thin steel plate. From these results they would not be capable of penetrating a standard US ESAPI or Enhanced Small Arms Protective Insert plate commonly worn in US Interceptor and similar vests, although the round would cut through the soft armour parts of the Interceptor which houses the ESAPI plates.

The 7N21 has a muzzle velocity of 1,508 feet per second, propelling an 82-grain bullet, whilst the 7N31 registers just over 1,900 feet per second with a lighter 65-grain slug. Even older Russian designs like the PSM in 5.45 × 18mm and the wartime TT-33 Tokarev in 7.62 × 25mm can easily penetrate a Level III vest. The 9 × 19mm NATO ball has some penetrative qualities, but is not engineered specifically to penetrate ballistic helmets and Level III or higher body armour, both of which are generally rated to stop such a round.

As noted, the Chinese PLA too followed a similar path with their 5.8 × 21mm. Designed as a hot load (meaning that it develops extremely high pressures within the weapon to propel the round at the velocity required) with a steel core, it was developed as part of the PDW programme that spawned the latest issue PLA submachine gun, the Type 05. The round is viewed with some suspicion from the perspective of terminal effectiveness, but it is reported to be able to penetrate 1.3mm of steel plate such as in a conventional, non-ballistic, steel helmet.

The PDW concept of a matched pistol and SMG is hardly new. As we will discuss in the next chapter, NATO looked for exactly such a pairing during the 1980s and early 90s. These programmes gave birth to the German 4.6 × 30mm fired from the MP7 and the cancelled P46 or UCP pistol and the Belgian 5.7 × 28mm used in the P90 and the FiveseveN. The 5.7 × 28mm has received much negative press in the United States due to its armour-piercing capability although the military load, the 32-grain SS190, is not available to civilians (the commercial SS197 loading available to US civilian shooters will not penetrate a standard PASGT helmet).

The issue with the design of the SS190 is two-fold. The round is designed with a steel penetrator with a heavier aluminium core. Whilst this design means it can reliably penetrate Level III armour and most ballistic helmets as it was designed to do, the design also means that it tends to tumble quickly within the target. The best that can be said about its terminal effectiveness is that the results are still out. The fact that the calibre is little used sees wildly contradictory accounts of its effectiveness.

Whether pistol rounds need an armour-piercing capability is an interesting question. In a scenario against peer or near-peer adversaries, it may be useful, but experience in the counter-insurgency and counter-terrorist operations of the past two decades would place the emphasis on an expanding design as the vast majority of opponents are not wearing any form of body armour. Also, again it must be stressed that the pistol in non-SOF military hands is purely a defensive weapon and will only be employed in the gravest of circumstances. Ball ammunition, with its admittedly light penetrative capacity, may be the best of an uncomfortable compromise.

With the .40 S&W largely out of the picture and the 5.7 × 28mm only adopted in a tiny handful of cases, the 9 × 19mm will continue as the dominant military combat pistol calibre until genuinely revolutionary steps are made, likely in the field of caseless or cased telescoped ammunition, a subject we will return to in a later chapter. In summary, 9 × 19mm benefits from manageable recoil characteristics, large magazine capacities and relatively light weight. It is also firmly entrenched within the NATO supply chain meaning ammunition is easily available, a not inconsiderate point when the battlefields of the future may well be focused on the Baltics.

## Current Trends

In military service the pistol has one simple but overriding requirement as we have stressed – it must go 'bang' when needed, every time. Reliability, swiftly followed by safety, are the keys to a successful general-issue military pistol design. No weapon is responsible for more negligent discharges than the pistol – it must be, in British Army parlance, 'squaddie proof'. Unit cost, of course, also plays its part.

As noted earlier in the chapter, pistols have seen something of a renaissance during the Global War on Terror and associated conflicts. There is, however, some evidence of soldiers dispensing with pistols, even after receiving them as a special issue. In Helmand, Afghanistan, it appears that after the initial novelty of the general issue of pistols to all, many left them at the forward operating base (FOB) when they went on patrol. Others however, like embedded teams training the Afghan National Army or Police, kept theirs close in case of a green-on-blue attack by disgruntled Afghan trainees or Taliban infiltrators.

There has been the occasional call to dispense with pistols altogether as largely unnecessary added weight, some arguing that the weight would better be served by additional magazines for the soldier's primary weapon. British Army veteran Doug Beattie was unequivocal when asked his opinion by the author:

> I believe every single soldier should have a secondary weapon and that should be in the form of a pistol. This gives the soldier the ability to lower his posture at various times but remain fully armed and able to engage enemy at short distances. The pistol also gives a crossover during close range engagements when it is not practical to stop to clear a stoppage or change magazine – as intended by UKSF.

A British Army 9 × 19mm Glock 17, the L131A1, in full recoil. *(USMC, Sgt. Gregory D. Boyd)*

The pistol also gives individuals who have section weapons the ability to engage within confined areas where they cannot bring their weapon to bear and in that it becomes a personal protection weapon. There is also a question of ballistics – as the SA80 [L85] has good penetration there are times on the battlefield when we do not want that overkill at short range – be that within buildings were others are operating or in crowds. To that end, the pistol gives you options.

It also provides the soldier with a weapon should their primary small arm be unavailable. As noted earlier, the pistol is very much a back-up weapon. Having said that, there are times when it comes to the fore, typically when a soldier's primary weapon has been disabled or lost, or when there is simply not enough room to effectively use an assault rifle or light machine gun.

Beattie found himself without his own L85A2 after leaving his vehicle in a hurry during a contact in Helmand and ended up clearing buildings with only his sidearm and hand grenade: *'Here I was, a 9mm pistol in my right hand, a grenade in my left hand, about to try and clear the house ahead of me.'* When he did make entry, he spotted a trio of Taliban attempting to flee, at least one of whom opened fire upon him with his AK-47. *'I staggered backwards, desperate to get away, firing eight, nine, perhaps ten shots from my pistol as I tried to escape. Had I hit him? Had I hit any of them?'*

Beattie managed to withdraw out of the room and posted in the fragmentation grenade before again entering with his pistol. The Taliban had escaped and were running across an adjacent field. He couldn't tell if any of them were wounded. He lamented: '*Already they were out of range of my Browning pistol. If only I had had my rifle.*'

The Australian Army agrees, with their professional journal noting in 2015:

Handguns are increasingly being recognised as a vital piece of equipment for the protection of deployed soldiers. With the correct holster, a handgun can be brought into action faster than the F88 and M4 rifles can be reloaded. Handguns thus play a critical back-up role in the event of catastrophic failure of the primary weapon. Indeed, in some circumstances, it makes sense for the handgun to supersede the rifle as the primary weapon.

It further states:

Internal data from Special Air Service Regiment (SASR) training courses indicate that, on average and with an appropriate holster, a handgun can be brought into action three seconds faster than the ADF's standard issue F88 Austeyr bullpup rifle can be reloaded, and two seconds faster than an M4 carbine. For most operators, this can be increased even further with a little extra training. These seconds are potentially the difference between life and death on the battlefield. And, of course, a soldier whose rifle suffers a catastrophic failure during combat, and who has no handgun to fall back on, is in a very difficult situation indeed (the analogy of a reserve parachute seems appropriate here).

A British soldier involved in the trials to select a new combat pistol for British forces added in a similar vein:

In the event of your main weapon failing, with the new Glock you can draw and shoot the enemy within two seconds. You need to know that wherever you are, whatever you're doing, if your main weapon fails, you have that secondary system – and that within seconds you and your comrades can draw your pistol and engage the enemy.

For some soldiers such as snipers however, it can be an unneeded burden, particularly as standard operating procedures (SOP) now call for snipers to carry a carbine or assault rifle in addition to their sniper platform, explained Nathan Vinson, former Master Sniper for the Australian Army and a veteran of Rwanda and Afghanistan:

To me the pistol was more of a hindrance to carry. Sometimes our sniper teams would carry the old 9mm (still in service) when we only had the one bolt action rifle [SR98] as a backup, which was fine. However, once we started carrying the SR25 and HK417 there was no reason. Furthermore, we encourage our teams to carry F88s when on patrol with the primary engagement weapon either strapped to pack or inside the pack. Once a target was acquired the F88 with the pack was cached and the long rifle was employed for the final stalk of the target and engagement.

The full issue kit for the new US Modular Handgun System – note the drop holster and adapter to mount on MOLLE, two different lower frame sizes (M17 and M18) and the standard 17-round magazine and two extended 21-round magazines. (*US Army*)

Many of these SOPs came into place after the ambush of US Marine sniper teams in Iraq. Sniper teams now go armed with both their principal sniper platform and an individual weapon, as the threat is simply too high to rely upon a pistol as back-up to a bolt-action sniper rifle. For example, Estonian snipers in Afghanistan carried shortened 5.56 × 45mm Galil SAR carbines, whilst German Army sniper spotters used the 4.6 × 30mm MP7A1, now often replaced by a G36 variant or even the 7.62 × 51mm G28. In US Army infantry sniper teams, all members will carry a 5.56 × 45mm M4A1, including one 40mm M203 launcher, along with their pistols.

The Israelis are an interesting case study in the use of pistols as, outside of their SOF and security services, they are rarely carried by Israeli Defence Force (IDF) personnel. The reasoning is apparently two-fold. One is that pistols are considered a dangerous weapon in the hands of conscript soldiers. Secondly, they believe that all personnel should be armed with a 5.56 × 45mm carbine, or in days gone by a 9 × 19mm UZI sub machine gun, as they may be called into action at a moment's notice.

After the rash of terrorist knife attacks and bombings in 2015, IDF officers were allowed to carry personally-owned sidearms on base. With the increase in pistols came a dramatic rise in negligent discharges. New rules now make it much harder for personally-owned pistols to be carried within the Israeli military.

\* \* \*

The method of carry of the pistol has also always been a challenge. The fashionable SAS-style drop-leg holster is difficult to use whilst seated and conversely is prone to banging around on the user's thigh if running. They are also certainly not the most secure of holsters. Many attach a lanyard to the pistol when employing a drop-leg holster in case the weapon becomes loose.

Another British veteran, Phil Boshier, who deployed on Operation Herrick VIII and XIII as a combat medic with UK forces, recounted to the author: '*As a medic I was issued a sidearm as well, [a] SIG P226 with a Blackhawk leg holster which I binned after two or three patrols as it was just a pain in a contact.*' Instead he went with a field-expedient solution: '*The Osprey* [body armour system] *single magazine pouch was a great SIG holster it turned out.*'

Along with vehicle drivers, many Special Forces began to mount their pistols directly on the chest of their body armour. This was arguably a faster location to draw from and kept the pistol from getting snagged on windows or door frames as they made entry. Many regular soldiers followed their lead. This type of placement of the pistol had its own unintended dangers however. Late in the Afghan campaign it was discovered that when struck by an IED, particularly the common pressure-plate victim-operated type favoured by the Taliban, pieces of whatever was attached to the front of a soldier's body armour could fly upwards and cause additional injuries to the face and neck. This included pistols and for British forces at least, a ban was quickly put in place.

Most first-world militaries now issue modern secure holsters intended to be worn on the belt at the hip. This is by far the safest and most reliable form of holster. Drop holsters were designed to allow SOF operators to draw their pistols whilst avoiding snagging on body armour groin protectors; less of an issue today as the trend is to reduce the size and weight of combat body armour. Chest holsters have their place and are likely the best option for soldiers operating in and around vehicles. Shoulder holsters are still occasionally seen, but almost exclusively worn by aviators rather than infantrymen. In the cockpit this method of carry makes sense as it keeps the pistol safely tucked away.

\* \* \*

In terms of shooting techniques, most militaries have followed their SOF and teach their soldiers to fire controlled pairs of rounds – the famous 'double-tap'. This maximises both the chance of a strike and of delivering a lethal hit. SOF by comparison have moved on as combat experience has shown that enemy may well require multiple hits before ceasing hostilities and thus SOF and elite light infantry units like the US Army Rangers will continue to engage a target until that target ceases all movement. For the infantryman who can only hope for such levels of training, the 'double-tap' remains the best compromise.

In technical terms, apart from a general move toward the use of polymer in pistol construction and the adoption of safety systems other than the standard external manual safety, there has been little real innovation in the field of combat pistols in the past two decades. Polymer and similar materials make sense to reduce weight, whilst external safeties are increasingly becoming something of a dying breed, led principally by the widespread adoption of Glock platforms that typically do not include a manual safety.

The fact that pistols, almost all fitted with external safeties, have been historically notorious for negligent or accidental discharges actually argues against the strict requirement for external safeties – it's never stopped soldiers making mistakes in the past. Defence departments have begun to realise that other safety mechanisms can be adopted which are effective, but which speed up the employment of the weapon. Under the incredible stresses of close combat, manually disengaging a safety catch is just one more challenge the soldier will be forced to face. Eliminating it arguably increases the likelihood of a successful conclusion to a close-quarters gunfight.

The biggest development in method of operation has been the striker-fired pistol. Put simply, this is a weapon that has no exposed hammer. It means that the weapon will always fire with a consistent trigger pull rather than the lighter single action (if the hammer is cocked to the rear when made ready) followed by the heavier double action pull of many traditional designs.

To complicate matters there are also double-action only pistols with exposed hammers, but these are typically aimed at the law enforcement market as they are designed to mitigate the risk of a negligent discharge. There are single-action only pistols too, like the Browning Hi-Power; these require the hammer to be cocked before firing.

Hammer-fired designs, like the SIG Sauer P226 for instance, either fire after the hammer is manually cocked to the rear, or the trigger is depressed in double action – this trigger action both cocks and releases the hammer. Striker fired means that the weapon is made ready when the slide is moved to the rear and released, engaging the internal striker. A common example is the Glock. With no standard external safety, the Glock is then ready to fire as long as the trigger is firmly grasped to engage the trigger safety. Many argue that striker-fired designs are slightly faster to get into action, with the added bonus of no exposed hammer to snag on clothing or webbing. The downside to most striker-fired designs is that to de-cock the weapon, you must eject the magazine and then pull the trigger to drop the hammer. With hammer-fired designs, the tension on the hammer can be manually released or done so by a de-cocking lever, again like on the P226.

For military purposes, both forms of design have their adherents. The hammer-fired has been traditionally considered safer due to the external safety (and de-cocking mechanisms) which reduce the risk of a negligent discharge. Others claim that striker-fired are just as safe as long as the user has been trained in basic

9 × 19mm Glock 17 stripped to its component parts – the simplicity of the design and resultant maintenance is obvious. (*Open Government License v3.0, Stuart Hill*)

pistol handling. With the widespread adoption of the Glock and the recent procurement of the M17 (P320) for the US military, it would seem that striker-fired designs are the likely future direction for issue combat pistols.

The addition of Picatinny style rails on pistols has been another relatively recent development and it's rare to see a new design without them. Infra-red and visible lasers, often combined with a white-light weapons light, is the most common adornment and has its place in assisting in low-light conditions. The infra-red can be used with night vision goggles, showing a green laser projection that is invisible to the naked eye.

Special operators have followed the lead of competition shooters and the US military's special mission units by mounting mini red dot optics to the frames of their weapons. The idea is to increase the speed it takes to acquire a target, something which the red dot certainly does in comparative testing versus iron sights. In a CQB environment where the pistol may be the primary weapon, for instance on a commuter train or airliner, this makes a lot of sense. For the infantryman, such situations would be far from a common occurrence. Red dots for general issue may improve the accuracy of the infantryman's shooting but is it a necessary added weight? The author argues against it purely on the basis of how rarely the conventional army, as opposed to SOF, actually employ their pistols. It's both an added weight and something more that can break!

*    *    *

A number of nations are currently replacing their issue pistols with more modern platforms. The Russians with their Grach 6P35, the Poles with their PR-15 and the Danes with the US M320. Making sense of Russian pistol acquisitions is a difficult task with each competing design bureau claiming that their latest and greatest will soon be adopted by the Russian military (in this, note similarities with the replacement for the AK-74M covered in a later chapter). It seems clear, however, that the Grach 6P35 (MP-443) is seeing combat service – including in Syria – and is intended to be the general-issue replacement for the Makarov PM.

Another new Russian pistol is also in the offing. Designed by Dmitry Lebedev for the famous Kalashnikov Concern, the PL-15 is a new design based on the previous PL-14 model. Chambered for $9 \times 19$mm and holding 16 rounds in its magazine, the PL-15 is a thoroughly modern design developed for use by Russian SOF who have shown serious interest in it.

The Poles have adopted the domestically designed and produced, thoroughly modern $9 \times 19$mm PR-15 RAGUN, a 15-round capacity combat pistol that bears a superficial resemblance to the P226, but weighs slightly less than even a Glock 17. It replaces the older $9 \times 19$mm WIST-94 Piryt, which itself replaced a number of Makarov based designs.

The M320 has also been recently selected to become the issue sidearm of the Danish armed forces replacing the M/49, their variant of the superb SIG Sauer P210. The M/49 has served since the 1960s, a pistol that whilst being astoundingly accurate and reliable, also suffered from an 8-round magazine. Faced with stiff opposition from the Glock 17M, the Smith & Wesson M&P M2.0 and 2.0 Compact, the Beretta APX and the Turkish Canik TP9 SF, the M320 was announced as the winner in April 2018 with deliveries scheduled to begin in 2019.

The Turkish Canik trialled for the competition deserves a special mention as it began as a licence produced Walter P99 and has, through a number of iterations, become the pistol that won the recent Turkish military contract for a new $9 \times 19$mm sidearm. This type of development, essentially product improving a foreign design for domestic production, has been also seen with Turkey's HK417 derivative, the MKEK MPT-76 battle rifle, which we will return to in a later chapter.

Polish snipers conducting building clearance drills using their newly issued 9 × 19mm PR-15 RAGUN pistols. (*US Army, Markus Rauchenberger*)

The French Army too is also looking to replace its mix of PAMAS G1 (a licence-produced Beretta M92) and their increasingly elderly MAC50 with a single issue 9 × 19mm sidearm, but no decision has yet been made. French SOF use both Glock and H&K variants so it is likely one of these manufacturers will win the eventual contract although the M320 will certainly be submitted.

## Individual Weapon Summaries

### Gryazev-Shipunov GSh-18

Adopted in small quantities by the Russian military, this 9 × 19mm pistol owes much to the Glock in terms of operation (even including its own variant of the Glock trigger safety). It is designed to fire the steel core 7N31 cartridge to provide armour-piercing capability, although it can operate a range of more standard 9 × 19mm loadings.

It is fed from a double-stack 18-round magazine of an unusual design, likely inspired by the Stechkin APS. Instead of funnelling the rounds into a single feed like most pistols, it has a literal double stack feeding alternatively from either side, increasing magazine reliability – although apparently loading the magazine is somewhat painful on the thumbs! Its polymer construction keeps its weight down to 580g, lighter even than the Glock 17.

### Grach 6P35 (MP-443)

In contrast to the GSh-18, the Grach (Rook) is noteworthy for its all metal construction rather than the more common polymers used in most modern pistols –

The new Russian 9 × 19mm PL-15 design from Kalashnikov Design fitted with detachable sound suppressor and laser aiming module. (*Kalashnikov Group/Kalashnikov Media*)

this is undoubtedly due to its intended round, the high pressure 7N31. The double-action Grach is slowly being phased into service as the standard issue sidearm of the Russian Army since 2003 replacing the venerable Makarov PM (although it is doubtful the PM will ever be fully replaced as there are so many of them). The Grach is more widely known within Russia as the Yarygin PYa.

Rather than continue with their own 9 × 18 and 9 × 21mmmm variants, the Russians wisely chose the common 9 × 19mm calibre, opening up foreign sales, although as noted the Grach was designed from the ground up to handle the hot 7N31 loading in the same manner as the GSh-18. Again, like its competitor, the Grach features an 18-round magazine. Its steel body keeps recoil manageable although it consequently weighs in at the heavier end of the spectrum at 850g. Along with the Russian Army who adopted the design in 2003, to date the Grach has also been adopted by Belarus, Kazakhstan and Armenia.

It seems clear that the Grach 6P35 (MP-443) is seeing combat service – including in Syria – and is intended to be the general-issue replacement for the Makarov PM. Their SOF may soon adopt the new PL-15 designed by Dmitry Lebedev for Kalashnikov Concern. Chambered for 9 × 19mm and holding 16 rounds in its magazine, the PL-15 is a thoroughly modern design. Other Russian SOF carry a range of commercially purchased Glocks.

## Makarov PM

The 9 × 18mm Makarov replaced the elderly 7.62 × 25mm TT-30 Tokarev in Russian Army service back in 1951. The Tokarev had served extensively throughout the Second World War and was well liked, although its lack of an external safety, other than a manually applied half-cock feature, meant that it was more dangerous to carry with a round chambered and the hammer back than other competing designs.

Based largely on the venerable Walther PP design, the PM equipped all units of the Russian military throughout the Cold War and was widely exported, particularly to client states in the Middle East. It is still one of the most common pistols encountered in conflict zones. An unremarkable design, its emphasis was on concealability rather than being an effective combat pistol, a fact reinforced by the choice of Spetsnaz units to acquire Czech CZ 75s whenever possible.

The PMM is a slightly modernised version of the PM, featuring a 12-round magazine and an improved 9 × 18mm loading. Although pitched to the Russian military, it was never adopted outside of domestic law enforcement. A similar sized pistol was also introduced in the form of the PSM which used a 5.45 × 18mm, but was only really issued to staff officers. Curiously, the 5.45 × 18mm was also designed to penetrate body armour with its admittedly diminutive steel core. The PSM found more favour with the Russian police and security services than the military who soldiered on with their Makarovs and the odd Stechkin APS.

## QSZ-92

Designed in the Chinese proprietary 5.8 × 21mm, the QSZ-92 holds an impressive 20 rounds in a similar manner to its Belgian cousin, the FN FiveseveN, in a double stack magazine. Adopted in the late 1990s by the PLA, it features an ambidextrous Beretta style de-cocker safety and magazine release allowing the weapon to be fired by left handed shooters. Somewhat unusually, it features a polymer lower and metal slide.

The QSZ-92 fires the PLA issue ball round, the 46-grain 5.8 × 21mm DAP-92, which includes a steel penetrator to increase armour penetration in a similar

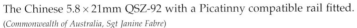

The Chinese 5.8 × 21mm QSZ-92 with a Picatinny compatible rail fitted.

*(Commonwealth of Australia, Sgt Janine Fabre)*

manner to the Russian $9 \times 19$mm 7N31. The $5.8 \times 21$mm round is fired from the QSZ-92 at approximately 1,500 feet per second. The results of any independent, and unclassified, testing of the round's effectiveness against body armour or helmets has been impossible to acquire. By all of the admittedly limited reports available, the round underperforms versus the similar Belgian $5.7 \times 28$mm, including in armour-piercing capability.

A 15-round capacity $9 \times 19$mm version (the CF-98) has also been produced for the export market which has been adopted by the Bangladesh and Pakistani militaries. Reports from shooters who have fired the more commonly available $9 \times 19$mm variant rate the weapon as nothing particularly outstanding and in line with what one would expect from a Chinese service weapon. Like Russian produced small arms, the PLA are looking for something which is straightforward, reasonably cheap to produce in large numbers and reliable. With these three factors in mind, the QSZ-92 can be considered a success.

### Heckler and Koch USP (P8)

The H&K Universal Self-loading Pistol (USP) was designed originally to target the police market during the early 1990s as sales of the then new .40 S&W chambering rapidly overtook more traditional calibres like the .45ACP and $9 \times 19$mm. The USP, a superbly made and accurate pistol based on design work for the Mk 23 Offensive Handgun Weapon System developed for US Special Operations Command, sold well to law enforcement in the .40 S&W chambering.

These sales were assisted by an extensive range of options with regard to the location of the external safety and single and double action offerings, allowing users to choose a pistol that suited their particular needs. The USP was also one of the first commercial designs to offer a frame-mounted rail under the barrel as standard allowing for the addition of tactical lights and lasers, another direct result of H&K's experiences developing the Mk 23.

With the release of the USP, Heckler and Koch undoubtedly also had their eyes on the then upcoming Bundeswehr pistol trials. The German Army was looking for a new service pistol to replace the venerable P1, itself based on the wartime Walther P38. The USP won the competition and the Bundeswehr subsequently adopted a USP variant in $9 \times 19$mm as the P8 in 1995, although the last P1 in German service was eventually retired in 2004.

The P8 has served with distinction on German deployments to Afghanistan and Iraq. It has a redesigned safety and sports 15-round translucent magazines, in a similar fashion to original G36 magazines, so that the user can see how many rounds are left (although with the magazine seated in the pistol grip, this appears to be a somewhat nebulous feature on the P8). Some user reports mention that the standard German $9 \times 19$mm ball intended for use in the MP5 submachine gun, the DM51 loading, is too hot for the pistol and reduces service life, resulting in hairline cracks to the slide. There have also been reports of problems with the plastic magazines in Afghanistan.

A new variant called the P8A1 was adopted by the Bundeswehr in 2017 with a reinforced frame to handle the DM51 loads and an anti-corrosion finish. Another

A US infantryman firing the Bundeswehr issue 9 × 19mm Heckler and Koch P8 during NATO competitions. (*US Army, Sgt. Apryl Bowman*)

variant is the P8C or Combat A1 used by German special operations forces which dispenses with the external safety. A .45ACP variant known as the P12 was also adopted by the Bundeswehr for their specialist reconnaissance troops. The .45ACP chambering was chosen as the pistol was intended to be used primarily with a sound suppressor; the .45ACP remains subsonic meaning there is no distinctive and betraying crack as the bullet breaks the sound barrier.

Variants of the USP have been adopted by Georgia, Lithuania and the Irish Defence Force. The largest user following Germany is Spain, with adoption occurring in 2011 to replace the Llama M-82 after beating off healthy competition from both the SIG SP2022M and the Beretta PX4. The USP has also been issued to Estonian forces since a 2005 decision to replace their Warsaw Pact era Makarov PMs, seeing action in Afghanistan with the Estonian contingent to ISAF. Germany has also recently adopted the P30 from Heckler and Koch for SOF and some specialist infantry units in the Feldjäger. It has no external safety unlike the P8, making it faster to get into action.

### Fabrique Nationale FiveseveN

The Belgian FiveseveN was developed following a 1989 NATO requirement for a personal defence weapon (PDW), a process we will look into in more detail in the next chapter. The futuristic looking FiveseveN pistol was meant as a partner weapon for the P90 PDW using the same round – the 5.7 × 28mm.

The FiveseveN fires its 5.7 × 28mm round at high velocities but generates up to a third less felt recoil than a comparable 9 × 19mm. The round was developed with the express purpose of penetrating a CRISAT (Collaborative Research into Small Arms Technology) target comprised of some twenty layers of Kevlar and a titanium plate, mimicking Russian body armour. The pistol can even fire specialist 5.7 × 28mm loadings such as the L191 tracer and the subsonic SB193. Like the Chinese QSZ-92, the FiveseveN features a 20-round magazine.

As noted previously, the terminal effectiveness of the military 5.7 × 28mm SS190 is still open to question. Law enforcement shootings in the United States seem to paint a perhaps less than stellar picture of its performance. It must be emphasised again though, as with any calibre, shot placement is everything. The FiveseveN has the advantage of being significantly easier to shoot than comparative 9 × 19mm designs thanks to its reduced recoil, meaning that, all other things being equal, it could result in better shot placement.

The FiveseveN has not surprisingly been adopted by the Belgian Army as its standard issue pistol, the only nation to date to adopt the pistol for military general issue. It has, however, been more widely employed by military and police special operations units across the globe. Even the Belgians initially procured it only for its special operators, but it is now intended to replace their Browning Hi-Powers more widely. More ominously, the Libyan Army purchased 367 examples of the pistol in 2009 (along with P90 PDWs and F2000 assault rifles) and was employed until the fall of Gaddafi's regime. At least some are now in insurgent hands.

## Fabrique Nationale Browning Hi-Power GP-35

The legendary Browning still remains the issued sidearm in a small and ever-decreasing number of armies. The Browning, although a proven design of noted reliability, is simply getting too old. Its 13-round magazine capacity, almost unique for many years, has today been eclipsed with smaller, lighter pistols offering greater capacity.

The Australian Army still maintain stocks of Brownings (officially the Self-Loading Pistol, 9mm Mk 3), many of which have been rebuilt several times over the years. Indeed, some examples in ADF service date back to the 1950s. The Indian Army continues to issue their own licence-produced version. A requirement for a replacement has apparently been issued, but there appears little news of any concrete advancements (this is not unusual in the maelstrom which is Indian small arms procurement).

A fascinating recent study was carried out for the Australian Army by their Special Air Service Regiment's Battle Wing which compared the Browning L9A1 (High Power), a Glock 19 fitted with a Trijicon RMR optic, a H&K USP (which is issued to Australian Special Forces), a Smith & Wesson M&P 9L again fitted with a Trijicon RMR and a Steyr M9A1. Surprisingly they found that the elderly Browning could still hold its own in the accuracy department, second only to the RMR equipped G19.

One of the biggest traditional users of the Browning was the British Army. The UK placed their last order for 2,000 L9A1s in 2001. Since then the British Army version, the L9A1, has been replaced in service by the L131A1 Glock 17.

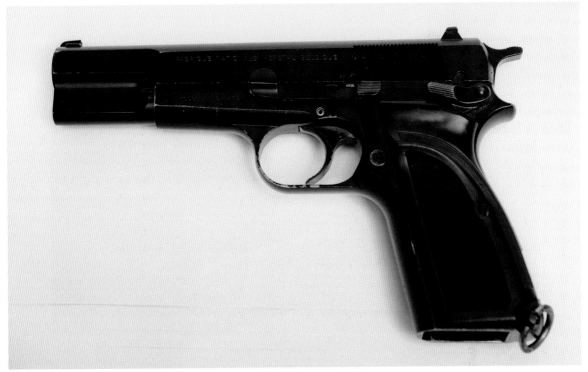

The legendary 9 × 19mm Browning Hi-Power, here in UK issue as the L9A1 before its replacement by the L131A1 Glock. *(Open Government License v3.0, LA (Phot) Brian Douglas)*

Production of the Hi-Power by FN Herstal itself sadly ended in 2018. The Israelis continue with the Browning as their official issue pistol, although even older Beretta M1951s, their first official issue pistol, still make an appearance. As noted earlier, the IDF do not generally issue sidearms outside of SOF.

The Browning was the favoured pistol of none other than Saddam Hussein, although when captured by special operations forces, he was armed with a rare fully automatic Glock 18 that was later presented to the then President George W. Bush. The Browning was common amongst Iraqi officers, but the Iraqi licence produced Beretta M1951, chambered for the 9 × 19mm and called the Tariq, was standard issue (confusingly a second Iraqi produced pistol was also known as the Tariq – another licenced Beretta copy, this time of the 7.65 × 17mm Model 70).

### SIG Sauer P226

Based on the P220 and P225 design, SIG Sauer first developed the 9 × 19mm P226 for the US JSSAP trials. It was known for its accuracy and was capable of accepting either the standard 15-round or extended 21-round magazine. The weapon found favour with a number of armies and SOF including the British SAS and US Navy SEALs (until recently replaced by both units by Glock 19 variants). Some nations, including Japan, still carry the earlier P220.

Elements of the Finnish Army still use the P226, it is standard issue for the Singaporean Army and the New Zealand Defense Force adopted the Swiss pistol as their issue sidearm for all combat arms in 1992, replacing their ageing stock of Browning Hi-Powers. In 2016, they announced the purchase of 1,900 fourth generation Glock 17s to replace the P226s.

The 9 × 19mm SIG Sauer P226R (L105A2) issued as a second tranche to the urgent operational requirement purchase of pistols for UK forces in Afghanistan.

(*Open Government License v3.0, Senior Aircraftsman Daniel Herrick*)

The British Army had purchased some 6,000 SIG Sauer pistols as part of several Urgent Operational Requirements (UORs) for the Afghanistan campaign (no doubt based on its use by both UKSF and the Royal Military Police). Initially these were P226s (type classified the L105A1 and with rails as the L105A2), but later both the more compact P228 (L107A1) and the modernised and rail equipped P229 (L117A2) – all in 9 × 19mm – were also ordered.

The UOR SIGs were surplus to requirements when the new L131A1 Glock arrived. Many of the SIGs were well-worn from the harsh conditions in Helmand and from constant use, tour after tour. A MoD statement on the matter read:

> It is wrong to suggest the MoD wasted money on SIG Sauer pistols, which were bought in 2008 to meet an urgent operational requirement and used by British forces in Iraq and Afghanistan for five years. By 2013, extensive tests showed the Glock pistol offered a better long term solution to replace the Browning in terms of its capability and value for money.

### SIG Sauer M320/M17

The M320 is best known as the winner of the US Army's MHS competition to replace the issue Beretta M9, as detailed at the beginning of this chapter. It is an outstanding example of a truly modular combat pistol. The M320 can be configured for concealment as a compact version (M18) or for general duty (M17) with different length slides and barrels and a range of grips to suit different sized hands. It is also designed to accept a mini red dot sight or similar optic. The M17 is being issued with three magazines – one 17-rounder and two extended 21-rounders.

Close up view of the 9 × 19mm M17 Modular Handgun System. (*US Army*)

Recently the M17 and M18 have run into problems with stoppages reported with the XM1152 issue ball ammunition. It does apparently feed reliably with the new XM1153 SP or Special Purpose expanding ammunition. Civilian M320s have also experienced an admittedly exceptionally rare condition in which the weapon may discharge if dropped. SIG announced a product recall and the issue was soon solved. The fix had already been applied to the MHS variant before it was issued. Indeed, in a statement an Army spokesperson confirmed: *'There is no drop test deficiency with the MHS. SIG Sauer corrected this issue prior to the start of testing, and the MHS passed the Army's drop test.'*

The US Marine Corps announced in 2018 that the M17/18 will be replacing the full gamut of sidearms in use by the Marines to include the M9, M9A1, .45ACP M45A1 and M007 (Glock 19 although Marine Raiders will be keeping their Glocks for the time being). The M17/18 will also be adopted by the US Air Force, Navy and Coast Guard. As previously noted, an M320 variant has now been adopted by the Danish Army, the first selection of the platform from outside of the US military. Others will likely follow.

### Beretta M92F/M9

The 9 × 19mm Beretta became the standard sidearm of the United States military in 1985 after the exhaustive and drawn-out selection process of the JSAAP we chronicled earlier. Featuring a 15-round magazine, the M9 was a modified M92. It served the US military until the 2018 adoption of the M17. It was often singled out for criticism by American Iraq and Afghan veterans, although many of these complaints related to the issue magazines which were not Beretta factory magazines and not manufactured to the same tolerances.

The M9 was also criticised for lack of terminal ballistics but the culprit for this lies firmly at the feet of the then issue M882 ball which, like any conventional 9 × 19mm ball ammunition, will punch through a target rather than expanding. The M9A1 saw a rail fitted to allow attachment of weapon lights and lasers for the Marine Corps. As noted previously, a modernised variant, the M9A3, was developed specifically for the MHS competition.

It remains the issue pistol for the majority of the Colombian, Egyptian, Italian, Jordanian armies amongst others. A copy of the Beretta M92, the Brazilian Taurus PT92, has seen widespread adoption in South America including by the armies of Brazil and Peru. The South Africans carry a Beretta copy, the Vektor Z-88 although it is being slowly replaced with the more modern Vektor SP-1. The Afghan National Army also issues surplus M9s as its standard issue pistol.

### Glock 17

There is little that can be said about the Glock family that has not been said before; they have earned a reputation for reliability under the most testing of conditions. The fact that they are the most common pistol to be found in the holsters of special operators is proof enough of the rugged, straightforward reputation of the Austrian pistol. It was a narrow defeat in the US MHS trials and the Glock MHS candidate was a firm favourite – uniquely it featured a frame-mounted external safety and a lanyard ring to secure the weapon.

The 4th generation 9 × 19mm Glock 17 as issued by the British Army.
(*Open Government License v3.0, Steve Dock*)

A Generation 4 Glock 17 type classified the L131A1 replaced the L9A1 Browning Hi-Power in UK service in 2014. An officer from the Infantry Trials and Development Unit noted that the L9A1 was reaching the end of its useful service: '*We began to lose a little bit of confidence in its reliability.*' Another commented of the trials: '*We started with eleven types, but a few were excluded along the way. Now we had five pistols in the final test, and in April (2012), the final option is checked.*' Unfortunately the full panel of competitors has not been publicly released, however the Glock was an excellent choice for the British Army.

The Serbian Army has purchased the G17, as have the Romanians, Dutch, Norwegians and the Lithuanians along with the Finns and the Swedes. Across all of Western Europe and into the Baltics, the Glock has become the most popular choice for issue sidearm. The Malaysians are also adopting the Glock, replacing a mix of H&K P9S and South African Vektors. New Zealand replaced their issue SIG P226 with the Glock 17 in 2015 and when the Australian Defence Force finally replaces their Brownings, it is the odds-on favourite, although again the SIG M17 may now give it a run for its money.

## Future Trends

With the step-away from .40 S&W due to the wear and tear on pistols chambered for the round and its questionable increase in lethality, the 9 × 19mm will remain the most common calibre for any future military service pistols. As previously noted, apart from some very limited special operations use, the .40 S&W never made any serious inroads within military procurement (although with the lack of a defined calibre in the recent US MHS trials, Glock did submit a .40 S&W entry alongside its 9 × 19mm offerings). The .45ACP will remain only within SOF for specialist suppressed applications; 10mm and similar calibres like the .357 SIG have never been seriously considered as a general issue calibre. The 9 × 19mm will rule the roost until a genuinely evolutionary pistol cartridge is developed – most likely some sort of hyper velocity caseless round.

Russian and Chinese efforts around high pressure, armour-piercing loads aside, both nations also continue a fascination with special purpose pistols, including integrally suppressed models like the iconic 7.62 × 17mm Type 64 and those designed specifically for underwater use. As these are in the realms of special operations rather than the infantryman we won't be looking at these designs in detail but suffice to say both have developed some intriguing but niche platforms for their national SOF.

One such weapon that deserves a mention is the Rsh-12 chambered for the massive 12.7 × 55mm. This large frame revolver holds 5 rounds and was reportedly designed to complement a bullpup assault rifle firing the same ammunition.

The Chinese PLA Type 92 or QSZ-92 in 5.8 × 21mm. (*Commonwealth of Australia, Sgt John Waddell*)

The Rsh-12 can apparently fire armour piercing ammunition which can penetrate even Level IV body armour and even subsonic loads, indicating a suppressor may be available for this little known revolver – although the effectiveness of any suppressor on a revolver without specialised 'sealed' ammunition is open to question.

Special operations units have been decking out their pistols with all manner of lights, lasers, suppressors and mini red dot sights over the past decade and indeed the US Special Operations Command recently placed a large order to equip all of their units with Trijicon mini red dots. Will these accessories make inroads with the infantry? Based on another recent US requirement document from Army Contracting Command looking for commercial off-the-shelf light units, officially termed the Pistol Aiming Light (PAiL), we could see them sooner than we think. The PAiL calls for both white light and infra-red spectrum laser capability but notes that a visible laser is not required. The requirement states: *'The PAiL program anticipates procuring between 2,000 and 20,000 (current total Acquisition Objective) systems)'* which would indicate issue to limited combat units only.

Apart from rail-mounted weapon lights, which make a lot of sense for combat engineers for example, most of the other gadgets are designed for extreme close quarter battle, the likes of which is only typically experienced by special operations. For conventional infantry forces, such accessories are just largely additional weight and it's difficult to envision a scenario when their use would justify that extra weight. That however doesn't mean they will not be adopted, at least in small scales (and note again the M17 features a slide cut to allow mini red dots to be mounted, although this wasn't a requirement). As we shall see in later chapters, the influence of the SOF community on the infantry is strong. Soldiers look up to and copy the equipment of operators, a fact that has been recognised, and indeed exploited, by some small arms manufacturers. Rail mounted IR lasers and mini red dots are only the latest in a long line of 'cool guy' gear to appear.

Nations that still issue pistols like the Browning Hi-Power and similar wartime relics will eventually move to more modern designs. As noted for instance, the Canadians are looking to replace their Brownings, but they are in little rush. Perhaps befitting the actual tactical importance of the pistol, the earliest the Canadians may see a new service pistol is 2026. The Australians too show no signs of retiring their Hi-Powers, although a Glock purchase has been mooted a number of times. Budgets being what they are – tight – the money will always be spent on higher priority equipment than pistols.

In terms of which pistols will gain prominence within the world's armies, the Glock will surely continue to be a firm favourite. In the author's opinion, Glock's entry into the MHS trials, now known commercially as the Glock 19X, is perhaps the perfect off-the-shelf choice for a general issue combat pistol. It offers utter reliability with simple handling and field stripping. The MHS variant of the Glock 19X is likely even a better choice as it features a manual safety to keep the traditionalists happy. Loaded with the new XM1153 Special Purpose hollow-points or similar, the 19X is the perfect sidearm for the infantry soldier.

The 9 × 19mm SIG Sauer P226 with Surefire weapons light. (*US Army, Capt. Charles Emmons*)

Royal Marines and US Marines firing the 9 × 19mm L1313A1 Glock. (*USMC, Lance Cpl Timothy Turner*)

## Breaking News

Canada has announced an 'Army Interim Pistol Program' due to recognition of the advanced age and thus wear on their issue Browning Hi-Powers. This will provide some 7,000 sidearms as a stop-gap measure. A full replacement programme is still not scheduled. Whilst the Glock is the obvious choice, the SIG-Sauer M17 will likely also compete.

The French Army has also finally announced a procurement programme to replace their issue G1 (Beretta 92 copy) with 75,000 new 9 × 19mm sidearms. The new pistols will be designated as either the PSA (Pistolet Semi-Automatique) or PANG (Pistolet Automatique de Nouvelle Generation). Interestingly, the requirement includes a line item for some 7000 suppressors, along with subsonic ammunition, for the new pistol.

Likely competition will be between Glock, Heckler and Koch, and SIG-Sauer. Both Glock and H&K have extensive ties to French military with numerous Glocks and H&K USPs in service with Army and Navy special operations units. SIG-Sauer arms the majority of general duties police in France and will be hoping to leverage this relationship as well as aggressively pricing their contender (which will be particularly difficult against Glock).

# CHAPTER TWO

# SUB MACHINE GUNS AND PERSONAL DEFENCE WEAPONS

## Overview

Sadly, the days of the military sub machine gun (SMG) are largely over. For many years the demise of the SMG was continually forecast but the platform held on, finding new, although admittedly niche, roles for itself as a Personal Defence Weapon (PDW) or in the hands of special operators. Today, however, the death knell has sounded loud and clear.

The cause of the SMG's demise amongst the infantry was the short-barrelled carbine, typically chambered for the more powerful 5.56 × 45mm round. As the late and much-lamented firearms authority Kevin O'Brien once noted: '*What killed the SMG is simple: AR-platform carbines began to approach the MP5 in size, while being miles ahead in capability.*' This is the story of the demise of the SMG in a nutshell. Short barrel 9 × 19mm SMGs simply cannot compete in a military environment versus an M4 or similar platform which eclipses the SMG in terms of both range and lethality. But firstly, let's take a quick look at the history of the SMG to understand how we have arrived at this point.

SMGs were first designed to equip soldiers with a handy fully automatic, blowback action weapon – using pistol calibre ammunition to help manage the recoil – that could be used in trench-clearing in the First World War, literally spraying huge volumes of rounds down the trench line. The Germans had already perfected the Mauser C96 machine pistol with its own detachable stock and soon developed the famous 9 × 19mm Bergmann MP18, the first true infantry SMG. Surprisingly, the allied nations had no counter and at war's end, Germany and Italy (with their Beretta M1918 firing the 9 × 19mm Glisenti rather than the German 9 × 19mm Parabellum) had the only functional designs that saw combat.

Both nations continued development, followed by the Spanish and Czechs and the Americans, although John Thompson's famous design was commercially produced without government support and until the outbreak of war, was better known as the principal armament of gangsters and G-men during the Prohibition. The advent of the Second World War was the golden era for SMGs. All nations deployed a wide range of designs, many of which were product improved based upon combat experience.

After the war, the SMG was still a popular platform thanks to its compactness and full automatic capability. The iconic 9 × 19mm UZI was designed and manufactured by the young nation state of Israel in the 1950s to provide a cheap and handy weapon for self defence, as well as arming paratroopers and similar troops who required a compact individual weapon.

US Army Cavalry soldier conducts small arms familiarization with Bundeswehr troops and the 4.6 × 30mm MP7A1. (*US Army, 1st Lt. Charles Morgan*)

Into the 1970s, the SMG was largely relegated to arming support troops or tank crews. With the development of such weapons as the 5.56 × 45mm CAR15, a carbine version of the standard M16, the writing was seemingly already on the wall. The rise of international terrorism, however, saved the SMG from extinction as it was soon seen as the perfect shoulder weapon for the fledgling counter-terrorist teams formed to combat the scourge. These different eras resulted in four distinct generations of SMGs.

First generation weapons, to include the inter-war .45ACP Thompson, were heavy and fired from an open bolt, lowering their accuracy at longer ranges. Most had no selector to allow semi-automatic fire, meaning the user would have to become adept at squeezing off short bursts, easier to do with the generally lower cyclic rates of these early weapons. This was not so much of an issue as their intended use was in close quarters urban, trench or jungle fighting.

Second generation comprised the SMGs of the Second World War, the famous 9 × 19mm MP40 and 9 Sten amongst them. These still fired from an open bolt but had been lightened with the use of stamped sheet metal rather than wood and collapsible or folding stocks, reducing overall length. The third generation, born in the Cold War, saw the rise of the telescoping bolt (meaning the bolt wrapped around the barrel) with the 9 × 19mm UZI which further reduced the weapon's overall length. The UZI and the Czech Vz23 also innovated with the use of a magazine that was fed through the pistol grip.

The fourth generation of SMG typically replaced the open bolt mechanism with a closed bolt. This led to far greater accuracy potential, although with prolonged automatic firing it also led to a greater risk of 'cook-offs' and similar malfunctions. Most SMGs, and PDWs, today would be classified as fourth generation. They are typified by the closed bolt action, selectors enabling semi-automatic or even burst along with full automatic, and a collapsible or folding stock as standard. Most also feature Picatinny rails to enable the mounting of optics and lights to the SMG.

Although some would argue that PDWs like the P90, the SIG Sauer MPX, or the commercial Kriss designs are examples of a fifth generation, and they certainly do include some very innovative features such as the magazine placement and feed device of the P90, but are these really evolutionary enough to term them genuinely fifth generation SMGs? The author would argue not. They still fire from a closed bolt and follow the general controls of previous, fourth generation weapons. The MPX for example, whilst being a superb SMG, is generally regarded as an update to the classic MP5.

The only still common military use for the SMG is as a suppressed SOF platform – carbines firing 5.56 × 45mm ammunition are simply not as quiet even with the latest generation of suppressors. Subsonic 9 × 19mm ammunition has also been much more commonly available in a large number of designs, whilst subsonic 5.56 × 45mm is a relatively recent development.

The Heckler & Koch 9 × 19mm MP5A3 in action on the range. (*US Army, Specialist Pierre-Etienne Courtejoie*)

The 5.56 × 45mm relies very much on its velocity to yaw and cause deep primary and secondary wound channels (something we will examine in the following chapter) and reducing its velocity under the speed of sound means reducing its terminal effectiveness. The recoil pulse of the typically light subsonic rounds also significantly decreases the reliability of 5.56 × 45mm weapons.

On a quick tangent – although suppressors are a common sight on military M4A1 carbines and the like carried by SOF, they are generally not using subsonic loads. The suppressor is intended to reduce their signature to the enemy by masking both the report and the muzzle blast. For true suppressed functions subsonics, which eliminate the tell-tale audio crack as the round breaks the sound barrier, are essential.

In this manner, the Heckler and Koch MP5 SD in various models has soldiered on across the world, but even the venerable SD is being replaced by the SIG Sauer MCX in the relatively new calibre of .300 Blackout or 7.62 × 35mm. The MCX has been adopted by numerous SOF units including the British SAS and as such further adoption is all but guaranteed, although intriguingly it was trialled by SOCOM and yet not adopted.

The .300 Blackout offers the capability of using subsonic ammunition when required and then with a magazine change can swap to full-power rounds that can be fired through the suppressor. As the author noted in his last book, *Guns of the Special Forces*, this allows operators to use subsonic ammunition whilst on an objective but gives them the increased range of full-power loads should a firefight in more open country break out. Of course, this is not something that most infantrymen will experience and the need for specialist suppressed weapons is thus largely restricted to SOF.

Where the SMG may still have some use is with military Personal Security Details (PSDs) who require a more compact weapon for use in and around vehicles and in some cases to be concealed upon their person. Whilst carbine length 5.56 × 45mm platforms can cover most needs, in PSD work the soldier may be firing from inside a vehicle or room and the compact carbines available – typically with a 9-inch or less barrel – produce intense muzzle blast, noise and pronounced recoil making them distinctly uncomfortable to shoot (the author has fired the HK53, a 5.56 × 45mm carbine in an MP5 sized chassis, and the muzzle blast was impressive to say the least!).

A 9 × 19mm or similar calibre compact selective-fire weapon, whether a traditional SMG or its more recent cousin, the PDW, offers a possible solution. Pistol calibre rounds produce far less recoil and muzzle blast, particularly in an SMG, than a rifle calibre short barrel carbine whilst being far more accurate than a pistol. Arguably the concept of the SMG and PDW may thus still warrant some examination with regard to the employment of the SMG by conventional military.

The NATO PDW programme of the 1980s and 1990s led to the development of new PDW calibres and new weapons, namely the 5.7 × 28mm and the 4.6 × 30mm fired from the Belgian Fabrique Nationale P90 and the German Heckler and Koch MP7 respectively. These were designed to bridge the gap between service pistols and general issue assault rifles and were intended for the likes of officers, vehicle crews and artillery gunners – all of whom did not require a full-size weapon but needed the ability to mount a defensive action should the need arise. With NATO thinking at the time firmly-on-peer or near-peer threats, the ability to penetrate body armour and Soviet pattern helmets was a foremost requirement.

A PDW variant of the futuristic Heckler and Koch XM-8, long seen as the possible successor to the M16 family, was even developed before the programme was ultimately scrapped. Although the P90 and MP7 garnered the headlines, they were not the first modern PDWs. The Poles for example had designed and issued the $9 \times 18$mm PM-63 back in 1962 for vehicle crews and officers. The PM-63 was notable for the fact that it featured a two-stage trigger in much the same way as the later Steyr AUG. Press to the first stop position and the weapon fires semi-automatically, depress the trigger fully and the PM-63 fires in full-auto.

The PM-63 was replaced by the PM-84 in 1984, a redesigned variant rechambered for $9 \times 19$mm (but also produced in $9 \times 18$mm for domestic use within the Eastern Bloc) and dispensing with the two-stage trigger selector. The PM-84 was itself superseded by the PM-98 and the PM-06 variant that added a Picatinny rail and new adjustable stock but was not adopted by the regular Polish Army, instead being issued to SOF and Border Guard units. Today the PM-84P has been replaced by the $5.56 \times 45$mm Mini-Beryl assault rifle that will be discussed in the next chapter (which itself is being now replaced by the MSBS-5.56B).

A Polish Cavalry soldier fires his $9 \times 19$mm PM-84P Glauberyt SMG/PDW on a NATO range. (*US Army, Pfc. Emily Houdershieldt*)

| | Calibre | Magazine | Weight Unloaded | Length |
|---|---|---|---|---|
| FN P90 | 5.7 × 28mm | 50 | 2.5kg | 500mm |
| SIG Sauer MPX | 9 × 19mm | 30 | 2.7kg | 425/610mm |
| Heckler and Koch MP7A2 | 4.6 × 30mm | 20/40 | 1.5kg | 340/540mm |
| Heckler and Koch MP5A3 | 9 × 19mm | 30 | 2.8kg | 490/660mm |
| Heckler and Koch MP5K | 9 × 19mm | 15/30 | 2.0kg | 315mm |

The Czechs too issued a PDW of sorts to their tank crews – the venerable Vz61 or Skorpion which straddles the definition of SMG and machine pistol. This was produced in the tiny 7.65 × 17mm (.32ACP) and featured a skeleton folding stock. Suppressed models were sometimes encountered with Eastern Bloc SOF but the weapon today is a Cold War relic.

## Calibres and Ammunition

As we have noted, the PDW calibres were designed primarily to penetrate body armour and helmets, not to produce incapacitating rounds in an adversary. Anecdotal evidence from US Navy special operations personnel who have used suppressed MP7s extensively in Afghanistan notes that the 4.6 × 30mm requires multiple hits to be effective, although their quietness was unmatched. Rumours abound that the Navy special mission unit SEAL Team 6 has all but returned to the 9 × 19mm MP5SD series, with the MP7A1 now only used by SEAL support personnel whose primary role is not combat but who need a true PDW such as dog handlers and EOD operators.

One of the chief advantages of the 4.6 × 30mm is the light recoil of the MP7 – it has been compared to the .22LR by some qualified users, making it easier to achieve hits even during extended full-auto fire. The MP7 typically fires a tiny 31-grain round but at a high velocity of around 2,300 feet per second. The standard round, the DM11, features a steel core penetrator but a number of bullet designs are available including a solid copper reduced penetration round and a traditional hollowpoint.

The .300 Blackout is the new kid on the block. Along with offering very quiet subsonic operation in a package of a similar size to an MP5, it gives increased range capability, particularly with standard supersonic ammunition. As noted, the calibre was developed for US special mission units to give them a low-profile suppressed weapon that could be used at close or intermediate engagement ranges beyond the capabilities of the MP5SD series or the MP7.

Will the .300 Blackout gain any traction outside of these limited SOF applications? The author believes not, for a general issue PDW weapon for the infantry it doesn't do anything the 5.56 × 45mm firing a decent round like the M855A1 or Mk 318 cannot from an M4A1 or G36K. For suppressed or clandestine applications, the calibre makes a lot of sense; for anything else it is simply adding yet another calibre to the supply chain. A good case in point is the US Army PSD

A US Marine handling a 4.6 × 30mm Heckler and Koch MP7A1 during joint NATO exercises. Note B&T sound suppressor and Aimpoint red dot optic. *(USMC, Cpl. Clarence L. Wimberly)*

requirement – 9 × 19mm is the stated calibre. For ultra-short SMGs/PDWs, this is really the only choice if the user wants to achieve any degree of accuracy without being deafened and blinded by the report of a compact 5.56 × 45mm.

Questions about its terminal effectiveness have also plagued the 5.7 × 28mm as we have described in the previous chapter. It is difficult to sort the wheat from the chaff as the round is in such limited use that the amount of data that can be collected is minute in comparison to 9 × 19mm or 5.56 × 45mm. Again, where the calibre seems to have a genuine advantage is in suppressed weapons – note a number of European counter-terrorist units issue the weapon to their point-men, presumably with subsonic ammunition. It is in service with a handful of military PSD teams but as a general-issue PDW cartridge, the 9 × 19mm is a far better known quantity.

The great advantage of the 9 × 19mm is that a vast array of ammunition types have been developed for it, both for competition and law enforcement and civilian self-defence application. Whilst most military issue 9 × 19mm SMGs are still fed the standard full-metal-jacket ball round, with the recent adoption of the XM1153 hollowpoint, we may see military SMGs and PDWs finally firing a potent hollowpoint or expanding round. Not to be forgotten is the commonality of 9 × 19mm training ammunition to include frangible and Simunition projectiles. These are stocked by all NATO members and is another good example of NATO standards in small arms ammunition.

## Current Trends

As mentioned, the US Army issued a 2018 requirement for trial weapons for a new PDW or what they are terming an SCW or Sub Compact Weapon. Curiously it calls for 9 × 19mm rather than allowing inclusion of the likes of the 4.6 × 30mm or 5.7 × 28mm. The details are scant and seem to paint a picture of confusion – the Army doesn't seem to actually know what it wants or needs in this new SCW platform, a not uncommon feature of small arms Request for Information (RFI), many of which are more of scoping exercises to understand the requirement than anything designed to lead to adoption.

The RFI mentions Picatinny rails naturally and suppressors are referred to but they are not spelt out as a requirement. The SCW is to be *'capable of engaging threat personnel with a high volume of lethal and accurate fires at close range with minimal collateral damage,'* which means accurate fully-automatic fire with no overpenetration. The ultimate recipients of the SCW will be Army personal security details or PSDs. *'Currently, personal security detail military personnel utilize pistols and rifles; however, there is an operational need for additional concealability and lethality.'*

As many as ten firms initially submitted weapons. These included Beretta with their PMX; Colt with a variant of their M4 based SMG; CZ with the Scorpion EVO 3 A1; LMT with the MARS-L9 suppressed 9 × 19mm variant of their successful 5.56 × 45mm MARS assault rifle; SIG Sauer with the excellent MPX and Trident Rifles acting for B&T with an APC9 variant. There were also four lesser known firms: CMMG with their Ultra PDW (something along the lines of the Colt SMG); Quarter Circle 10 with their CLT and QV5 platforms (AR based but using MP5 magazines); PTR with an MP5 clone and Zenith Firearms with the Z-5RD, Z-5P and Z-5K, these last are again clones of the MP5, this time produced in Turkey under licence from H&K.

Three further firms were later added to the list: the famous Noveske Rifleworks with an AR-based design; Angstadt Arms with their UDP-9 which feeds from Glock magazines and again resembles a miniaturised AR platform; and finally Heckler and Koch who were visibly and confusingly absent from the initial list. H&K submitted their UMP9, a lighter, polymer-based variant of the base MP5.

Not surprisingly, the programme was cancelled in mid-2018 but relaunched mere weeks later with a new emphasis placed on concealability – a *'highly concealable SCW system'*. The focus on concealability means the weapon must be no longer than 15 inches with the stock collapsed (folding stocks are allowable but 'telescopically collapsible' seems to be the preferred option).

There was further detail in the form of a requirement for the weapon to fire a 147-grain round (perhaps the XM1152 ball adopted with the new M17 pistol), be able to be fed from either a 20- or 30-round magazine (the 20 round makes sense if concealability is really the deciding factor) and it must be able to fire up to 60 rounds per minute on full automatic for five minutes (thus 300 rounds) without failure. Certainly, the known designs from H&K, CZ and the SIG should be able to easily meet these requirements.

A US Army Personal Security Detail NCO in Iraq armed with a 9 × 19mm Heckler and Koch MP5PDW. (*US Army, Pvt 1st Class Jesus J. Aranda*)

Who will win the contract? The author believes SIG Sauer are best placed from a position of (a) fit for purpose design with the MPX, (b) M4 based controls meaning minimal retraining, and (c) recent history of wins of US government contracts with the M320 pistol in the M17 competition and adoption of the .300 Blackout MCX by Joint Special Operations Command (JSOC), along with their involvement in the SOCOM PDW requirement which we'll cover in a moment. Other likely contenders are of course H&K and CZ with their proven designs, although LMT may be the dark horse that surprises everyone, having quietly made something of a name for themselves in quality military small arms.

This is not the first time the US Army has looked at a PDW issue. Both the P90 and MP7 have been trialled by both the Army and USMC as far back as the early 1990s and more recently, the Army was publicly looking at the PDW concept in 2007 – likely spurred on by the nature of the war in Iraq. At the time, the head of the programme office mentioned a platform that was *'larger than a pistol and smaller than a carbine'*, designed primarily for vehicle crews: *'When you get all your soldiers geared up in an up-armoured Humvee, there's not a lot of room.'* Suffice to say, again the programme went nowhere.

SOCOM are also investigating a PDW, although this will be chambered in the .300 Blackout calibre and likely has been influenced heavily by the JSOC adoption of the .300 Blackout SIG Sauer MCX for its Low-Visibility Assault Weapon requirement. A compact variant of the MCX is the presumed winner, known commercially as the Rattler which is about the same size as an MP5K. Muzzle blast and recoil are likely to be significant without the use of a suppressor. The SOCOM requirement was for a kit that could be employed with an in-service M4A1 lower rather than a complete weapon (and includes a suppressor option). Whether this PDW will end up being adopted is open to question although field trials are apparently imminent.

The Bundeswehr is one of the few NATO nations to actually issue a PDW in the role that it was intended for, in their case the H&K MP7. It has been widely employed in Afghanistan by support personnel (most specifically drivers), military police and is issued to infantry officers and NCOs. One German company commander, however, mentioned to the author that he swapped his MP7 for a G36 as soon as he practicably could after arrival in Afghanistan, understandably preferring the larger 5.56 × 45mm calibre and the longer-range capability of the rifle.

The employment of the MP7 by vehicle crews in the Bundeswehr makes much sense and really ratifies the concept of the PDW – a compact, lightweight weapon that can be easily transported within a vehicle. Although some German soldiers have argued that the short barrel, folding stock G36C would be a better choice, the MP7 seems to have been successful in this admittedly niche capacity. Prior to the MP7 adoption, the Bundeswehr used the MP2, their classification for the MP5, some of which still soldiered on in NATO deployments to the Baltics as late as 2005 as the MP7 adoption rolled-out. The MP2 was employed in much the same manner and was widely used by field police. Intriguingly, in 2018, the Bundeswehr loaned forty MP7s to a Berlin police authority as there was an

Bundeswehr infantry patrol supporting a Belgian Army psy-ops team in Afghanistan 2012. Note the 4.6 × 30mm MP7A1s carried by the officer and radio operator in the centre – one with extended 30-round magazine. The Belgians carry the standard 5.56 × 45mm FNC rifle, the other Germans a mix of 5.56 × 45mm G36A2, 7.62 × 51mm G3A3ZF and just visible to the rear, a 5.56 × 45mm Heckler & Koch MG4. *(ISAF, Andrea Bienert)*

apparent delay in delivery of their own MP7s (the German Army now has over 5,000 in their armouries).

The Japanese Ground Self-Defense Force adopted the Minebea Mitsumi M9 based on the IMI Mini-Uzi in 1999 as a PDW for vehicle and tank crews, aviation, logistics and artillery personnel (prior to the M9's adoption, Japanese tank crews still carried the Second World War relic M3A1 'Grease Gun' in .45ACP, incidentally as did many US Army AFV crews until the M4 became more widely available). It was also intended to serve as a PDW for officers in much the same way as the MP7 was in German service. Although it features a forward grip, it is entirely stockless and, combined with its reported rate of fire of 1,100 rounds per minute, makes the weapon notoriously inaccurate over anything but the closest ranges.

Taurus recently developed the 9 × 19mm SMT9 which has been adopted by the Brazilian Army. It features a curved 30-round magazine and visually recalls the HK UMP and the Czech Scorpion Evo. Although primarily destined for special operations forces, some SMT9s appear to have been fielded by Brazilian paratrooper units.

The Chinese military also embarked on the PDW journey beginning in the 1980s. The PLA has a number of submachine guns in inventory, although mainly integrally suppressed models for SOF use. The general issue SMG is the bullpup Type 05 produced in the Chinese proprietary calibre, the 5.8 × 21mm, replacing the 7.62 × 25mm Type 85.

The round is also used in the QSZ-92 or Type 92 general issue PLA pistol, following similar thinking to FN's P90 and FiveseveN pairing and the proposed

A rare Japanese 9 × 19mm PM-9 Minebea, a curious Mini UZI variant. (*Creative Commons*)

matching of Heckler and Koch's MP7 and their unfortunately defunct UCP or P46 pistol. The PLA view the Type 05 as a true PDW, replacing the assault rifle for officers and certain infantry roles. The competing model was the CF05, originally produced in 5.8 × 21mm but now offered for export and to police in 9 × 19mm. An integrally suppressed variant is also produced known as the CS06.

## Individual Weapon Summaries

### Heckler and Koch MP5 Series

The MP5 is perhaps the gold standard of SMGs. Like the Israeli UZI before it, the development of the MP5 was a game-changer. It was one of the first SMGs to fire from a closed bolt, increasing its accuracy, and scaling down a number of features from its parent, the G3 battle rifle. Its original stick magazine was replaced in the late 1970s for the familiar curved version to better feed hollowpoints and frangible ammunition. With its adoption by many of the world's leading SOF, it was inevitable that the MP5 would trickle down to infantrymen.

In the West German Bundeswehr, it was adopted as the MP2 and served as a PDW for weapons crews, officers and vehicle crewmen. In many other armies it was adopted for the tasks of close personal protection. The core MP5A2 and A3 with fixed and collapsible stocks respectively, were joined by the integrally suppressed SD series and the ultra-compact MP5K or Kurtz (short) designed for body-guarding work.

The MP5 undertook a significant series of modifications in the 1980s for a variant intended to equip US special operations units with the SMG I, the SMG II,

MP2000 and the MP5 PIP. The only successful design began life as the HK54A1 (the original production name for the MP5 was HK54) but was later known as the SMG II. It was optimised for use with a suppressor including a pressure switch that allowed the user to adapt the weapon from firing supersonic to subsonic reliably and cleanly when specialist subsonic ammunition was not available. Original versions also featured a bolt-lock position that would allow single shots to be fired without the bolt reciprocating and significantly lightened the weight of the weapon with a new fully-collapsible stock and angled foregrip. It also allowed the single base weapon to be configured by the user in at least three ways – as a conventional MP5 without suppressor, as an SD model with suppressor and as an MP5K style compact SMG (a 50-round drum was also produced).

The SMG II was never produced in quantities apart from a small order of 60 or so for the US Army special mission unit, Delta Force. These were basically hand-built and were used extensively by that unit on Aztec counter-terrorism drills. A former operator explained to the author that the SMG II was well-liked and used alongside regular MP5s ('it was the operator's choice') until both were replaced in the role by short barrel 5.56 × 45mm Colt carbines.

The most successful variant in US military service was the MP5N (Navy) first adopted by the SEALs and featuring a titanium forward sight, ambidextrous fire selector (which later became standard on all MP5 models) and a threaded barrel for suppressor use. Both 10mm and .40S&W versions were launched for the law enforcement market but made little in-roads with the 9 × 19mm model reigning supreme. A slightly modernised and lightened version, the UMP, was launched in 9 × 19mm, .40 S&W and .45 ACP but outside of police and some SOF sales, it didn't make a huge impact. The UMP in 9 × 19mm is currently amongst the competitors in the US Army SCW trial.

The MP5 is still the most likely to be encountered SMG in military hands, simply as so many have been produced. The Royal Marines issued a variant with

The classic 9 × 19mm Heckler and Koch MP5A3 with Navy selector (adding 3-round burst). (*Heckler and Koch*)

British Royal Marine Commandos conduct drills with their railed 9 × 19mm MP5A3s (rails likely FAB Defense or B&T). Note the two MP5s at the end of the line featuring vertical foregrips. (*USMC, Sgt. Esdras Ruano*)

a Picatinny rail kit for the specialised role of boarding and clearing suspect vessels as the 9 × 19mm provides less of a danger of ricochets and splashback when operating around bulkheads, particularly when using frangible CQB ammunition. It is also still in use by US Army PSD teams in a number of guises including the MP5K PDW which adds a side-folding stock to the shortened MP5.

### Heckler and Koch MP7 Series

We have spoken at length about the MP7 earlier in this chapter but the principal features of the MP7 family are its ultra-compact length, its relative quietness when used with a suppressor, and its light weight – even drop holsters have been designed for the platform to allow it to be carried like an over-sized pistol.

H&K market a proprietary rig as their marketing notes:

The MP7 multi-purpose ambidextrous holster can be carried on the thigh, it can be secured to the belt at the hip, carried on the shoulder or concealed by a reversible vest. The weapon is secured to the holster using the lateral Picatinny rail of the MP7 whilst the locking mechanism ensures that the fire selector has to be in the SAFE position before the weapon can be holstered. This added safety feature eliminates the chance of accidentally firing the holstered weapon.

Its portability is its key and really only attraction to non SOF users as it fires a still controversial round, the 4.6 × 30mm, and suffers from a limited maximum range

A close up view of the 4.6 × 30mm Heckler and Koch MP7A1. *(Heckler and Koch)*

(in practical terms, 50–100 metres in combat conditions is the best one can expect from any SMG including the MP7 series). Pitched originally as the natural successor to the MP5 after NATO interest in the PDW concept waned, the MP7 has not unfortunately achieved anything like the same levels of adoption outside of European specialist police and a handful of military SOF units.

The latest variant, the MP7A2, is coated in H&K's distinctive dark yellow (almost reminiscent of Second World War Dunkelgelb) RAL 8000 finish and now features a non-folding forward grip. Instead it is attached by an underbarrel rail. Additional Picatinny rails have also been added to either side of the barrel; 20-, 30- and 40-round magazines are available for both the A1 and A2 variants with the 20 routinely seen in MP7A1s in Bundeswehr service.

### CZ Scorpion EVO 3

Adopted in small numbers by the Czech Army in 2012, the EVO 3 also sees service with the Afghan National Directorate of Security intelligence agency and numerous police and paramilitary groups in countries as disparate as Kenya and Egypt. It is an entirely conventional design featuring a side-folding stock which reduces its length to just over the size of an MP5K. Chambered for the universal 9 × 19mm, it fires from a standard 30-round magazine or can be fitted with shortened 10- or 20-round magazines when concealed. Like the MP5, it is a pleasure to shoot and easy to shoot well.

### P90

We have covered the development of this Belgian design in depth so suffice to say here that the P90 has seen very limited military service. Although it is often stated that the Mexican Army adopted the P90 as a general issue SMG, it was in fact only purchased by their SOF. Where the weapon has found favour is in its suppressed form. Using the subsonic SB193 round, it is carried by a number of

European police counter-terrorist units, who appreciate the massive firepower available in such a compact package.

## Type 05

The Chinese PLA issue the Type 05 as their standard issue PDW. A bullpup design that resembles the PLA's issue rifle, the QBZ-95, it is fed from a 50-round magazine in its original $5.8 \times 21$mm chambering, common to the QSZ-92 service pistol (not to be confused with the longer $5.8 \times 42$mm of the QBZ-95). A $9 \times 19$mm variant has been produced for law enforcement and export sales that sneakily uses the same magazine design as the MP5.

Although looking futuristic, the weapon is surprisingly simplistic. It features basic iron sights and instead of a common Picatinny rail, has a fixed optics mount above the carrying handle. Additionally, it fires from an open bolt, somewhat compromising its accuracy. The Type 05 is available with a quick-detach suppressor matched with subsonic $5.8 \times 21$mm ammunition.

## SIG Sauer MPX

SIG Sauer saw the potential in the SMG both as a PDW and suppressed platform for SOF. They took the two leading platforms in both areas – namely the M4 and the MP5 – and combined the best elements of each to come up with the $9 \times 19$mm MPX. Modularity being the key word in twenty-first century small arms design, SIG Sauer fully adopted the principle with the MPX allowing users to easily

$9 \times 19$mm SIG MPX with sound suppressor and SIG Romeo reflex sight. (*Creative Commons, Gar2chan*)

configure different stock types and barrel lengths (an 8-inch barrel is standard) without recourse to a unit armourer.

Conversion kits aimed at law enforcement allow rechambering to the proprietary .357 SIG or the .40 S&W. It is suppressor ready, although an integrally suppression variant, the MPX-SD, is also available as is the shortened MPX-K. Firing from the closed bolt, the MPX is firmly pitched as an obvious successor to the MP5 family, even mimicking their naming conventions, but handily follows standard M4/M16 controls so anyone trained on an M4 or M16 platform will be able to easily transition to the MPX.

The weapon is new to market and has yet to generate any significant military sales although police and civilian sales of the semi-automatic only variant appear robust. SIG Sauer are surely betting on winning the US Army SCW procurement although a US Army Contracting Command order for up to 2,000 MPXs has already been placed in 2018.

The intended end users for this purchase, which also includes large quantities of $7.62 \times 51$mm 716G2 rifles, .300 Blackout MCXs and $9 \times 19$mm SP2022 pistols, is unknown although the Army did make a bulk purchase of SP2022s in the late 2000s which were transferred to the Iraqi Police, so supplying partner nations is the most likely reason for this latest purchase.

## Future Trends

Despite all of the doom and gloom, the PDW may be in for something of a revival with the increased threat of Russian 'hybrid warfare' tactics. Following the example of Ukraine, the Russians may well deploy their 'Little Green Men', as their SOF in unmarked uniforms are termed, in support of similar expansionist missions in the Baltics.

The Russian model means that non-frontline units could quickly find themselves facing Russian SOF, a situation that certainly calls for something more robust than a $9 \times 19$mm pistol with which to defend themselves. It could be argued that even an Iraq scenario of predominantly urban insurgency may foster a return to the PDW, although shortened $5.56 \times 45$mm carbines like the M4 served admirably during the long insurgency following the 2003 invasion.

New models do appear, but these are aimed predominantly at the police market – the excellent $9 \times 19$mm B&T APC9 for instance is in service with the Austrian counter-terrorist unit EKO Cobra and was developed with their input. The Russians have adopted the Vityaz-SN, but again primarily in the hands of internal security and SOF.

Along with the 'Little Green Men' threat, the biggest likely impact on the future of SMGs and PDWs is the US Army SCW contract. The perceived need for such a platform still puzzles the author as, unless these will be concealed on-person (like the famous MP5K covert shoulder rig) or carried in 'man-bags' or similar, a $5.56 \times 45$mm platform with a side-folding stock would be much more preferable. A G36C or an MCX with its original skeletonised side-folding stock would offer much greater capability within a package only marginally larger than an MP5.

The Russian 9 × 19mm Vityaz-SN standard issue SMG based on the AK74 assault rifle.
*(Kalashnikov Group/Kalashnikov Media)*

Whatever weapon is adopted will be on its way to becoming the future MP5 although in a far, far reduced marketplace. The SMG may just have a little more life in it yet.

## Breaking News

As we go to press, the US Army has announced their down-select to six competitors for the SCW contract. Still in the running are Angstadt Arms with their AR based UDP-9, SIG Sauer with their MPX-K and Trident with their own B&T submission (which could be the MP9 but more likely another APC9 variant as the requirement seems to rule out weapons featuring a magazine fed through the pistol grip).

Three new entrants have been added and passed the down-select: B&T USA with an unknown platform but likely the APC9K; Global Ordnance with another new platform, the AP9A3S based on a Slovakian design (and looking rather like an APC9 at first glance); and Shield Arms with their SA-9K (a design so new there are as yet no images of it available, however, it too is believed to be AR based).

Beretta, Colt, CZ, Heckler and Koch, LMT and Noveske have been withdrawn, as have CMMG, Quarter Circle 10, PTR and Zenith Firearms. The smart money is still on the MPX-K with SIG's recent procurement wins in mind (along with very competitive pricing) but the APC9K may still surprise … and it did. The APC9K was successful in winning the SCW contract with an initial purchase of 350 weapons announced in April 2019.

# CHAPTER THREE

# ASSAULT RIFLES AND CARBINES

## Overview

The principal individual weapon carried by today's infantry soldier is the assault rifle. The term is widely considered to denote a weapon capable of selective fire – semi and fully automatic or burst modes – firing an intermediate calibre rifle round. Intermediate rounds have less range and recoil than full power rifle calibres like the $7.62 \times 54$mm or $7.62 \times 51$mm, but with greater range and terminal effects than the $9 \times 19$mm used in sub-machine guns and pistols.

The greatest recent evolution in the assault rifle is currently at hand as the US develops a new intermediate calibre which will likely then be adopted by NATO and become the twenty-first century's $5.56 \times 45$mm. It is thus worth taking a moment to examine the fascinating, and frustrating, history of the development of the assault rifle and the intermediate calibre round to understand the current focus on the new 6.5mm CT, the most likely successor.

A US Army soldier returns fire during a contact with insurgents in Mosul, Iraq 2008. He carries the $5.56 \times 45$mm M4 with M68 Aimpoint red dot and PEQ-2A infrared illuminator.
(*US Army, Spc. Kieran Cuddihy*)

The Germans conducted extensive operational research into infantry combat during the First World War and concluded that the vast majority of contacts with the enemy were within 300 metres. This spurred development of the intermediate calibre with their initial efforts focusing on 7mm. The concept was developed into what is commonly understood to be the first true assault rifle used by the German Army during the Second World War in the form of the 7.92 × 33mm Sturmgewehr 44 or StG44.

The 7.92 × 33mm was known as the *'Infanteriepatrone Kurz'* or 'infantry cartridge short', being a necked-down version of the 7.92 × 57mm used in the issue machine guns and K98 bolt action rifles. The production Stg44, which followed a number of trials weapons, fired the new cartridge from a relatively short, selective-fire rifle that was fed from a 30-round curved magazine, reminiscent of the later AK-47.

The Stg44 was intended to be used on semi-automatic at range whilst the 500 round-per-minute cyclic rate would be handy when assaulting buildings or trenches. German tactical doctrine placed much significance on suppressive fire and the StG44 was seen as the perfect accompaniment to their MG34 and MG42 medium machine guns.

The Russian 6.5 × 50mm Fedorov Avtomat actually pre-dated the famous German weapon by several decades, being first issued in 1916 and used in the latter stages of the First World War and the Russian Civil War. The Fedorov Avtomat was actually designed for the Russian 7.62 × 54mm but was rechambered to fire the Japanese 6.5 × 50mm which was available in abundance from captured stocks.

In 1942, the Russians captured a number of examples of the early prototype German Mk b42 that was undergoing combat trials on the Eastern Front. Russian engineers began work on developing a similar intermediate calibre round and by the close of 1943, they had one ready for testing – the 7.62 × 41mm, and by the following year a weapon to fire it had been developed. Fielding of the AS-44 was too late for combat operations, although some were issued for post-war field trials.

The AS-44 was of a similar weight to its contemporaries at 5 kilograms. Initial versions also featured a folding bipod which increased the weight of the weapon, but increased stability and accuracy when firing full-auto. It offered a detachable 30-round curved magazine, inspired by the Mk b42, which resembled the design eventually chosen for the AK-47. Although the AS-44 performed well in testing, it failed to match the accuracy of the issued bolt action Mosin Nagant 91/30.

Other similar designs were developed by the Russians for weapons trials, including a second weapon designated the AS-44 but designed by the developer of the famous PPSH-41 sub-machine gun. The Bulkin AB-46 was another, a design that directly impacted on the final production version of the AK-47. At a glance it appears to be the bastard offspring of an AK-47 and the original Stg44.

Another design was the Korobov TKB-408. It was unique in that it was a bull-pup design, meaning that the magazine well was placed behind the pistol grip to reduce the overall length of the weapon. The TKB-408 was undoubtedly one of the first bullpup designs, a concept that would later heavily inspire British post-war small arms design.

Competitive trials held in 1946 led to the selection of Mikhail Kalashnikov's AK-46. Following several years of refinements to Kalashnikov's design, it was officially adopted in 1949 as the AK-47. Firing the intermediate 7.62 × 39mm round, the AK-47 featured a fixed wooden stock, fired from a detachable 30-round magazine and could fire both semi and full automatic. The AK-47 was phased in to replace the Simonov SKS semi-automatic carbine that the Russians had adopted as an interim measure.

Other nations were following suit after studying infantry combat in the Second World War. A number of reports supported the contention that most infantry combat occurred within the golden 275–300 metre mark, at least in the European theatre of war, including Norman Hitchman's *Operational Requirements for an Infantry Hand Weapon* for Johns Hopkins University which studied rifle use in combat.

Hitchman noted in the declassified report: '*Battlefield visibility data show*[s] *why combat rifle fire is actually so limited in range by normal terrain obstructions to the line of sight as rarely to exceed 300 yards* [274 metres].' He also noted that beyond that range, marksmanship drastically worsened:

> Measurements of marksmanship show that performance is of a very low order beyond a range of 300 yards. For attack and defense in European actions, it was found that about 80 per cent of effective rifle and LMG fire takes place at less than 200 yards [182 meters] and 90 per cent at less than 300 yards, according to the estimates made by the men interviewed. About 90 per cent of the LMG fire was at less than 300 yards.

He had this to say about calibres: '*Wound ballistic data offer convincing evidence that small caliber, high velocity missiles* [bullets] *may be used profitably at such ranges, without loss in wounding effects and with significant logistical gains.*'

The British, whilst still agreeing with the move toward a lighter intermediate calibre, instead looked for a selective fire rifle chambered for a new round that could reach targets out to 600 metres. They came up with the .280 or more precisely the 7 × 43mm and a revolutionary assault rifle to fire it, the EM-2. This was one of the first bullpup designs (along with the Russian TKB-408) and featured a 1 × optical sight incorporated in the carrying handle.

Unfortunately the US, despite the Hitchman report (and Donald Hall's *An Effectiveness Study of the Infantry Rifle* for Aberdeen Proving Ground) and similar findings in UK operational research, had decided upon the 7.62 × 51mm as a replacement for their wartime .30-06 and placed pressure upon the newly formed NATO to adopt the 7.62 × 51mm as its standard rifle calibre. The British actually did end up going it alone and adopting the 7 × 43mm briefly with the EM-2 (as the Rifle, Automatic, No. 9 Mk 1) before a change of government cancelled the programme and instead adopted a semi-automatic only licenced version of the Fabrique Nationale FAL in 7.62 × 51mm (the L1A1 Self Loading Rifle). The history of infantry small arms would read rather differently if the EM-2, and more importantly its 7 × 43mm round, had been adopted. We will see later how modern developments point toward a calibre within the 6.5mm to 7mm range as the ideal assault rifle calibre.

The EM-2 was certainly forward thinking and not just in its calibre. As mentioned, it incorporated a magnified optic, one of the first designs to do so and something which became much in favour in the 1970s and 1980s before the advent of the Picatinny rail. (The Germans had incorporated an optic on early marks of their 7.92 × 57mm FG42 but this was later scrapped and the weapon itself was arguably closer to a battle or automatic rifle than a true assault rifle due to its calibre.) The EM-2 was also a bullpup which has proven to be one of the more interesting paths in post-war small arms design.

The origin of the name 'bullpup' is shrouded in the mists of time, but it is generally agreed that the earliest example was the Thorneycroft Carbine designed in 1905. The EM-2 was probably the most well known until the arrival of the Steyr AUG, the FAMAS and the L85A1. Essentially a bullpup places the magazine behind the working parts in the receiver, shortening the overall length of the weapon but maintaining a similar length barrel to more conventional designs. It was briefly heralded as the future for infantry rifles during the 1970s only to fade into almost obscurity until a recent flurry of designs has seen the likes of the Croatian VHS-2, the Israeli Tavor and the new Polish MSBS-5.56B reignite interest.

With the M14 adopted in the US and the FN FAL or H&K G3 across the rest of NATO, it took events in South-East Asia to force a re-examination of a smaller

The historical evolution to the L85; from left to right: the 5.56 × 45mm L85A2, the 4.85 × 49mm XL64E5 and the .280 British EM-2. Many argue that the .280 was the correct choice for a NATO standard assault rifle calibre. (*Open Government License v3.0, PO Phot Owen Cooban*)

Australian Army infantryman in Uruzgan Province, Afghanistan 2010. He is armed with the 5.56 × 45mm F88SA1 variant mounting a Trijicon ACOG. (*Commonwealth of Australia*)

calibre. As most readers will know, the AR-15 and later M16 series in 5.56 × 45mm were produced as lightweight, handy selective fire weapons initially for US Air Force security police and special operations personnel.

Amid much controversy and politicking (including the scrapping of the Army's much heralded SPIW or Special Purpose Individual Weapon which fired a 5.6 × 49mm fletchette round and looked something like a bullpup FG42), the M16, as the XM16E1, was adopted by the US military alongside the M14. By the late 1960s, however, the M14s had virtually disappeared from front-line service.

We will discuss later the inherent benefits and drawbacks of the 5.56 × 45mm itself but the success of the M16 eventually saw other NATO countries adopt the calibre, despite much groaning over yet another change foisted upon them by the US. In the Soviet Union, the AK-74 was developed, firing a similar small calibre but high velocity projectile, the 5.45 × 39mm. In developing nations, 7.62 × 51mm and 7.62 × 39mm would reign supreme and for many years to come (invariably fired from either the Heckler and Koch G3 or the Fabrique Nationale FAL).

\*   \*   \*

The next great attempt in innovation following the widespread adoption of the so-called SCHV or small calibre high velocity 5.56 × 45mm was the US Army Advanced Combat Rifle (ACR) programme. Maxim Popenker and Anthony G. Williams do an admirable job in describing the programme in their book *Assault Rifle: The Development of the Modern Military Rifle and its Ammunition* and readers

The Steyr ACR (Advanced Combat Rifle) prototype for the defunct ACR programme firing the 5.6mm fletchette. (*Defence Academy Shrivenham, Matthew Moss*)

are directed toward this work, however, a brief appraisal is required here to understand the impacts of the ACR.

The ACR programme, launched in 1985, aimed to develop a replacement for the M16A2 that would see '*an enhancement in hit probability of at least 100 per cent at combat ranges over the baseline performance of the M16A2 rifle ... at extended ranges, the improvement required will be considerably greater than 100 per cent. The weapon will be expected to enable the rifleman to detect targets at ranges greater than 400m in offensive action and at least 1,000m during the conduct of the defense,*' according to the programme summary.

With such ambitious objectives, the programme was all but doomed to failure, however it produced a number of interesting prototypes, all optimised to increase hit probability by smothering the target with projectiles. A number of companies pursued fletchette ammunition designs following the long defunct SPIW initiative, another developed a duplex round which improved short range accuracy, whilst Heckler and Koch famously developed the G11 with its caseless ammunition. The G11 offered a 3-round burst that fired at an incredible 2,000 rounds per minute, the unique design of the weapon's buffer ensuring the recoil was not felt by the shooter until after the 3 rounds had left the barrel.

Although appearing the most conventional of the prototype designs for the ACR, the Colt ACR fired a 5.56 × 45mm duplex round. (*Defence Academy Shrivenham, Matthew Moss*)

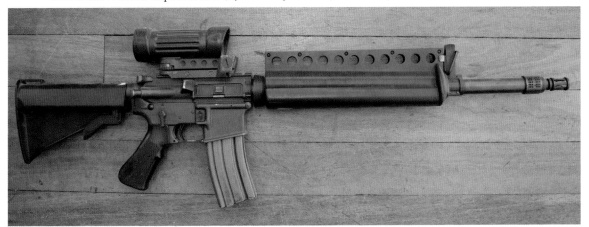

The 4.7mm caseless Heckler and Koch G11 prototype for the ACR programme.
(*Defence Academy Shrivenham, Matthew Moss*)

Despite some genuine innovation, none of the examples could meet the lofty aims of the programme. Some of the developments would be seen in later rifles however, particularly with regard to multi-position collapsible stocks, integral and railed combat optics and caseless ammunition. Next was the Objective Individual Combat Weapon (OICW) which again aimed to increase hit probability at similar ranges to the ACR. The method called for an integrated grenade launcher using high tech systems which could airburst grenades above the target; one programme officer explained: '*It knows where to blow up. The fire control has a ballistic computer with a range finder allowing it to program the round to within one meter of its target.*'

Heckler and Koch developed the XM-29, a monstrous looking weapon that featured a 20mm grenade launcher mounted above an XM-8 5.56 × 45mm rifle which was based on the G36. Mounted above the grenade launcher was a laser range finder and optical sight which increased the bulkiness of the weapon. Trying to combine so many requirements into an infantry weapon ensured that none were ultimately acceptable – the assault rifle component only had a 9-inch barrel, leading to poor accuracy at longer ranges, and the 20mm rounds were not considered lethal enough.

The OICW programme, although a failure like the ACR, did lead to a number of developments that were later incorporated into new weapon designs. The assault rifle component, the XM-8, looked to be a contender as a possible replacement for the M16A2 and was even trialled in limited numbers in Iraq. It appeared again during a 2007 test to compare the reliability of the M4 in dusty conditions in which it performed admirably. The grenade launcher went on to become the ultimately doomed XM-25 Punisher which we will detail in a later chapter.

\* \* \*

Perhaps the biggest recent development in assault rifle ammunition in recent years has arrived in the form of the US Army LSAT or Lightweight Small Arms Technologies programme which spent almost a decade from 2008 working

The final competitor in the ACR trials, the AAI ACR, firing 5.56 × 45mm fletchette ammunition. (*Defence Academy Shrivenham, Matthew Moss*)

on new concepts to reduce the weight of standard issue ammunition including the 5.56 × 45mm and 7.62 × 51mm. Partnering with commercial specialists such as Textron/AAI, LSAT produced cased telescoped or CT ammunition for both calibres. Cased telescoped ammunition uses a polymer casing to hold the bullet rather than the traditional brass or steel casing. By eliminating the metal, this can reduce the weight of CT ammunition by more than a third in comparison with brass.

The LSAT programme has now been subsumed by the Next Generation Weapons System (NGWS) programme which, whilst initially focused on a squad automatic weapon replacement (the Next Generation Squad Automatic Rifle set to be issued in 2022), will also look a Next Generation Squad Weapon (Carbine). Five firms are working on the SAW replacement and at least some of these will continue onto the carbine development.

Army Lieutenant General Paul Ostrowski has been quoted as saying: '*We know that the 5.56mm is not going to be the round of the future because we have issues associated with adversaries' body armor,*' but what that ammunition will look like and its calibre is undecided: '*Some will probably come with a polymer case that looks just like a current 5.56mm round except there won't be as much brass, some will come with a polymer case that is of the non-traditional form.*'

## Calibres and Ammunition

Assault rifle calibres are perhaps the biggest bone of contention amongst firearms enthusiasts, but the harsh reality is that lower calibre ammunition translates into a lighter combat load. The terminal effectiveness and range capabilities of the lower calibre round must however be optimised to ensure the best compromise for the infantryman.

Thomas Ehrhart, the author of the influential study *Increasing Small Arms Lethality in Afghanistan: Taking Back the Infantry Half-Kilometer* explained to the author that all such all arguments boil down to: '*What we learned in the various studies of combat performance with small arms following WWII and Korea is what led to our current use of 5.56. Soldiers can shoot better with 5.56 than they can with 7.62, and they can carry twice the amount of ammunition for the same weight.*' The late 'Hognose', Kevin O'Brien, perhaps put it best when he said: '*You can carry it all day, or you can shoot it all day, but not both.*'

Balanced against the weight calculation is effectiveness. The ideal military bullet needs to have the capability of penetrating through whatever clothing or

|  | Calibre | Magazine | Weight Unloaded | Length |
|---|---|---|---|---|
| EF88 | 5.56 × 45mm | 30 | 3.39kg | 802mm |
| HK416 (with 14.5in barrel) | 5.56 × 45mm | 30 | 3.56kg | 900/804mm |
| AK-12 | 5.45 × 39mm | 30 | 3.3kg | 945/725mm |
| AK-74M | 5.45 × 39mm | 30 | 3.6kg | 943/705mm |
| X-95 | 5.56 × 45mm | 30 | 2.95kg | 590mm |
| M16A4 | 5.56 × 45mm | 30 | 3.9kg | 1,006mm |
| M4A1 | 5.56 × 45mm | 30 | 3.51kg | 840/756mm |
| L85A3 | 5.56 × 45mm | 30 | 4kg | 785mm |
| Type 95 | 5.8 × 42mm | 30 | 3.3kg | 743mm |
| G36 | 5.56 × 45mm | 30 | 3.6kg | 998/758mm |

body armour the target is wearing, penetrate into the body and then expand or fragment to cause the largest possible permanent wound channel, hopefully without overpenetrating to exit the body. As we have noted earlier, the velocity of the round will increase the effects of the temporary wound channel – a round that is largely spent, meaning that it has lost most of its velocity for instance at extended ranges, will cause a minimal temporary wound channel, even if it fragments and expands.

A Czech Republic soldier in pre-deployment training for Afghanistan in 2012, armed with the 5.56 × 45mm CZ805A2 carbine. (*US Army, Spc Tristan Bolden*)

The bullet needs to be able to penetrate far enough through tissue and muscle to destroy vital organs that are located deeper in the body. Thus, a round such as some frangible designs intended to expend their energy upon initially striking the body, will not always reliably incapacitate an adversary. To do so requires some amount of penetration to reach the vital organs and/or create a massive wound channel.

Other rounds, typically those designed with a requirement to penetrate helmets and light body armour, including most standard issue military assault rifle rounds, may instead 'zip' through the target's body without expanding or fragmenting and often exiting, creating a narrow permanent wound channel. If such a round destroys a vital organ on its path, it may well incapacitate the target, but the consistency of any such incapacitation relies purely on the chance of such a round hitting a vital organ. Glenn Dean, a US Army officer involved in the development of the M855A1 enhanced 5.56 × 45mm round, explained: '... *destruction of central nervous system tissue so that the body can no longer control function, or reduction in ability to function over time through blood loss. The closest things the human body has to an "off switch" are the brain, brain stem, and upper spinal cord, which are small and well-protected targets. Even a heart shot allows a person to function for a period of time before finally succumbing to blood loss.*'

What is needed is a round that will penetrate deep enough before expanding and/or fragmenting to ensure the best chance of destroying these organs (this will also limit the likelihood of over-penetration that can be dangerous in densely populated urban areas). The round also needs to be barrier-blind to some extent, meaning that it will not be deflected or prematurely expand/fragment when it strikes an intermediate object on its path to the target (car window glass, for example, or even heavy foliage). The same round ideally will also be able to penetrate the body armour and helmets of likely peer or near peer enemies, all the while doing so with acceptable accuracy and reliability. A tall order by any measure.

The original M855 issued by the US military since the early 1980s was a 62-grain round encased in a copper jacket with a lead core surrounding a steel penetrator. This steel penetrator was designed from the outset to penetrate Soviet Army issue helmets and body armour, examples of which had been recovered from Afghanistan and used in the ballistic testing of the round. It was actually adopted in 1982 to replace the M193 primarily to improve the performance of the M249 SAW at longer engagement ranges (the M193 was a lighter 55-grain full metal jacket round). The M855 was known across NATO as the SS109. Amongst users in the US military it was informally known as the 'Green Tip' on account of its distinctive colouring.

In overly simplistic terms, a well-placed 5.56 × 45mm round to the head is far better than a 7.62 × 51mm to the extremities. Shot placement is key and effective shot placement only occurs through regular and rigorous training with the individual weapon. However, having said that, obviously the design of a bullet and the selection of an appropriate calibre should be aimed toward maximising the potential for that round to cause the largest temporary and permanent wound

A Danish infantryman pulling security in Helmand Province, Afghanistan 2009. He carries the Danish issue 5.56 × 45mm M/95 (Colt Canada C7) fitted with an Elcan M145 optic. The M/95 is being replaced with the M/10 (C8 IUR). (*ISAF, Petty Officer 2nd Class Aramis X. Ramirez*)

channels to offer the greatest chance of ensuring the targeted enemy combatant ceases to be a threat in the least amount of time possible.

An M855 fired from an M16A2 or M16A4 leaves the muzzle at approximately 3,000 feet per second. The M855, in common with all 5.56 × 45mm designs, rotates upon its axis as it travels toward the target. At extended ranges, it loses velocity and will deviate from its trajectory, resulting in inaccuracy at ranges beyond 600 metres. This effect is increased as the barrel of the weapon is reduced in length. A 5.56 × 45mm round will ideally tumble as it strikes its target, creating what is known as yaw. If the target is struck by a round with enough residual velocity, it will likely break apart, causing larger and more devastating temporary and permanent wound channels. The round, or these fragments, needs to be able to penetrate deeply enough to effect major organs whilst not over-penetrating. Over-penetration may result in a smaller permanent wound channel and poses risks to non-combatants and fellow soldiers.

No bullet can meet all of the criteria for an ideal round – one that can penetrate any intervening light cover, pass through heavy clothing and/or body armour with minimal decrease in velocity, and strike deep enough within the target to endanger major organs, whilst expending all of its residual energy to eliminate over-penetration. Even a round specifically designed to yaw, which will increase the damage caused to the target, will not perform well if it has to pass through any intervening cover, body armour or even heavy clothing. Shooting aimed pairs, the famed double-tap, is a simple and obvious way of maximising incapacitation chances by increasing the likelihood of at least one of the rounds yawing correctly.

There is always mention of the Somalia experience when detractors of the 5.56 × 45mm – and in particular the M855 'Green Tip' – need an example of its supposed inadequacy. The author has had the opportunity to speak with a dozen Delta Force veterans and a similar number of Ranger veterans from the Battle of Mogadishu in 1993. None mentioned any particular issue with the M855 round. There were numerous cases of enemy being shot multiple times but that was not considered unusual and there was contentment with the round. One Delta Force operator, Dr Norman Hooten, even mentioned his preference for the M855 as he was very used to it and could trust it to perform as advertised if he did his part with shot placement.

The Somalia stories seem to stem from one particular operator who was dissatisfied by the M855 passing through enemy and has been very publicly quoted in his dissatisfaction. This over-penetration was likely due to its armour-piercing core and the build and clothing of the average Somali militiaman (the M855 typically penetrates *'up to 7 inches before beginning to yaw, and will already have exited the body before yaw or fragmentation occur'*, according to a US Army evaluation – the same issue would be experienced in Iraq and Afghanistan where, anecdotally at least, 'through and through' or 'ice-pick' wounds were also encountered with the M855).

Remember the M855 was designed to improve the accuracy of the M249 and defeat Soviet body armour of the time. Dean suggests: *'The same bullet fired against*

An excellent close up of the working parts of the 5.56 × 45mm M249 SAW. Note the 'green tip' M855 ammunition. (*US Air Force, Justin Connaher*)

*a large, thick, well-conditioned person has a very different reaction than that fired against a thin, malnourished opponent.'*

Delta had other ammunition available (for their Aztec counter-terrorist missions for example) but chose to stay with the M855 in Somalia. It was not the best possible round, something like the later Mk 262 would have likely performed far better, but it was what was available and what they had trained with. It is telling that the accounts of failures to stop with the 5.56 × 45mm have seemingly dried up since the adoption of the vastly improved M855A1 in 2010.

US Army Major Glenn Dean provides one of the best explanations of yaw, the essential element of the terminal effectiveness of light, high velocity bullets like the 5.56 × 45mm:

> Rifle rounds in flight experience a certain swing known as yaw, as they rotate about their axis in flight to the target. This yaw is not enough to effect the accuracy of the round, but it does change its effects when it strikes the target. A slightly yawed round will tend to tumble and fragment more than a round that strikes the target with no yaw. It is the tumbling and fragmentation that causes the majority of tissue damage that results in target incapacitation.

Specifically, with regard to the M855:

> The yaw behaviour of the M855 tended to vary unpredictably with range, and especially at close-quarters battle ranges, such that two soldiers shooting the same target at the same range could see very different results. In essence, all of the anecdotal evidence was correct – the M855 could be highly lethal,

or highly ineffective, depending on circumstances which the user could not control.

Herein lies the core of the oft-reported failings of the $5.56 \times 45$mm in Iraq and Afghanistan, at least in terms of lethality. The M855 wasn't a bad round *per se*, it was simply too inconsistent. Soldiers needed a bullet which would increase the likelihood of the round yawing when it struck a human target and thus increase the chances of immediate incapacitation of the enemy. Low yaw bullets perform better at armour penetration and barrier blindness, whilst high yaw has a far greater chance of incapacitation.

An Army test of the M855 highlighted its inconsistent yaw:

> At a low angle of yaw, the bullet reacts more slowly, causing the inconsistent effects observed in the field. The location and amount of yaw depend upon the speed of the bullet at impact, angle of impact, and density of tissue.

The same study continued:

> At a high angle of yaw, the projectile typically strikes a soft target without exiting the body. In doing so, the bullet transfers all of its energy within that target, which increases the severity of tissue damage and therefore, the likelihood of incapacitation. Conversely, at a low angle of yaw, the bullet may pass through a soft target. If it does not puncture a vital area, such as an

A British Territorial Army soldier patrolling the outskirts of Kabul, Afghanistan 2008. He carries the older $5.56 \times 45$mm L85A1 with a Maglite flashlight mounted under the barrel – an unusual combination. Newer L85A2s were prioritised to Task Force Helmand. (*ISAF, Tech. Sgt. Laura Smith*)

organ, the through-and-through hit will only cause minimal damage because the projectile traverses the body without expending significant energy.

Users such as SOCOM were working with Naval Surface Warfare Centre Crane, who conduct much of the development and enhancement of small arms and ammunition for American SOF units, to produce an enhanced round for both carbines and for 5.56 × 45mm designated marksman rifles like the Mk 12 and SEAL 'Recce Rifles'. The outbreak of conflict in Afghanistan spurred on that development and saw two separate loads eventually offered – the Mk 262 for the Mk 12 and similar platforms and the Mk 318 as an enhanced M855 replacement, offering far more consistent fragmentation.

The Mk 262 was being used by select units of the Marines and Army along with SOF (and later surprisingly by the New Zealand Army) and was performing well. The Mk 262 did seem to offer greater accuracy at range and improved terminal effects from carbine-length barrels and reports from units in the field were encouraging, however cost virtually eliminated it from widespread adoption. The cost of the Mk 262, four times that of the old M855, led to the USMC initially adopting the Mk 318 rather than the Mk 262. The Mk 262 is roughly twice as expensive as the new M855A1.

Both the Mk 262 and the Mk 318 were built using an Open Tip Match or OTM design. This is a legally handy way of creating a round designed to fragment consistently without using a hollowpoint design, (which we have seen in earlier

A US Army soldier scans with his Trijicon ACOG equipped M4 – note GripPod vertical foregrip that incorporates a collapsible bipod. (*US Army*)

chapters is still a grey area for the US and NATO forces) although the OTM design was primarily used to enhance accuracy in both rounds. It was not however designed to consistently penetrate body armour, the likes of which would be seen equipping any future peer or near peer adversary.

The M855A1 Enhanced Performance Round was originally conceived as a 'green' or environmentally friendly 'lead free' round to minimise lead pollution on small arms ranges. In Glenn Dean's eye-opening account of the development of the M885A1, he notes that both the infantry and SOCOM participants on the 'lead free' programme expressed concerns that focus should instead be placed on improving the M855 in combat rather than on environmental concerns. Dean says that: '*What started as a program to be more environmentally friendly became a significant upgrade in military small arms capability.*'

The arguments of the infantry and SOF representatives resonated and the programme was altered, largely in secret, to develop an improved M855 which would offer similar capabilities as the Mk 262 along with improved light armour penetration AND be a 'green bullet'. The eventual result was the M855A1 which mated a steel tip penetrator to a copper slug – the penetrator elevated armour penetration and increased barrier blindness (for instance through glass or car doors).

The only real down side to the M855A1 is the increased wear on the bolt and barrel of weapons firing the projectile due to the high pressures generated by this hot load. There was also a reliability issue with using the new round with older STANAG magazines, forcing the introduction of a new Enhanced Performance Magazine for use with the M855A1. Although this has been leapt upon by its detractors, who are clamouring for the adoption of a new calibre rather than wringing every last bit of capability from the 5.56 × 45mm, most fail to mention that new magazines are also a likely requirement for any calibre change using existing M16/M4 platforms.

Lieutenant Colonel J.K. Woods, Product Manager for Small Caliber Ammunition in the Office of the Project Manager Maneuver Ammunition Systems, PEO Ammo, gave an excellent summary of the advantages of the M855A1 as the round was adopted into general service in 2010 and is worth quoting at length:

> This is not to imply that the EPR [Enhanced Penetration Round] increases the maximum effective range of the M4 or M16. Its trajectory matches the M855's, which aids in training, lessens the need to re-zero the weapon, and allows it to link to the current tracer round (the M856) for eventual use in the M249 SAW. So while the maximum effective range does not increase, effectiveness at range does, meaning the round greatly extends the range of desired effects along its trajectory.
>
>     The Army tackled the consistency issue by focusing on the yaw of a projectile and how differences in yaw can influence results when striking soft targets. The M855 round, similar to the Army's M80 (7.62mm ball round), is a 'yaw-dependent' bullet. As any bullet travels along its trajectory, it 'wobbles' in both pitch and yaw, causing the projectile to strike its target at different attitudes with virtually every shot.

An Italian Lagunari 'Serenissima' Regiment reconnaissance soldier is pictured on exercise with the newly issued 5.56 × 45mm Beretta ARX160A3 with carbine length 11-inch barrel.
(*Canadian Forces, Sgt. Sebastien Frechette*)

For a yaw-dependent bullet such as the M855 or M80, this results in varying performance, depending upon where in the yaw/pitch cycle the bullet strikes its target. For example, at a high angle of yaw, the M855 performs very well, transferring its energy to the target in short order. At a low angle of yaw, however, the bullet reacts more slowly, causing the inconsistent effects observed in the field.

The M855A1 is not yaw-dependent. Like any other bullet, it 'wobbles' along its trajectory. However, the EPR provides the same effects when striking its target, regardless of the angle of yaw. This means the EPR provides the same desired effects every time, whether in close combat situations or longer engagements. In fact, the U.S. Army Research Laboratory (ARL) verified through live-fire tests against soft targets that, on average, the M855A1 surpassed the M80 7.62mm round. The 7.62mm, although a larger caliber, suffers from the same consistency issue as the M855, but to a higher degree.

Hard-target performance is a second area where the EPR really shines. The exposed, heavier, and sharper penetrator, along with a higher velocity, allows soldiers to penetrate tougher battlefield barriers than is possible with the current M855. Although it's not an armor-piercing round, the EPR can penetrate 0.375-inch-thick mild steel at distances approaching 400 meters (based on the range at which 50 per cent of the rounds can pass through the barrier). The M855 only penetrates this material out to approximately 160 meters.

Not only is this performance much better than the M855's with its smaller steel penetrator, it is vastly better than the M80 7.62mm round. Additionally, the EPR can penetrate concrete masonry units at ranges out to 80 meters with the M16 and 40 meters with the M4. The M855 can't penetrate this type of battlefield barrier at any range.

Also notable is the EPR's excellent performance against softer inter-mediate barriers such as car doors, windshields, or Kevlar fabric. The thinner metal found on car doors poses no problem. When engaging targets behind windshields with the EPR, ARL has shown an increase in the probability of hitting the occupant, due to both the steel penetrator and the copper slug remaining intact through the glass. Furthermore, ARL tested the round against 24 layers of Kevlar fabric out to 1,000 meters, but discontinued the test as the Kevlar showed no sign of being able to stop the EPR. The EPR also penetrates some lesser-quality body armors designed to stop 7.62mm ball rounds. Another benefit soldiers will see from the new round is its effective-ness when engaging soft targets at longer ranges. As a small-caliber projec-tile's velocity decreases, it eventually will reach a point at which it can no longer transfer most of its energy to its target. Below this velocity, which equates to range, the round is more likely to pass through its target with little effect. The M855A1 can maintain consistent, desired effects at a much lower velocity, resulting in excellent effectiveness at far greater ranges along its trajectory.

In addition to the above-mentioned performance improvements, the EPR is more accurate than the M855. Accuracy testing during production lot acceptance has shown that, on average, 95 per cent of the rounds will hit within an $8 \times 8$-inch target at 600 meters. It also uses a flash-reduced pro-pellant optimized for the M4's shorter barrel.

When discussing soft target performance, Woods fails to mention in his other-wise excellent summary that the M855A1 will fragment in the human body within a reported 3 inches causing an extensive and deep permanent wound channel. The velocity of the round creates a secondary or temporary wound channel as organs are displaced by the fragmenting bullet.

Lieutenant General William Phillips, Military Deputy to the Assistant Secretary of the Army for Acquisition, Logistics and Technology argued:

Since the early days of the Iraq War, when you used to hear about 'through and throughs' and they would pull the trigger and someone would fall down, or not fall down and keep coming – with this round that essentially stops. When you hit someone with this round they essentially go down. And the feedback we get from our soldiers, time and time again in combat, using this new round, is exactly that. It's providing great lethality for our soldiers and our squads on the ground.

The issue 5.56 × 45mm M4 carbine with rail covers, magazine, sling and vertical foregrip. All Army M4s are being upgraded to M4A1s, recognizable for their heavier profile barrel. (*US Army*)

Thomas Ehrhart confirmed that he believes the rounds are a step-forward and alleviate many of the concerns he addressed in his study:

> The improvement in consistency of fragmentation in M855A1, which began widespread fielding in 2012, has largely mitigated my previous concerns with the limitations of 5.56. Shot placement still trumps all, but we have largely eliminated the known problems of M855 'green tip' when fired in carbines with 14.5″ barrels.
>
> I am comfortable with the 'consistency' of M855A1. Mk 318 also works well. Precision of M855A1 is greater than M855, but there are considerations such as greater pressure and wear on the system (higher velocity, more pressure/wear and exposed hardened penetrator tip can gouge feed ramps). I'm not sure about the compatibility with other NATO 5.56 systems.

With the heavier barreled M4A1, the reliability of the M855A1 also seems to have improved with PEO Sergeant Major Doug Maddi stating that the weapon has been observed firing '58 basic loads mean rounds between stoppages'. As pointed out by Eric Graves of Soldier Systems, that would be some 12,180 rounds fired between stoppages.

\* \* \*

The M855A1 seems to be performing very well indeed as a general-purpose round – that is one which can penetrate light armour/helmets, is barrier-blind to most impediments in its path and offers consistent terminal effects with its fragmentation in human targets from both rifle and carbine length barrels. The British Army is also adopting a new bullet for the 5.56 × 45mm weapons to replace their SS109 variant, the L15A1. Termed the L31A1, the new round is a 62-grain solid hardened steel-core round that appears, from what little information is available, to be optimised for long-range penetration rather than fragmentation. Australia has also recently introduced a modified variant of their SS109 loading, the F1.

A Japanese Ground Self-Defense Force paratrooper fixes a bayonet to his 5.56 × 45mm Howa Type 89. (*US Air Force, Justin Connaher*)

Termed the F1A1, the new round is to all intents and purposes an M855 enhanced for accuracy at extended ranges.

The Israelis announced a new contender in 2018, the APM or Armour Piercing Match round. The APM is a heavy (73 grain) 5.56 × 45mm full metal jacket design with an unknown penetrator. Its manufacturer, Israeli Military Industries, claims that the round solves the issue of issuing both 5.56 × 45mm and 7.62 × 51mm in that the APM allegedly outperforms the US M80 7.62 × 51mm in both accuracy and penetration of body armour out to 800 metres. No detail has been released regarding comparison with the M885A1 EPR.

If the APM performs as advertised, we may have a solution both for the enhancement of the 5.56 × 45mm to allay any overmatch concerns and extend the capabilities of the perennially popular but short-ranged LMGs like the Minimi, whilst simplifying the supply chain. It, of course, remains to be seen how the APM performs in terms of terminal effects, but the concept sounds promising. Such innovations also negate the costly, in both terms of procurement and retraining, adoption of a new standard rifle calibre.

In terms of defeating current Russian body armour with trauma plates, only the Swedes issue rounds with this specific capacity in the form of the 7.62 × 51mm M993 and the 5.56 × 45mm M995, both featuring tungsten cores but, according to noted firearms authority Anthony G. Williams, are prohibitively expensive to field in any numbers. What their effectiveness against soft targets (i.e. those not

The newly issued Australian Army 5.56 × 45mm F88 equipped with Elcan Specter DR optic and GripPod vertical grip. (*Commonwealth of Australia, LSIS Peter Thompson*)

Indian Paratroopers carrying the Israeli Tavor 5.56 × 45mm TAR-21 and GTAR-21 fitted with M203 grenade launcher. (*Creative Commons, Panky2sharma*)

The export variant of the AK-74M in 7.62 × 39mm, the AK-103, has been adopted by a growing number of nations including Pakistan and Saudi Arabia. (*Kalashnikov Group/Kalashnikov Media*)

wearing heavy body armour) is unknown but likely to be similar to the problems which faced the M855 and armour piercing rounds in general.

The Russian 5.45 × 39mm is an interesting design that really should gain greater appreciation. As noted small arms researcher Christopher R. Bartocci explained in *Small Arms Review*:

> Like its 7.62 × 39mm counterpart, the 5.45 × 39mm projectile consists of a steel jacket, steel penetrator core, lead alloy around the sides and on top of the steel penetrator. However, there is an empty space between the tip of the lead and the tip of the projectile. What this does is greatly increase its terminal performance over that of the 7.62 × 39mm cartridge.
>
> When the projectile hits tissue the lead core shifts in the tip causing the projectile to yaw in about 4 inches consistently opposed to the 7.62 × 39mm projectile beginning to yaw at nearly 10 inches in depth. In many cases that could be thicker than a body it strikes. This is consistent and repeatable. The length of the projectile and keeping the center of gravity in the rear of the projectile, plus the velocity, keep this performance repeatable and reliable.

The 5.45 × 39mm also displays a far flatter trajectory than the 7.62 × 39mm, an advantage shared with the 5.56 × 45mm.

The Russians have also developed the 9 × 39mm as a calibre designed for a range of curious Russian platforms which serve as suppressed assault rifles and sniper rifles. The two most common weapons chambering the round, the AS Val and the VSS Vintorez, are both suppressed and were originally designed for SOF use (the VSS for instance breaks down into a specially designed briefcase for covert actions). Surprisingly, both offer selective fire.

The 9 × 39mm was designed solely for use with suppressed weapons and was actually the result of Russian experiments with subsonic 7.62 × 39mm loads for use in the AKM. Two variants are commonly issued – SP5 ball and SP6 armour piercing. Both are designed to be effective out to 400 metres. The 9 × 39mm is a powerful and relatively quiet round and for its niche application, it may even out-perform the .300 Blackout. It is unlikely however to be seen in the hands of infantrymen, so we will limit our discussion of it here.

Along with the recent arguments about overmatch described in the introduction is an often-paired disparagement of the 5.56 × 45mm in terms of the mythical 'stopping power'. Spend five minutes on the internet and you will read any number of claims about the ineffectiveness of the 5.56 × 45mm; it is a 'pipsqueak' round, a 'varmint' calibre rather than a true combat round like the 7.62 × 51mm (or insert the latest flavour of the month calibre here: 6.5mm Grendel, 6.8 × 43mm Remington *et al.*).

The 7.62 × 51mm is a fine calibre and is perfect for its role in sniper and designated marksman rifles or in medium machine guns. It traditionally offers greater range, less ballistic drop and increased penetration over the 5.56 × 45mm – it is also a better calibre to employ in Arctic conditions as at temperatures below freezing, propellant powder burns much more slowly, reducing velocity and range. It has also offered, anecdotally at least, greater terminal effects on human targets. Where the shine begins to dull on the 7.62 × 51mm are two other equally important factors: weight and recoil.

Firstly, let's consider weight. The oft-quoted maxim of an infantryman is that he or she can carry double the 5.56 × 45mm than the 7.62 × 51mm and it's pretty accurate. A standard issue rate of six magazines (plus the seventh in the rifle) is around 4 kilograms lighter with 5.56 × 45mm. As we have noted back in the introduction when we discussed the ever-increasing combat load of the infantryman, this is not to be dismissed lightly. A 7.62 × 51mm rifle will also be 1–2 kilograms heavier than a similar weapon in the smaller calibre. For the sake of argument, we can say that perhaps 6 kilograms of combat weight can be saved with the issue of a 5.56 × 45mm individual weapon.

Now, recoil. The 7.62 × 51mm, unless fired from a relatively heavy, full stocked rifle (and certainly not in bursts or on full automatic), is not the easiest calibre to gain proficiency with. Recoil is typically sharp for the average soldier. It is slower to re-acquire a sight picture, particularly if fired rapidly, and produces a sizeable muzzle blast which reduces accuracy in low light shooting. Most modern soldiers are not adept with firearms when they join their respective militaries, unlike during the Second World War when a far greater percentage had some familiarity, particularly those from rural communities. It is obvious that teaching someone to shoot proficiently enough to pass basic qualification is easier with a smaller calibre rifle, doubly so if that weapon is equipped with a good combat optic.

A third point is magazine capacity; the vast majority of 7.62 × 51mm platforms are fed from 20-round magazines due to the larger physical size of the round.

The 5.56 × 45mm Colt Canada C8A3 is the standard issue carbine of the Canadian military, seen here fitted with an EOTech optic. (*Kelly Stumpf, Colt Canada*)

Most 5.56 × 45mm rifles have another third up their sleeve. Even the newer generation calibres (and most are not all that new) like the 6.5 Grendel lose a few rounds in M16 sized magazines. And then there is the question of the physical dimensions of an M4A1 or similar sized rifle firing the larger round.

From a 14.5-inch barrel like that used in the current M4A1, the muzzle blast and report would be greatly accentuated making a short-barrelled 7.62 × 51mm platform rather uncomfortable to shoot. This also plays into the combat accuracy question. If a soldier is comfortable with the recoil, muzzle blast and report of his or her service rifle, if they are not nervously anticipating the result of pressing the trigger, they will shoot more accurately – particularly under stress. Consider the FBI trials of pistol rounds which found that any minute increase in potential terminal effectiveness of larger calibres was far outweighed by the lighter and more comfortable shooting characteristics of the 9 × 19mm. The less felt recoil, the better the agent (or the soldier) will shoot. So does this mean we should be retreating to .17 Hornady Magnum as our desired assault rifle calibre? Of course not. What it does mean is that 7.62 × 51mm isn't the answer for the majority of infantry roles. To wring the best from the 7.62 × 51mm, a short-barrelled carbine is certainly not the best platform – it will only marginally increase range and lethality thanks in part to the velocity lost from the reduced barrel length.

Use the 7.62 × 51mm in a 16in to 18in or even longer barrelled rifle, match it with a variable power combat optic such as the excellent 6 × Trijicon, and you are looking at a weapon platform that can harness the best from the 7.62 × 51mm. Remember also, as we also touched upon in the introduction, you need to be able to see the target to shoot it. A 7.62 × 51mm without decent optics will mean only hitting targets at the ranges the pundits claim is the edge of the envelope for the 'puny' 5.56 × 45mm.

Both calibres begin to exhibit bullet drop from about 250 to 300 metres dependant on barrel length and load, but the 5.56 × 45mm invariably loses velocity faster as it packs less propellant than the larger 7.62 × 51mm casing. This can result in bullet drop of 3 metres or more at extended ranges. This is increased with shorter barrelled carbines. The 7.62 × 51mm is certainly a better performer at extended ranges but is that what an infantryman needs?

Ehrhart noted to the author:

> The recipe for a successful small arms engagement is rather simple. Only hits count and those hits must penetrate deep enough in a vital area to cause massive, rapid blood loss and/or destroy a component of the central nervous system (brain or spine). 5.56 accomplishes this primarily through fragmentation, which occurs if velocity is sufficiently high at the impact range.

William F. Owen was equally clear and direct:

> Bullets are what kill. Get into the science of wound ballistics and avoid the 'oh 5.56mm is useless' bullshit. It's a really good killer, but not all 5.56mm is the same.

*    *    *

Along with the Russians, the Chinese have also transitioned to a smaller calibre general service round, the 5.8 × 42mm. The PLA have asserted that the new calibre is superior in both range and terminal effects to both the 5.56 × 45mm SS109 used by most NATO armies and the 5.45 × 399mm 7N6 round employed by the Russians and anecdotal evidence at least suggests that the round is superior to the SS109 in terms of retained velocity, but is apparently designed for penetration of body armour rather than optimising terminal effectiveness.

The Chinese were the first to truly grasp both the idea of an intermediate calibre that could be used by a family of weapons systems – from short barrel carbines to squad automatic rifles and medium machine guns – and to have the production might to actually produce the goods. The resulting bullpup 5.8 × 42mm Type 95 assault rifle was made in a number of versions including a carbine and a light support weapon featuring a 75-round drum which will be covered in a later chapter.

The US Army was keenly aware of this and noted in their Soldier Weapons Strategy 2014 report:

> Near-peer threats are moving towards a common, intermediate caliber to maximize fire-power and efficiencies for the squad in an attempt to increase lethality at close range and accuracy at long-range. Potential adversaries have begun to field common intermediate caliber, advanced performance

An unusual pairing. A Japanese soldier with the Japanese Ground Self-Defense Force and a Chinese soldier with the People's Liberation Army on exercise armed with a (borrowed) 7.62 × 39mm AKM and 5.8 × 42mm Type 95 assault rifle respectively. (*USMC, SSgt Christopher Giannetti*)

A Chinese sailor armed with the 5.8 × 42mm QBZ-95-1 (Type 95-1) carbine. (*Chinese Navy, Xingjian Zeng*)

ammunition with a max effective range of 600m for the improved rifle; 800m for the light machine gun.

The first iterations of the 5.8 × 42mm saw two different cartridges issued. One was the DBP87 for use in assault rifles and carbines. The other was the DBP88 which had a slightly longer casing to prevent it being loaded in the Type 95 and designed for use in designated marksman rifles and medium machine guns. Both were eventually replaced by the 71-grain DBP10 which can be fired through all 5.8 × 42mm weapons, partly due to the propellant used in the earlier version which caused excessive fumes and carbon build-up from unburnt particles. This leads us to a problem experienced by all ammunition fired from assault rifles and carbines. All assault rifles are designed to be fired in short bursts or semi-automatically. Indeed, all major armies now teach aimed semi-automatic fire as the standard, with automatic reserved for trench and building clearing only.

The US Army's manual on marksmanship, snappily titled *Rifle Marksmanship M16/M4 Series Weapons* spells this out:

When applying automatic or burst fire, Soldiers deliver the maximum number of rounds (1 to 3 rounds per second) into a designated target area while rapidly applying the four fundamentals. This specialized technique of delivering suppressive fire may not apply to most combat engagements. Automatic weapon fire may be necessary to maximize violence of action or gain fire superiority when gaining a foothold in a room, building, or trench.

Rifles are not machine guns and will overheat and ultimately fail to fire if subjected to lengthy periods of sustained fire. Rapidly firing magazine after

An Australian soldier fires a Chinese PLA 5.8 × 42mm Type 95 with unknown scope.
(*Commonwealth of Australia, Sgt John Waddell*)

magazine on semi-automatic will also cause heat dissipation problems that may lead to catastrophic stoppages – 'cook-offs' – where the weapon becomes so over-heated it ignites rounds in the chamber, seizing up the action resulting in a stoppage that cannot be immediately cleared, or even the destruction of the gas tube or barrel which will render the weapon inoperable.

A recent well publicised example of assault rifles suffering such failures was the insurgent attack against Combat Outpost Kahler (COP) at Wanat in eastern Afghanistan. COP Kahler was attacked on 3 October 2009 by a numerically superior insurgent force that made the best use of the terrain to rain RPG and recoilless rifle fire down upon the exposed US Army outpost and an adjacent Observation Post (OP). Reports appearing soon after the battle detailed multiple failures to fire, including catastrophic stoppages.

There were three rifle squads, all understrength at between five and seven members, armed with the usual issue rate of 5.56 × 45mm M4 carbines, 40mm M203 launchers and 5.56 × 45m M249 SAWs. One paratrooper was armed with a 7.62 × 51mm M21 serving as a designated marksman rifle. In addition, two 7.62 × 51mm M240 medium machine guns were present, crewed by a similarly understrength weapons squad. Both M240s were deployed at the OP nicknamed the 'Crow's Nest'. There was also an understrength platoon of Afghan National Army present, armed with Soviet pattern small arms, and a three-man Marine Corps mentoring team equipped with M4s and an M240. Additionally, there were a number of heavy weapons platforms at the COP. A mortar squad manned two 120mm and one 60mm mortar. On the rifle platoon's HMMWVs were mounted two .50cal heavy machine guns and two Mk19 automatic grenade launchers. A single TOW II anti-tank guided missile platform was also present, again mounted on a HMMWV. These heavy weapon systems were targeted, and the TOW disabled, in the initial fusillade of insurgent fire.

One of the soldiers suffered catastrophic failures with a succession of three M4s that he used to defend his position. According to an Army report from the Combat Studies Institute (CSI) he fired all three at '*maximum rate of fire simply to suppress the enemy in order to survive*'. All three failed, likely due to overheating, and eventually seizing up as the soldier fired magazine after magazine through the weapon.

The M4 will overheat after as relatively few as 140 rounds are fired, either semi-automatically or in burst mode. US Army guidance calls for a maximum practical rate of fire of 12–15 rounds per minute. The guidance explicitly notes: '*This is the actual rate of fire that a weapon can continue to be fired for an indefinite length of time without serious overheating.*' In extremis, it can fire rapidly in burst function to a maximum of three consecutive magazines (90 rounds) before the weapon needs to cool down or face a catastrophic failure:

> Firing 140 rounds, rapidly and continuously, will raise the temperature of the barrel to the cook-off point. At this temperature, any live round remaining in the chamber for any reason may cook-off (detonate) in as short a period as 10 seconds.

A Latvian soldier armed with a 5.56 × 45mm Heckler and Koch G36KV carbine with AG36 grenade launcher. (*US Army, Sgt. Rob Summitt*)

A US Army soldier firing a very dusty and well-worn 5.56 × 45mm M249 Para PIP fitted with ACOG optic. Note the use of the cumbersome plastic 200-round box rather than the 50- or 100-round soft fabric pouches which are generally preferred in combat due to their lighter weight. (*US Air Force, Tech. Sgt. Barry Loo*)

One of the soldiers fighting for his life at the OP later recounted:

> My weapon was overheating. I had shot about 12 magazines by this point already and it had only been about a half hour or so into the fight. I couldn't charge my weapon and put another round in because it was too hot, so I got mad and threw my weapon down.

The same soldier who had used and discarded a number of M4s later attempted to fire a discarded M249 SAW to no avail, unaware that it was jammed earlier. Apparently, a round had become jammed in the barrel and the weapon was only brought back into action with a later barrel change. The CSI report again notes, '*2d Platoon paratroopers were forced to fire their small arms at the maximum cyclic rate*'. The result of this rapid firing was that '*the SAWs and, in particular, the M4s, experienced difficulty maintaining such a rate after the barrels got excessively hot. When that occurred, the weapons would jam*'.

The SAWs were being fired at ferocious rates. One participant noted he '*grabbed the engineer's weapon that was left at our position and which was a SAW and ... started laying down about 800–1,000 rounds at the bazaar and wood line around the mosque.*' This kind of prolonged firing, even in machine guns designed for rapid automatic fire, will inevitably result in stoppages.

\* \* \*

Beginning in 2010, reports surfaced from the German Army ISAF contingent of 5.56 × 45mm G36s suffering failures to fire during a protracted firefight in Kunduz where G36s were employed in rapid fire to suppress nearby insurgents. The contact lasted for nine hours whilst a Bundeswehr Fallschirmjäger was surrounded by Taliban. According to some reports, the G36s were being fired on full auto, dumping magazine after magazine, and with the prolonged automatic fire the barrels not surprisingly heated up resulting in some loss of accuracy.

One press report from Reuters, relying upon leaked data from three separate scientific investigations, including those from the Ernst Mach Institute and the German Army's Technical Center for Weapons and Ammunition, claimed that the overheating saw a shift in zero by as much as half a metre at 100 metres and as much as 6 metres at 500 metres (which is well beyond the likely engagement ranges typically experienced). Again however, the G36, nor any assault rifle is designed to be used like a machine gun. One of the key roles of infantry NCOs is to issue fire control orders to limit over-heating from prolonged firing.

The alleged issue with the G36 became public in 2015 and led to the announcement of an immediate replacement of G36s in German Army special operations use (with another H&K model, the HK416) and a programme to replace the G36 in the wider Army with a new weapon by 2019. Moving to a short-stroke piston operating system like the 416 will certainly reduce the amount of carbon build-up and reduces the amount of heat generated in the cycling of the weapon's action but is not a panacea.

An infantryman with Bermuda Regiment firing his 5.56 × 45mm Heckler & Koch G36C carbine. (*USMC, Cpl. Ryan G. Coleman*)

A Spanish Marine practising close quarter battle shooting with a 5.56 × 45mm G36E with EOTech optic. *(USMC, Sgt. Kassie L. McDole)*

From the author's own investigations into the circumstances and veracity of the claims against the G36, one can assume that such shifts to the weapon's zero did occur as it was being used in a manner never intended, nor taught, by the Bundeswehr. Like the M4, the G36 is designed to be able to fire rapid semi-automatic shots for short periods or a limited number of bursts.

It seems that the whole G36 controversy was politically motivated and knee-jerk reactions to abandon the G36 and launch a replacement programme were announced before the full facts were known. Heckler and Koch even took the German government to court over the potentially defamatory claims made by some politicians which could easily harm the manufacturer's business. It is also telling that the G36 was slated for replacement in 2020 anyway.

Bundeswehr soldiers who have served in Afghanistan and used the G36 in combat are overwhelmingly positive about the rifle. As veteran end users, they also understand the limitations of using an assault rifle as a light machine gun, a role it was never designed or intended for. One German soldier quoted by H&K noted *'that a rifle subjected to continuous automatic fire no longer maintains its accuracy, should be known to everyone'*.

The G36 has been in German service since 1995 and has been deployed in combat numerous times in the Balkans, Africa, Iraq and Afghanistan. If the issue was something more than overheating from rapid fire, one would suspect there would have been at least some reports or rumour that the rifle was not up to scratch. Additionally, the weapon has been widely adopted by European special operations and counter terrorist units who have also seen significant action – surely one of these organisations would have raised the alarm if the weapon was less than suitable due to some inherent problem?

What does appear to be true is that in extreme temperatures like those experienced in Afghanistan, and after being fired on fully automatic for extended periods, the G36 may suffer some loss of zero. H&K has rightly pointed out that the Bundeswehr trials for the then new rifle in the early 1990s did not include any such torture tests examining this specific scenario.

## Current Trends

We mention optics a lot as a crucial part of the effectiveness equation. It must be remembered that combat optics, from non-magnified red dots to variable magnification telescopic models once more at home on high end competition rifles, are a relatively recent phenomenon. SOF began to experiment with red dot sights in the late 1980s until they became commonplace with such units in the 1990s. For the infantryman, the wait was a little longer as most US Army units didn't see their first close combat sights until the invasion of Iraq or shortly after. These were generally Aimpoints designated the M68 which displayed a LED red dot in the tube. The aim was to improve target acquisition times and for this the red dot is superb. It can also be used with both eyes open, unlike most magnified optics.

The USMC had adopted a magnified option – the Trijicon ACOG or Advanced Combat Optical Gunsight. The Marine version was of fixed four-power

A New Zealand Army soldier firing the Canadian issue 5.56 × 45mm C8A3 with Elcan m145 optic.
(*USMC, Sgt. Sarah Dietz*)

A US Marine Lance Corporal firing his ACOG equipped 5.56 × 45mm M16A4 in Helmand
Province, Afghanistan 2013. His M16A4 mounts an M203 grenade launcher under the barrel.
(*USMC, Sgt. Bobby J. Yarbrough*)

magnification which displayed a tritium illuminated red chevron reticle which neatly incorporated a bullet drop compensator zeroed for the issue M16A4 and M855 round so that the shooter could adjust for the drop at longer ranges. Most Marines who participated in the 2004 Operation Phantom Fury in Fallujah carried ACOG equipped M16A4s. Results were impressive with journalists raising the issue as so many insurgent corpses were found with head wounds. A Marine Major was quoted at the time as saying: *'In Fallujah, Marines with ACOG equipped M16A4s created a stir by taking so many head shots that until the wounds were closely examined, some observers thought the insurgents had been executed.'*

The ACOG was, and remains, a very popular optic for the Corps. General James Mattis even called them *'the biggest improvement in lethality for the Marine infantryman since the introduction of the M1 Garand in WWII'*. The only area where improvement was needed was for close quarter battle shooting as the ACOG was

The 5.56 × 45mm L85A2 at the top is equipped with the issue Elcan Specter OS 4 × optic and Shield CQS procured to replace the interim Trijicon ACOG purchased for Afghanistan. The L85A2 at the bottom has the older SUSAT optic. (*Open Government License v3.0, Stuart Hill*)

a poor substitute for an Aimpoint when clearing buildings. Marines instead fell back on their training and shot their M16A4s using instinctive shooting instead.

Trijicon solved this issue quickly with a mount on top of the ACOG which allowed a mini red dot, such as their own RMR, to be fitted. For longer range shots or PIDing targets, the Marine used the ACOG. For CQB shooting, he or she simply looked up through the mini red dot and acquired a sight picture that way. The ACOG/RMR combination proved immediately popular and was adopted by UK Special Forces.

Several years later, with UK forces fighting vicious infantry firefights with the Taliban in Helmand, the issue L9A1 SUSAT (a fixed four-power design that had been fitted on L85A1s since the 1980s) was showing its inadequacies. The SUSATs were well worn and needed a modern replacement. The ACOG with a Docter red dot was chosen as the interim replacement for units bound for Afghanistan.

The ACOG has now been replaced in UK service with the Elcan Spectre OS4x which is another fixed four-power design. Australia has also adopted the Spectre in another variant, the DR1-4x which offers two fixed switchable magnifications, one for close quarter shooting, the other for longer ranges (an early variant of which was part of the US SOPMOD Block 2 kit for SOF).

*   *   *

Elsewhere around the world, Aimpoints and illicitly produced copies are the number one combat optic. Russia now produces its own versions including the PK-A which allows mounting on older style AKs without rails by using a side mount directly onto the receiver and the Axion Kobra which operates in a similar way to the US EOTech holographic weapons sights. Like Aimpoints these have no magnification but instead display an illuminated reticle to improve the speed of target acquisition.

Rails on which to mount such optics are now commonplace. There are even rails kits available for older AK series rifles; for newer designs like the AK-12 and AK-200 they come standard. Most modern rifles will feature a Picatinny rail along the top of its upper receiver (or even along the receiver and barrel in a design known as a monolithic rail) and at least one and often as many as three or four on the foregrip. The introduction of rails has also increased the combat load of the infantryman as many now mount an optic, a weapon light, an infrared laser and a forward grip to their weapons.

The US Army's M4s are currently undergoing an upgrade programme to bring them to M4A1 standard under the 'M4A1 Carbine Product Improvement Program'. The idea here is to bridge the gap between the basic M4 and incorporate many of the changes that have been available on SOF carbines since the mid-1990s, including the replacement of the 3-round burst function with fully automatic capability. The heavier profile barrel will also assist in reducing weapon failures caused by excessive firing. It also neatly sets up the M4 to serve a few more years before the next generation weapon is hopefully available.

A Romanian ISAF soldier in Zabul Province, Afghanistan 2011 firing his 5.45 × 39mm md.86, a domestically produced AKM variant. (*US Army, Spc. Jason Nolte*)

Responding to the overmatch hyperbole, the US Army even launched a programme to field 50,000 7.62 × 51mm rifles, bought off the shelf to replace M4A1s and tide over infantry units until the Next Generation Squad Weapon (NGSW) and associated rifle/carbine (the NGSW-R programme) were fielded. The programme, known as the Interim Combat Service Rifle, ran briefly in 2017 until it was cancelled in favour of the NGSW and a new squad designated marksman rifle (SDMR) in 7.62 × 51mm, based on the Heckler and Koch G28E, along with a new enhanced performance 7.62 × 51mm load.

Returning to the overmatch discussion, it's worth recording the experiences of a number of servicemen and their thoughts on overmatch by the enemy. An American veteran of both Iraq and Afghanistan said that he had never experienced overmatch despite being in a large number of contacts with the enemy: '*No, biggest enemy threat in my opinion was RPGs, however, they were very unreliable. On average I would say engagements were usually within 200 meters but sometimes we would get engaged from the other side of a valley almost a kilometer away in Afghanistan.*' Another added: '*The bad guys kick it off with an RPG, then run away while we chase them with everything we have. I was never impressed by what the fighters in Afghanistan could bring to bear.*'

Doug Beattie mentioned his observations from three tours in Helmand Province, Southern Afghanistan:

Using small arms my engagements ranged from 500 meters to 0 metres and everything in between. I normally found the average range was about

200 metres but I did encounter a lot of enemy at less than 100 metres. I think the environment really dictates this. The enemy used the PKM at this range to great effect but less so the RPG – this was normally fired into the air to create an airburst effect. RPGs at closer ranges; 150–200 [metres] were far more effective.

I was outgunned on multiple occasions but this was more based on troop mass than weapon distribution. Small groups of soldiers really did rely on indirect fire support and CAS as the enemy strength was normally greater. The sniper was a force multiplier but then at close ranges it became ineffectual – the sharp shooter rifle was more versatile as was the GPMG.

Another British platoon commander explained a novel reaction to being under suppressive fires:

Yes, I was fixed on many occasions by PKM and RPG however, believe it or not, accurate smoke worked very well as they knew we had marked their position but they did not know with what – this frightened them. This then would make them cease fire, giving us time to manoeuvre towards or away from the enemy depending on the situation. TB would always use civilian houses as cover so we could not bring down a heavy weight of fire onto the compounds as we were told to suspect all compounds would have civilians in.

Yes, we were sometimes fixed mainly by SAF [small arms fire], I found that the PKM or RPG would always go high and in the contacts we were involved in (around 2–3 contacts per day over a 6 month period) weren't that accurate, clearly that could be down to many reasons from poor handling to poor firing postions. With the L129A1/GPMG/LMG and UGL etc I never once felt we were outgunned by the TB [Taliban]. In regards to 5.56mm the SA80A2 is a good accurate weapon system with ACOG or LDS sights fitted. The general contact would be no more than 300–400 metres so range was never an issue. The closest contact would typically be 30–50 metres with a natural obstacle in the way.

A telling quote from a Norwegian soldier after the adoption of the $5.56 \times 45$mm HK416N:

Our experience is that our current group of soldiers become better marksmen quicker than previous groups who used the G3. On KD [known distance] ranges with pop-up targets, there are no issues knocking down targets at 400 meters consistently. We have had hits at further distances than that in Afghanistan with Comp M4's and $3 \times$ magnifiers. In my experience the inherent accuracy in the rifle is better than what most shooters can accomplish.

Herein lies the rub with the idea of overmatch with regards to service rifles. Despite some commentators loudly arguing for a new calibre to allow targets to be engaged beyond 400 metres, as this Norwegian soldier ably articulates, most modern service rifles in $5.56 \times 45$mm are more accurate than the shooter. Even

Members of the Norwegian Home Guard training with their 5.56 × 45mm Heckler and Koch HK416S, a modified variant produced in Norway for designated marksmen.
(*Minnesota National Guard, Tech. Sgt. Amy M. Lovgren*)

with optics, in this case a three-power magnifier operating in concert with an Aimpoint red dot sight, targets are being hit at 400 metres and beyond, and this with the much-maligned standard NATO SS109.

Just because a weapon has the capacity to strike a target at a given range does not mean that the individual soldier is able to – it's easy when discussing the finer points of calibres and ballistics to mistake capacity for capability. The training provided today to even the best first world armies does not necessarily equate in terms of increased accuracy and range in a combat environment and making the most of the capacities of their issued weapon.

Another serving British soldier explained to the author:

The SA80 in a section of eight has an effective range of 600 metres. Only on a few occasions was I engaged from a greater distance by SA fire. On those occasions their fire was not accurate but we still brought in AH [Attack Helicopter] or vehicle mounted .50 cal and GMG [Grenade Machine Gun] however, these were not always available. So I think it depends on what organic weapon systems you have at your disposal, whatever weapon we have they need to be light and accurate. In terms of optimum issues, I don't really think I had one but in a rural environment range and accuracy is what you need depending on your enemy, TB [Taliban] to North Korea/Russia are a different beast altogether.

*    *    *

Turning away from the overmatch question, a resurgent trend in assault rifles and carbines has been the bullpup design. Long considered a product of the 1970s, bullpups are increasingly returning to the front line. Many designers have noted their key advantage – reduced length whilst maintaining a longer, often rifle-length barrel. The Israelis in particular have been at the forefront with their Tavor family including the Mini Tavor now known as the X-95. The Tavor family and the Croatian VHS family have both sold very well on the international arms market. Other, mainly older designs have seen less success.

Belgium's Fabrique Nationale produced their own 5.56 × 45mm bullpup in the form of the F2000. It has unfortunately seen little adoption by any larger militaries (although Slovenia recently adopted it as their standard issue rifle noting, '*it took a quite a lot of courage to choose a weapon that was still not proven with other armies but as we tested it, it proved quite reliable and gave us all the capabilities that a modern assault rifle should have*'), whilst the French FAMAS has recently been retired in favour of a more modern but conventional design in the form of the HK416F.

The Singaporean bullpup design 5.56 × 45mm SAR-21 assault rifle. (*US Army, Sgt. Eric A. Rutherford*)

A Slovenian soldier firing his 5.56 × 45mm FN F2000 with Aimpoint optic in a NATO exercise. Note the blank-firing barrel adaptor. (*US Army, Spc. Derek Hamilton*)

The Steyr AUG remains in service in a handful of nations including Saudi Arabia (where it is being replaced by domestically produced AK-103s) with the Australians showing the only recent innovation with the weapon, developing the newly issued EF88. By modifying an existing weapon like the Australians, an army eliminates a new training regime by switching to a totally new weapon system and thus the requirement to re-train all of their soldiers.

Along with re-training, procuring new weapons is a costly and often time-consuming endeavour. The US has had a number of failed attempts to replace the M16A2 and later the M4 and M4A1. The XM-8 was an early example as part of the US Army's Objective Individual Combat Weapon. It was eventually cancelled in 2005. It was touted at the time as being a replacement for both the M4 and M16 series, and, in a light machine gun variant, the M249. Trial samples were even deployed for combat testing in Iraq.

The US Army's Individual Carbine competition was another example, looking for an improved M4. It was cancelled in 2013 after only two years of trials of the Colt M901, the FN SCAR-L, the H&K 416 and a Remington entry known as the Adaptive Combat Rifle.

If the trials and tribulations associated with replacing a weapons platform within a Western military like the US Army seem extreme, one needs to also consider how a developing nation fares with a far smaller budget. India is a good recent case in point. For many years, the Indian military were equipped with a mix of Second World War era bolt-action .303 Lee Enfields and a licence-

A US Marine examines a New Zealand Defense Force 5.56 × 45mm IW Steyr with integral 1.5 power optic which has been recently replaced by the LMT MARS-L. (*USMC, Sgt. Sarah Dietz*)

produced variant of the British L1A1 Self Loading Rifle (SLR) known locally as the 1A1 and manufactured by India's Ordnance Factory Board. In the 1980s, India decided to replace these Lee Enfields and 1A1s with a domestically designed and produced modern assault rifle chambered for the ubiquitous 5.56 × 45mm round. Over a decade the resulting weapon was developed and christened the Insas standing for Indian Small Arms System. The Insas was a curious blend of design features – the placement and operation of the cocking handle clearly owed much to H&K designs (as it was placed alongside the barrel above the hand-guard in the manner of the G3 or HK33), whilst the design of the receiver itself was very reminiscent of a Kalashnikov design. Two versions were designed, the 1B1 with a fixed polymer stock and the 2B with a FN FAL Para style side folding stock.

Although capable of accepting M16 STANAG magazines, the issue magazine was a translucent design à la the Steyr AUG but mystifyingly was designed to hold only 20 rounds. Following the fashion of the day, the Insas' selector offered both semi-auto and 3-round bursts. It could mount optics but used an outdated Russian-style side mount to do so. Perhaps most curiously, it also featured a butt plate from the Lee Enfield Mark III with compartments for a pull-through and oil bottle! It did however offer the capability of mounting a domestically designed underbarrel grenade launcher or launching NATO standard rifle grenades, something that was uncommon in a single design of the time.

The first examples of the Insas were issued in 1998 although issue was delayed due to a lack of 5.56 × 45mm SS109 ammunition (so much so that a large quantity

Soldiers from the Indian Army train alongside US soldiers with their current issue 5.56 × 45mm INSAS assault rifles. A prolonged procurement continues to replace the weapon with the AK-103 and/or the Tavor series appearing likely. (*US Army, Capt. Casey Martin*)

of Romanian 7.62 × 39mm AKMs were purchased as an interim replacement for the 1A1). Finally in the hands of the Indian Army, the Insas immediately ran into serious operational problems in the 1999 Kargil conflict between India and Pakistan. Questions arose around reliability and the weapon suffered poorly in sub-zero temperatures with the receiver apparently locking up in the cold and magazines cracking. The 3-round burst setting also malfunctioned, instead firing fully automatic bursts. The extended ranges encountered in the mountains in which they fought also highlighted the range limitations of the 5.56 × 45mm including its propensity to be affected by crosswinds. Many Indian soldiers in the Kargil yearned for the return of the 7.62 × 51mm 1A1.

By the millennium, only half of the planned purchase of Insas rifles had been delivered. Looking for another interim fix, India ordered a quantity of Israeli 5.56 × 45mm TAR-21 Tavor bullpup rifles to take up the shortfall. The reliability issues plaguing the Insas saw further procurement halted. The Insas was also now being criticised for being more expensive to produce than competing commercial designs. Eventually another version of the Insas called the Excalibur, that was being offered for export sale, was mooted as a possible replacement but this too was rejected.

In 2012 the Indian Army decided it wanted a modular assault rifle capable of firing either the 5.56 × 45mm or the 7.62 × 39mm, including options on barrel length and stock. A competitive tender was held with the Beretta ARX 160, the SIG 551, the Galil ACE, the CZ 805 and a modified M16A1 based design from Colt. After several rounds of evaluation, only the Galil and the Beretta remained in the running until the programme was officially cancelled in June 2015.

The 5.56 × 45mm Excalibur surfaced once more as a possible Insas replacement (now known as the MIR for Modified Insas Rifle with the 3-round burst mechanism dropped and an integral Picatinny rail added) and was apparently successfully trialled, however the Indian military then decided to revert to a 7.62 × 51mm calibre platform. A locally developed platform in 7.62 × 51mm was dismissed from the running in June 2017.

The Indians have also been looking for a short barrel CQB carbine since 2010 after they retired the 9 × 19mm Sterling L2A3 sub-machine gun that had served in that role since the 1950s. A tender was issued for almost 45,000 carbines with the M4, the Beretta ARX 160 and the Galil ACE all in the running, but again was cancelled. All up, the Indian military has issued a new tender every two years between 2011 and 2017. The latest as we go to press is that the Indian government has approved a new acquisition of some 72,400 7.62 × 51mm assault rifles and 93,895 5.56 × 45mm 'close quarter battle carbines'. As with a similar procurement decision for their new LMG, the decision has apparently been made that a commercial off-the-shelf option will be selected rather than again attempt to develop a home-grown weapon. These newly acquired weapons will be supplied only to frontline units whilst a domestic design will equip the rest of the military. In all likelihood the Insas will remain in service for these non-frontline units.

Big manufacturers like Beretta, Colt, H&K, and Fabrique Nationale have declined to enter the latest bout of trials, likely due to the restrictive conditions of the eventual contract. Thales has partnered with the Indian firm MKU to offer the F90CQB which is a variant of the new Australian EF88, specifically for the 'close quarter battle carbine' requirement. Israeli Weapons Industries (IWI) have opened a domestic production facility in India to manufacture a range of small

An Israeli soldier with the 5.56 × 45mm Tavor GTAR-21 with attached 40mm M203 grenade launcher and ITL MARS red dot sight. (*Creative Commons, IDF*)

arms to include the bullpup Tavor family, the Negev LMG and the 7.62 × 51mm Galil sniper variant, the Galatz.

IWI is currently also the only firm who are bidding on both the battle rifle and carbine, and the new LMG. With both the X95 and TAR-21 already in limited service with Indian police and SOF, and with the announcement of the domestic factory, IWI must be very well placed to finally scoop up the contracts.

Latest reports indicate that for the larger, non-frontline requirement (circa 760,000 rifles, although other reports indicate that budget cuts may result in only a third of this number being purchased), the adoption of the Russian AK-103 in 7.62 × 39mm is looking increasingly likely. A 7.62 × 39mm calibre platform would allow India to use the vast stocks of that calibre already in their supply chain. The Indian government and Kalashnikov Concern are negotiating for a joint venture that would see AK-103s domestically produced, although this process has been plagued by political interference. To further muddy the water, UAE's Caracal International had agreed a deal which would see their 7.62 × 51mm CAR 817AR domestically produced in India and offered as a contender for the 7.62 × 51mm assault rifle requirement, although they now appear to have been eliminated from the competition.

S&T Motiv (formerly Daewoo) of South Korea also entered the fray with an unknown platform but apparently a variant of their 5.56 × 45mm K2. They too have been declared non-compliant and are out of the running. SIG Sauer are also allegedly involved with pitching their 716 battle rifle. In all likelihood however, the AK-103 will win the non-front line contract whilst IWI will likely scoop the front-line battle rifle, carbine and LMG contracts.

*    *    *

Other developing nations are forging ahead with assault rifle replacement programmes. Portugal are replacing some 31,000 locally manufactured Indep G3s that have served as the standard issue for many years. The new standard issue is the Belgian FN SCAR family whilst their Rapid Reaction Brigade of airborne forces are equipped with a bewildering range of platforms including the 5.56 × 45mm G36KV, the HK416A5, the SIG 543 and the Galil ARM. Venezuela are adopting the AK-103 with production due to start domestically in 2019, replacing their own 7.62 × 51mm, the FAL and the 5.56 × 45mm FNC.

In developing countries, the FALs and G3s still soldier on, although an increasing number are adopting more modern designs in 7.62 × 39mm or 5.56 × 45mm. Iran for instance is also purchasing AK-103s. The weapon is being domestically produced in Ethiopia and Vietnam (and potentially soon the Philippines although competition is fierce from an Israeli munitions firm also looking to establish a domestic factory), in joint ventures with Kalashnikov Concern.

European nations are also re-arming. As previously mentioned, the French have recently adopted the HK416A5 over their veteran FAMAS bullpup design. Five competing designs entered the trials which began in 2014: the Beretta ARX160A3, the Croatian HS Produkt VHS-2 (another bullpup design), the Fabrique Nationale SCAR 16, the SIG Sauer MCX and the H&K HK416. The eventual winner, announced in late 2016, was the Heckler and Koch entry, the HK416F, which resembles the then latest HK416A5 but with a number of improvements including the capability of accepting NATO STANAG magazines and ambidextrous controls, eliminating the need for any conversion for left-handed shooters.

New Zealand also recently replaced their IW Steyr (Individual Weapon Steyr) in 2017 with a surprise contender, the American Lewis Machine and Tool (LMT) MARS-L (Modular Ambidextrous Rifle System-Light), again in 5.56 × 45mm. The MARS-L, a version of their CQB16 offering, is an AR based design that visually resembles the HK416. It features a 16-inch barrel which offers a good compromise between accuracy and compactness.

Reports from NZDF (New Zealand Defense Force) indicate qualification scores have doubled versus the IW with the introduction of the MARS-L fitted with the four power ACOG and the new Mk262 ammunition. The introduction of the MARS-L has not been without its challenges. In 2018, the NZDF identified issues with '*. . . the firing pins, trigger mechanisms and cracked bolt carriers. During introduction into service training a number of firing pins suffered breakages and to ensure all rifles are now at the highest standard, LMT has replaced all firing pins under warranty.*'

Broadly speaking what we are seeing currently is developing nations upgrading their base assault rifles with the likes of more modernised platforms such as the AK-103, the MARS-L, VH-2 and the X-95 in a mix of calibres dependent on the

New Zealand soldiers during an exercise carrying the recently issued 5.56 × 45mm LMT MARS-L fitted with Trijicon ACOG which replaced the IW Steyr (AUG) in New Zealand Army service. (*US Air Force, Master Sgt. Barry Loo*)

local threat environment. The 7.62 × 39mm is not going away thanks to the huge volumes of ammunition available and many countries will retain AK family platforms for the foreseeable future.

For first world nations, most are either upgrading to piston-driven designs like the HK416 to replace ageing and often war-worn G36s and similar weapons, whilst the likes of the United Kingdom and Australia decide to continue with upgraded variants of their issue weapon until a truly evolutionary development occurs. This will be the eventual US decision on a calibre in the 6.5mm region, whether in a caseless or cased telescoped format.

## Individual Weapon Summaries

### SCAR-L (Mk 16)

The SCAR or Special Forces Combat Rifle was Fabrique Nationale's much heralded replacement for the M4 and M4A1, developed in part to a brief from SOCOM which was looking for a new modular rifle that could serve as a marksman's rifle, sniper rifle or assault rifle. It was originally scheduled to replace the carbine within SOCOM, however the adoption of the 5.56 × 45mm SCAR-L (Light) was cancelled in 2010 and the 850-odd examples of the 5.56 × 45mm version were recalled in what was a serious blow to the stature of the SCAR platform.

The reason was related to budgets and to the performance of the SCAR-L (officially the Mk 16 Mod0) in the hands of Rangers in Afghanistan in 2009. SOCOM noted: *'The Mk 16 does not provide enough of a performance advantage over the M4 to justify spending limited USSOCOM funds when competing priorities are taken into consideration.'* This all but crushed any potential for the SCAR to be purchased by the US Army and only limited numbers of the SCAR-L remain in service with Naval Special Warfare.

Although adopted in small quantities by the Serbian Army and Chilean Marines, although principally for SOF, the biggest procurement has been by the Belgian Army which is slowly replacing their FN FNCs with the SCAR Mk 16. The SCAR platform has formed the basis for the HAMR (Heat Adaptive Modular Rifle) a variant of which looks set to compete in the US Army's NGSW- Rifle programme.

### HK433

Anticipated by many to replace the G36 in German service, the HK433 is the latest general issue rifle offered by Heckler and Koch. Taking into account the momentum for modularity, the gas piston 433 features an easily switchable barrel which gives soldiers (or more likely their armourers) the option of a range of barrel lengths based on their role. For urban house clearing, a compact 11-inch barrel is available whilst for the DMR role, a 20-inch is also offered.

H&K have proposed variants of the 433 in both 7.62 × 51mm and 7.62 × 39mm, the HK231 and HK123, although at the time of writing these have yet to be publicly unveiled. A model in the fashionable .300 Blackout is also mooted as the HK437. Most importantly, unlike early versions of the HK416 and the current G36 family, the 433 allows the use of any STANAG M16 pattern magazine meaning that a nation that adopted it could use magazines that are already in their inventory should they be using an M16 variant or compatible platform.

## HK416

The HK416 is a short-stroke gas piston design which was originally developed for an American SOF requirement to build better M4A1. The piston system means that the 416 doesn't generate the same amount of fouling as a regular gas impingement system. It is also better suited for use with a suppressor. It has been this reliability that has sold the HK416 to numerous armies, looking to upgrade their service rifles.

Outside of special operations forces, the first large scale military adoption of the HK416 was by the Norwegian Army in 2006. Their variant, the 416N, is issued in both the 16.5-inch and 10.5-inch barrel configurations and has seen extensive combat in Afghanistan since 2008. Heckler and Koch of course won the French Future Individual Weapon tender for the replacement for the venerable FAMAS with a variant of the HK416A5, the HK416F. Along with the rifle, the French Army ordered more than 10,000 40mm HK269 launchers for their 416Fs. The French Army received the first examples of their new 416F in May 2017 and it is slowly replacing the FAMAS, although many combat units in Mali are still equipped with the older bullpup design.

The USMC also adopted the HK416 as the M27 IAR initially to supplement and in many cases replace the M249 SAW. The M27 has now seen a far larger rate of fielding than originally communicated, with every Marine rifleman being issued

A French solder firing the 57.45 × 45mm Heckler and Koch HK416 fitted with EOTech sight at a range in Djibouti. (*USMC, Gunnery Sgt. James Frank*)

A relatively rare shot of a 5.56 × 45mm M27 IAR sans optics and fitted with a KAC QD sound suppressor and using the relatively recently introduced Magpul PMAG in Coyote Tan. (*USMC, Lance Cpl. Michaela R. Gregory*)

an M27 as his or her standard individual weapon from 2018 onward. Critics argue that the M27 is far more expensive than the M4A1 but a USMC spokesperson responded that economies of scale have reduced the ticket price of the H&K rifle: '*The price for that rifle is comparable to what we paid for the M4s the riflemen currently have. These companies are competing against each other. And we now have bought the finest infantry rifle for the same price the current infantry rifle is.*'

The Marines are continuing to innovate beyond the base M27 (and now the new designated marksman variant the M38 which we will consider in the next chapter) with a programme to trial suppressors across whole platoons, including individual weapons like the M27 but also the M240B medium machine gun. Another trial piece of equipment is a variable magnification optic on every rifleman's M27 which, with the proper training, would increase the accuracy and range of the majority of the squad's weapons. We will return to the concept of a general-issue variable optic at the close of this chapter.

The latest variant of the rifle, the 416A7 has been recently adopted by Bundeswehr special operations. Their variant includes the novel addition of a RFID that tracks the number of rounds fired by a particular weapon to ease maintenance, for example telling armourers when new barrels are required. The HK416 is hotly tipped to be the winner in the current German rifle trials to replace another H&K design, the G36.

The domestically produced 5.56 × 45mm Mexican FX-05 Xiuhcoatl replacing the 7.62 × 51mm G3 in Mexican service. (*Creative Commons*)

## FX-05 Xiuhcoatl

The Mexican military adopted the domestically designed and produced FX-05 Xiuhcoatl in 2006 after a licencing agreement with H&K to domestically produce the G36 fell apart. The physical similarity of the FX-05 to the G36 led to an investigation by H&K that found that although outwardly similar, the FX-05 was internally a different design. The FX-05 is intended to replace the Army's G3 stocks but production delays have resulted in many G3s remaining in service.

## IMBEL IA2

The IA2 is a Brazilian design that features a side folding stock, monolithic rail and accepts STANAG magazines. Domestically designed and produced by the state owned Indústria de Material Bélico do Brasil (Imbel), the IA2 began to replace Brazilian licence-produced FAL variants that have been serving the Brazilian Army since the 1960s, although the FALs will continue to soldier on as the IA2 is intended to supplement rather than wholly replace the battle rifle. A 7.62 × 51mm version which uses FAL magazines is also available which has been adopted by some Brazilian police units.

An earlier attempt to adopt a 5.56 × 45mm, the MD97, was based on the FAL and had a high proportion of common components. The IA2 is an entirely new design, physically somewhat resembling a SIG 552 carbine; 1,500 IA2s were trialled in 2013 before full adoption. In 2018, the Brazilian military placed an order for a further 8,000 IA2s.

A Brazilian general officer commented:

Imbel IA2 is a national project with the goal of replacing the old FAL and PARA-FAL rifles … the new 5.56mm version, which is lighter, more sophisticated, polymer-based, and highly reliable, as it was proven during the tests in different scenarios. These weapons may be used with different accessories produced in the country, such as laser sights, infrared thermal sights, 40mm-grenade launcher, bayonets, etc. We are positive that the Imbel IA2 will be the perfect substitute for the FAL, a weapon that has become a legend in the Brazilian Army.

## Daewoo (S&T Motiv) K1/K2

The first variant officially adopted of this South Korean rifle was the so-called K1 SMG, a 5.56 × 45mm carbine that had been rushed into production to meet an urgent requirement from South Korean special operators. Its rifle variant, the K2,

A Republic of Korea infantryman with the Daewoo/S&T Motiv 5.56 × 45mm K2C1 variant which added quad Picatinny rails and a collapsible stock to the standard issue K2. The optic is the domestically produced TDB M9. (*Commonwealth of Australia, Cpl Nunu Campos*)

was adopted in 1986 by the South Korean Army replacing the M16A1. The K2 is a fairly basic but reliable design using a long stroke gas piston modelled from the AK family while also incorporating elements from the M16A1 and the FAL whilst physically resembling the rifle version of the Vietnam-era Stoner 63.

The latest variant that is in limited use is the K2C1 which has modernised the original K2 design with the addition of a flat-top receiver allowing easy mounting of optics, a number of Picatinny rails on the forearm and a SOPMOD style collapsible stock. The K2 family has seen some overseas sales, mainly to SOF units, although the Nigerian, Lebanese and Malawian militaries have made significant purchases to equip their infantry.

As an aside, the Nigerian Army must have some very clever logisticians as along with the K2 they issue to various units the Beretta AR70, the FAL, the AK, the G3, the Tavor, the Polish M762, the Indonesian Pindad SS1 and the Chinese Type 81!

### Howa Type 89

This Japanese design was adopted in 1989 to replace the $7.62 \times 51$mm Type 64 in Japanese Ground Self Defense Force (JGSDF) service. Based upon the AR-18 that was licence produced by Howa in Japan but somewhat resembling an FNC in outward appearance, it features that favourite of the eighties, the 3-round burst setting and has an integral folding bipod along with the capability to launch rifle grenades.

### MSBS (Modułowy System Broni Strzeleckiej – Modular Firearms System) 16C FB-M1 and FB-M2 Grot

First issued in 2018 to elements of the Polish Army, the MSBS, or Grot as it is known, is now the standard issue rifle of Polish forces. Designed from the start as a modular system, the various models available share widely and the basic weapon can be quickly reconfigured.

The Grot features a full-length rail for optics, back-up iron sights and lasers with additional rails on the forearm for lights and vertical grips. It has also been widely fitted with an adjustable gas regulator to allow the use of suppressors. Importantly, it also accepts NATO STANAG magazines increasing interoperability with partner nations.

The head of Poland's Territorial Defence explained the naming convention and intention with the Grot in a 2017 interview with Defence 24:

> At the stage when the procurement was being designed, it was a dogma for us to assume that there would be a need to continuously perfect the weapon, similarly as it is done by armed forces of other countries. Thus, the rifle name is going to feature an 'M' suffix. In this way, the first batch of the weapons procured is to bear the designation of GROT 16C FB-M1, but at the moment we have assumed that within the framework of the agreement implemented it would be possible to modify the weapon even up to the M3 standard.
>
> What information is included in the designation? 16 refers to the barrel length, in inches, C refers to classic (conventional) rifle layout, while M and

A Japanese Ground Self-Defense Force with 5.56 × 45mm Type 89 mounting an Aimpoint red dot optic and weapon light. (*USMC, Gunnery Sgt. Robert Brown*)

the number refer to the modification designation. Today we also expect that a situation would emerge in which a need may arise to upgrade the rifle from M1 up to M3 standard for example. We are creating a system, within which conditions are inspiring the manufacturer to continuously perfect the weapon, in line with the requests submitted by the soldier.

Its partner, the MSBS-5.56B, is a radical redesign of the base weapon, turning it into a compact bullpup design. At the time of writing this has yet to be adopted, but rumour suggests it may be procured for Polish SOF but would also be eminently suitable as a PDW style weapon for AFV crews and the like.

## Beryl M556 and M762

The Beryl M556, known within the Polish military as the wz.96C, is a 5.56 × 45mm platform developed to replace both the 5.45 × 39mm wz.88 Tantal and legacy 7.62 × 39mm AKMs in Polish service. Adopted in 1997, it features triple Picatinny rails along the forearm and a collapsible stock but retains much of the look and feel of the traditional AK it is based upon including the clunky AK pattern selector. Surprisingly, the weapon was designed to launch rifle grenades as well as accept an under-barrel grenade launcher, although rifle grenades have fallen from favour amongst most NATO nations.

Polish Army soldier in Ghazni Province, Afghanistan 2010. The soldier in the foreground carries a 5.56 × 45mm Mini-Beryl with EOTech optic. The soldier to his left carries the standard issue Beryl with a wz.1974 Pallad grenade launcher attached under the barrel.
(*US Navy, Petty Officer 1st Class Mark O'Donald*)

A Polish soldier firing his 5.56 × 45mm Mini-Beryl (wz.1996C) with EOTech optic.
(*US Army, Capt. Charles Emmons*)

The M556 also has a carbine variant, the aptly named Mini Beryl. The M762 is a rechambered version of the M556 in 7.62 × 39mm and uses standard AK magazines. Like its 5.56 × 45mm little brother, the M762 features a selector that includes 3-round burst and triple Picatinny rails along the forearm and a further rail mounted atop the receiver. Although both the M556 and M762 are being replaced by the Grot series, examples of the M762 will likely soldier on in non-frontline units for some time to come.

Nigeria adopted the M762 in 2015 and has recently signed an agreement to domestically produce the M762 for further sales throughout Africa (they will also likely produce the Polish OBJ-006). The weapon the M556 replaced, the wz.88 Tantal, is now a common sight in the Middle East with stocks donated to Kurdish forces and the Iraqi military. Examples have also inevitably appeared in Syria.

### Colt Canada C7/C8

The C7 is a domestically produced version of the M16A2 manufactured by Diemaco – now Colt Canada. The C7 replaced the C1, a licenced FAL variant, when the Canadian Army decided to adopt the 5.56 × 45mm SS109. The C7 however has a number of interesting traits not found on a US M16A2 including the ability to fire full automatic rather than 3-round bursts.

The C7 was upgraded in the 1990s with the addition of a flat-top receiver featuring the by now standard Picatinny rail and christened the C7A1. Based on their early experiences in Afghanistan, Canadian forces received an updated variant, the C7A2, with collapsible multi-position stock and foregrip rail system. The C7A2 is commonly issued with the Elcan fixed 3.4 power magnification optic.

The Canadian Army notes:

> The C7A2 automatic rifle is an evolutionary or mid-life program upgrade from the C7 and C7A1 rifle variants. The upgrade is equipped with ambidextrous controls, low infrared signature and an extendable butt. In addition, the rifle can be fitted with a bayonet for close combat. Its primary sighting system is an optical sight, which is supplemented by an adjustable front sight and an adjustable backup sight.

A replacement for the C7 series is being examined under the Canadian Future Small Arms Research programme which is examining both conventional and bullpup designs along with ancillary equipment such as optics and lasers. This will also be influenced by any US decision on the NGSW programme.

Variants of the C7 have been adopted by the Netherlands and Denmark whilst the carbine version, the C8 and C8SFW, has found favour with numerous SOF units (some Canadian Army units now use the C8A3, the latest iteration of the carbine version). A new family of infantry rifles was introduced by Colt Canada in 2016 based around the Modular Rail Rifle (MRR) which has a modernised M-LOK mounting system and an integrated upper featuring a full-length rail.

A Danish soldier carrying the recently issued 5.56 × 45mm Canadian C8 IUR known as the M/10 in Danish service. This rifle is equipped with an Elcan M145 optic and PEQ-15 infrared illuminator. (*US Army, Specialist Markus Rauchenberger*)

## Galil Family

The domestically designed and produced Israeli Galil is based on the Finnish Valmet M62, itself based on the AK. Beating out competition from the M16A1, the HK33, the Stoner 63A1 and even a number of AK variants, the Galil was adopted by the Israel Defense Force in 1972. Rumours suggest a number apparently even saw action in the 1973 Yom Kippur War, although the principal IDF rifle for that conflict remained the FN FAL. Its first major combat debut was Operation Peace for Galilee in 1982.

Three principal 5.56 × 45mm variants were produced for the Israeli military: the AR as the standard issue service rifle; the SAR, its carbine equivalent; and the ARM as a type of light automatic rifle. This followed in the footsteps of the heavy barrel FN FAL Makle'a Kal carried by the IDF as their section support weapon during both the Six Day War and Yom Kippur War. It was a solid and reliable weapon with better accuracy than an AKM. All three variants could use M16 magazines but needed an adaptor to do so, a design oversight. Famously, the Galil included a bottle opener as experience had shown that Israeli troops would otherwise sometimes use the edge of the magazine well or the magazines themselves, potentially increasing the chances of a stoppage.

The Galil was never widely issued and was replaced in frontline service by American supplied M16A1s and Colt carbines in the late 1980s. A number of theories have been floated – and unfortunately the Israelis aren't telling – but its demise was likely from a number of factors. It suffered from weighing more than most of its contemporaries and the original version of its stock had to be replaced after performance issues were raised following operations in Beirut. Additionally, the 50-round magazine designed for the ARM light support variant could not be used when prone. Compared to the M16s that were arriving under US aid agreements, the Galil was also expensive for a small army like Israel to produce.

It was also never adopted by IDF special operations forces, who like most militaries, lead the way in defining the infantry's view of a particular weapon. Along with its lighter weight, and potentially slightly greater accuracy, the SOF preference for their Colt 653 carbines (and AKs) meant that the Galil never won the 'hearts and minds' of the Israeli infantryman.

The weapon went on to greater success with South Africa licence-producing the Galil as the R4 and R5 (carbine). The R4 remains the SADF's issue individual weapon. The Galil is today issued by a number of African countries including Botswana, Democratic Republic of Congo, Djibouti, Lesotho, Rwanda and Swaziland. After the AK family, the Galil is certainly the most widespread modern assault rifle in use in Africa.

The weapon family realised similar success in Central and South America. Colombia (who now domestically produce the Galil ACE – see below), Portugal and Guatemala, all already customers of the then Israeli Defense Industries, purchased the Galil in a number of variants as did Bolivia, Costa Rica, El Salvador, Haiti, Nicaragua and Peru. The Philippines also issues the Galil along with the M16A1.

Estonian Scouts in Baghdad, Iraq 2005 carry the 5.56 × 45mm Galil ARM fitted with M68 Aimpoint red dots. (*US Army, Sgt. David Foley*)

Estonia still issues the Galil in its AR, SAR and ARM guises, all in 5.56 × 45mm. The SAR is employed as a carbine whilst the ARM is used as a kind of IAR or automatic rifle with bipod deployed and fed from the Galil proprietary 35-round magazine. First adopted in 1994, Brügger & Thomet (B&T) were granted the contract to modernize Estonia's fleet of Galils in 2008 with rails systems based on feedback from Estonian deployments to Iraq and Afghanistan. Estonian Galils now mount both Aimpoint and EOTech optics, vertical foregrips and tactical lights. Brügger & Thomet also provided a number of 40mm B&T under-barrel launchers. Until the B&T upgrade, rifle grenades were standard issue.

The Estonian military are currently trialling a number of new rifles in a competitive tender to replace their issue Galils (and G3 variant 7.62 × 51mm AK4s, originally donated to Estonia by Sweden and upgraded by B&T with collapsible stocks). A number of platforms from H&K, CZ, SIG and LMT are in the running: the HK416, the SIG Sauer MCX and the LMT with their monolithic rail MLCPS – all in 5.56 × 45mm.

The Galil ACE is a modernised version of the Galil family that features a full-length top rail and collapsible stock. Variants are available in 5.56 × 45mm, 7.62 × 39mm and 7.62 × 51mm. Carbine models in each calibre are also produced. The ACE has replaced the licence-produced SIG 540 built by domestic arms manufacturer FAMAE in Chilean Army service and has rather surprisingly replaced a range of AKs in Vietnamese service.

## FAMAS

*'Le Clarion'* or 'The Bugle' is the famous French bullpup design adopted by the French military in 1975. More than 400,000 of the original FAMAS F1 (Fusil Automatique MAS Modele F1) were produced and the rifle saw combat service from Djibouti and Chad to Afghanistan and Mali. Widely respected within France, it unfortunately saw few export customers and is currently being replaced by the HK416F.

The FAMAS F1 had a number of features which were ground-breaking at the time that have only recently been acknowledged. For instance, almost uniquely, it featured a free-floating barrel. As we will explain later when we discuss designated marksman and sniper rifles, a free-floating barrel can greatly aid in a weapon's inherent accuracy. It simply means that the barrel is only attached to the rest of the weapon at the receiver and not at the hand-guard as is more commonly encountered. Less contact points translates to less vibration to the barrel that will affect accuracy, although primarily at longer ranges.

Because of the timing of its development cycle, the F1 was unfortunately designed to accommodate the US M193 5.56 × 45mm ball round rather than the later NATO SS109 and thus featured a 1 in 12″ barrel twist. Accuracy of the SS109 fired from an F1 suffered terribly and the French military was forced to issue their version of the M193 for the rifle, whilst the SS109 was issued for their Minimi light machine guns, unnecessarily complicating the supply chain. Anecdotally, the weapon also required a particular domestically-produced version of the M193 with a much stronger steel casing to operate reliably, although this was likely a problem with older issue weapons.

The F1 featured an integral folding bipod and an integrated rifle-grenade launching capability. Chiefly through this feature, the humble rifle grenade has remained in widespread service with the French military. Conversely, the original F1 version was also handicapped by its inability to easily attach an under-barrel grenade launcher like the American M203, placing an even greater reliance on the rifle-grenade capability. Intriguingly, the rifle is still carried today, equipped with all manner of modern optics and accessories, by French counter-terrorist units like the GIGN who deploy the FAMAS to launch the Israeli Simon door-breaching rifle grenade.

The design also had the 3-round burst setting that was popular in designs from the 1970s and 1980s (see the M16A2 and Daewoo K2 for other examples), however the selector for the burst option was, again uniquely, located behind the trigger and separate from the primary selector that offered the standard safe, semi and fully-automatic settings.

Additionally, the FAMAS was designed specifically from the ground up to be ambidextrous and capable of switching ejection ports to accommodate both left- and right-handed shooters. Ambidextrous controls are a recurring issue with most bullpups as the typical bullpup design places the weapon's receiver behind the pistol grip, meaning that hot expended casings will often strike a left-handed shooter in the face. The British L85A1 and later A2 designs are notorious for

A French Marine armed with the 5.56 × 45mm FAMAS with EOTech optic. This FAMAS features a number of upgrades from a 2010 programme (including rails and redesigned stock) which was cancelled in 2014 in favour of adopting the HK416F. *(USMC, Cpl. Timothy Turner)*

this. Others like the Austrian AUG offer a simple conversion for left-handed operation.

Unusually, the FAMAS was equipped with a straight-line 25-round rather than the more standard 30-round capacity magazine of its contemporaries. Apparently, this was related to going prone with the weapon – a longer magazine stuck out too far requiring the infantryman to risk crouching higher over the rifle. The magazine was rather short-sightedly a proprietary design and thus NATO STANAG magazines were not usable with the FAMAS F1.

A second version, the G2, was trialled but only adopted by the French Navy and some SOF. It featured a 1 in 7″ twist barrel suitable for the SS109 and able to accommodate STANAG magazines. Another version, the FELIN (*Fantassin à Équipement et Liaisons Intégrés* or Integrated Infantryman Equipment and Communications) added a 1 in 9″ twist barrel, accommodating both the French M193 variant and the SS109. The FELIN variant was developed as part of the French version of the Future Warrior programme and featured an integrated video camera and various optics.

### CZ805/807 Bren

Both rifles were developed to meet a Czech Army requirement for a phased replacement of their domestically-produced 7.62 × 39mm Vz58s, an AK based design dating from the 1950s. According to some accounts, more than twenty different designs were submitted by a range of manufacturers which were down-selected to two – the 805 and Fabrique Nationale's SCAR-L (in US service the Mk 16).

The Czech design won the competition and both the 805A1 and its 10.9-inch barrel carbine variant, the 805A2, were adopted into service from 2011. A third variant, the lighter 806, was purchased in 2016 in smaller numbers. The 806 is a product improved version of the 805 with a number of refinements made directly from the feedback of Czech soldiers who had used the 805 in Afghanistan. The 14.2-inch barrel, CZ805, is chambered for the $5.56 \times 45$mm whilst its bigger brother, the 807, is chambered for the $7.62 \times 39$mm Soviet round.

The 807 also allows the use of $5.56 \times 45$mm with a conversion kit. The 805 was designed with an innovative detachable magazine housing that can be swapped out by the user to accommodate M16 style or G36 magazines, if required, rather than the proprietary CZ polymer 30-round magazines that come standard with the weapon. This is a rare example of a manufacturer, and client, looking seriously to enable NATO interchangeability. The Slovakian Army followed suit with the Czechs and adopted the 805 to replace their own elderly Vz58s.

CZ small arms have seen increasing use with Egyptian forces, culminating with the 2018 announcement of a CZ manufacturing presence in Egypt. It looks increasingly likely that the CZ 807 will see general issue ahead of the Beretta ARX160 which looked to be the replacement for Egypt's mix of AK pattern rifles.

A Czech Republic soldier scans for enemy in Parwan Province, Afghanistan 2014 with his $5.56 \times 45$mm CZ805A1 Bren fitted with Aimpoint and magnifier. *(US Army, Staff Sgt. Daniel Luksan)*

The 807 in 7.62 × 39mm also looks set to become the new standard rifle of the Pakistani Army with domestic producer Pakistan Ordnance Factory manufacturing, although at the time of writing no official statement had been made (a new 7.62 × 51mm variant is also in the running).

Both Fabrique Nationale with the SCAR-H and Beretta with the ARX160 are competing against the CZ. A quantity of AK-103s in 7.62 × 39mm have been procured and rumour indicates that Kalashnikov Concern may have their new 7.62 × 51mm version available for testing (the AK-308). Whoever wins the contract will replace both the Chinese 7.62 × 39mm Type 56 and the 7.62 × 51mm H&K G3 in Pakistani service.

## BD-08

The BD-08 is a domestically-produced version of the Chinese Type 81 which is slowly replacing the Type 56 and Type 63 assault rifles issued by the Bangladesh Army. It features a side-folding stock and accepts standard 7.62 × 39mm AK magazines, but is otherwise a fairly prosaic design which physically resembles the Finnish Valmet M76. It replaces a collection of legacy Type 56s, G3s and FALs.

## L85 Series (SA80A2/A3)

The history of the L85 series is reasonably well known and we won't dwell too much on it here. There are several works as previously mentioned that cover the debacle which was the SA80 procurement. For an inexpensive and quick read on the subject, the author recommends *SA80 Assault Rifles* by Neil Grant as an excellent primer on the subject.

Instead the author spoke to British veteran of Iraq and Afghanistan, Doug Beattie, who kindly agreed for the author to include the following passage which eloquently documents both the service history of the L85 and Beattie's relationship with it:

> Our initial encounter took place when, as a Junior Non-Commissioned Officer, I attended the very first Section Commanders' Battle Course along with seventy-nine other men. The weapon was the replacement to the much heavier SLR. Because the magazine was behind the pistol grip, the SA80 was a much shorter rifle than its predecessor but its barrel length remained roughly the same, ensuring accuracy. It's fully automatic capability was a direct result of experience from the Falklands war where the Argentinians use of the FN version of the SLR – complete with auto fire function – often left the British floundering in engagements.
>
> On paper the SA80 seemed to mark a major advancement for the 'poor bloody infantry', but as I and my colleagues soon discovered the reality was rather less impressive. The fielding of the new weapon was done without adequate equipment checks, field trials and thought as to how it might integrate with other technological developments in fighting systems. In the jargon of this age it was a weapon not fit for purpose.
>
> The SA80's flaws were extensive. The magazine wouldn't stay on the weapon – as you patrolled, should your body brush against the magazine

release catch the magazine would fall off and rounds would be sent spinning all over the floor. The low-tech solution was to tie the magazine in place with a bit of string and a small locally purchased clip. If you wore mosquito repellent the rubber cheek-piece on the weapon would melt. The bayonet didn't attach correctly. The bolt and recoil spring assembly were under-engineered and not strong enough to do the robust job they needed to. This led to major stoppages and soon it became known as an unreliable weapon in the heat of battle.

It was common for the strength of the spring to be insufficient to force the bolt carrier rearwards and so a new round was not picked up and fed into the breach after the previous one had been fired. This was assuming the spent cartridge case had been ejected at all, as it was also common for the extractor to rip off the base of the round so preventing its successful disposal.

Add in the fact that the weapon could only be fired by a right-handed soldier – if a 'southpaw' pulled the trigger he could expect a face-full of brass or at least the man beside him could – and it was unsurprising that the answer to all the British Army's problems soon gained a questionable reputation, one that has proved hard to shake off even with the subsequent arrival of the new improved model, the SA80A2, that came without the faults which bedevilled its earlier namesake.

What the SA80A2 does retain is the accuracy of the original version, something that has only been enhanced by the ACOG sight. Add to this the development of an under slung grenade launcher allowing it to fire 40mm HE grenades, a Picatinny rail so the weapon can now except a down-grip for close quarter battle, laser light module for night engagements and various other gadgets and gizmos that would embarrass the US military, then you can see that the weapon has been developed into a seriously versatile fighting system.

Yet despite the changes the stigma remains. Performance might have improved but the new version looks like the old and essentially has the same name. It is all about confidence and that is something that is still missing after all these years. Many of my colleagues look longingly at the American M4 as an alternative to what they believe they are burdened with. In fact UK Special Forces already use the M4 or the C8 rather than the SA80A2 but then they always tend to have something other than standard issue kit regardless if it is better or not. It sets them apart from the average 'green troops' and underlines their elevated status by being different.

But to pine after the M4 ignores the facts. In side-by-side trials the UK weapon comes out on top almost every time. It has better accuracy; better penetration; better resilience to the harsh conditions found in both the desert and the jungle. Stoppages are low and it now does what it should always have done – combine a reliable, fast-rate of fire with the characteristics to make it a formidable weapon in the closest proximity to the enemy.

During the six months I spent in Afghanistan in 2010–11 I fired over 900 rounds without any stoppages. In 2008 I fired thousands of rounds, again without a single stoppage, not one. It was the same back in 2006 on my first tour of Helmand.

I am happy to fight with whatever I am given, as are most soldiers because that is what we do – dare I say it the Irish more than most! We like to fight – we find excuses allowing us to engage the enemy, rather than excuses not to. But still we are soldiers and as such we will always moan about something or other. And if there is one thing that has been moaned about more than others over the past 25 years it is the SA80. My fighting life is probably over. Perhaps it is time now for the SA80 to also leave the battlefield quietly after 27 years.

There are some other platforms in use but mainly with SOF, as Beattie relates. A Royal Marine unit with responsibility for protecting nuclear facilities and conducting maritime counter-terrorism and counter-piracy missions – 43 Commando Fleet Protection Group – recently purchased the Canadian L119A2 to replace their issue L85A2s, principally due to the L119A2's ambidextrous controls (and its improved ability to reliably cycle specialist fragmenting and Simunition training ammunition). A RM spokesperson virtually confirmed this, mentioning its increased capability for 'reduced ricochet, limited collateral damage'.

A British infantryman from 1st Battalion, Duke of Lancaster's Regiment deployed in Helmand Province, Afghanistan 2010. His 5.56 × 45mm 'Theatre Entry Standard' L85A2 mounts a Trijicon ACOG with back-up RMR, GripPod bipod and Laser Light Module.
*(Open Government License v3.0, Corporal Barry Lloyd)*

When will the L85 be retired? A 2012 tender for a Modular Assault Rifle System was issued with the ambitious target of introducing the first new weapons by 2014, but instead ground to a halt two years later. This would have likely seen the HK416 or even the SCAR well placed to become the new British infantry rifle. Instead the L85A2 was upgraded and is expected to remain in service until 2025.

The 2018 upgrade featured mainly cosmetic changes but saw a full-length top rail added along with a new H&K designed foregrip with rails, which attaches to the receiver rather than the barrel, offering a potential further increase in accuracy. Additionally, the Ministry of Defence noted:

- A more durable hardwearing coating in a 'Flat Dark Earth' colour offering better camouflage in a range of environments.
- The A3 is 100g lighter than the A2 and has a more streamlined fore grip making the weapon easier to handle.
- The A3 rifle has a bracket to secure new innovative low light sights which can clip on or in front of the day sight without the need to remove it. These sights are smaller, lighter and require fewer batteries whilst operating just as effectively in low light/night conditions.

## G36 Series

The G36 rose from the ashes of the cancelled G11 programme that saw West Germany develop a new caseless round, the $4.7 \times 33$mm, and a futuristic platform to fire it from. Sadly, the G11 was scrapped after the fall of the Berlin Wall and the resulting defence budget pressures from unification. Instead the Bundeswehr held a competition between the HK50 and the Steyr AUG, both $5.56 \times 45$mm designs for NATO commonality. The HK50 triumphed and was accepted into German service as the G36 in 1996.

The basic weapon itself is fitted with an integral 3-power magnification optic with a reflex sight mounted above it for close range shooting and was the first to integrate both magnified and reflex optics in the one package, in this case both fitted to the G36's carrying handle. More recent versions have dispensed with the integrated optics in favour of a Picatinny rail over the receiver or attached to a newer low-profile carrying handle.

The German Army (Heer) currently uses the following variants: G36A2 with rails and Zeiss RSA reflex sight; G36KA1 with rails and EOTech holographic weapons sight; and the G36KA2 with additional rails. A G36KA3 is also in service with IdZ-ES modifications as part of Germany's own Future Soldier programme. The System Sturmgewehr Bundeswehr programme to identify a successor to the G36 was announced in April 2017 by the German government. It is expected to enter service from 2019. As we go to press, no decision has been made but speculation indicates that there has been a down-select to two weapons, the HK433 and the short-stroke piston Haenel MK556.

Spain and Saudi Arabia both licence-produce the G36. The Spanish used the $7.62 \times 51$mm CETME C from which the famous G3 evolved. It was replaced by two $5.56 \times 45$mm platforms in 1985, the CETME L and its carbine variant the LC both of which somewhat mirrored the HK33. In 1999, the Spanish Army adopted

A Heckler and Koch 5.56 × 45mm G36KA4 rifle with EOTech sight and magnifier. A version of this rifle is used by the Lithuanian Land Force called the G36KA4M1.
(*US Army, Specialist Pierre-Etienne Courtejoie*)

the G36E and G36EK (the G36E, now known as the G36V, represents an export model and lacks the in-built reflex sight), both domestically-licence produced.

The Latvian military are the latest purchasers of the G36 family, replacing the current issue Swedish licence-produced G3 variant, the AK4, and old 7.62 × 39mm AKMs. For the first time, all of Latvia's armed forces will be armed with a 5.56 × 45mm individual weapon, simplifying training, maintenance and logistics.

## AK5

The AK5 (also known as the CGA5) is the Swedish issue variant of the venerable Belgian 5.56 × 45mm FN FNC. It was adopted in 1986 replacing the 7.62 × 51mm AK4, a licenced locally-produced G3. The FNC beat stiff competition from the HK33, the M16A1 and the Galil to be adopted in a modified form as the AK5. These modifications were principally to do with improving the weapon's resilience against the Swedish winter, but also replaced the fire selector that offered 3-round bursts with a more conventional semi, auto and safe.

A modified version, the AK5B, served for many years as a type of designated marksman rifle with one assigned to each squad and featured the British SUSAT optic. The current variant in service is the AK5C with an improved collapsible stock, ambidextrous fire controls and the addition of a Picatinny rail to modernise the design (a red dot optic has recently been procured). The Swedes are currently

Belgian soldiers carrying 5.56 × 45mm FN FNC M2 assault rifles during European Union exercises. (*US Army, Specialist Gerhard Seuffert*)

evaluating a replacement for the AK5C, but little is known of the models that are being trialled.

### AN-94

There has been a confusing proliferation of competing AK pattern designs emerging from Russia over the past couple of decades. The AN-94 was one of those handful of genuinely innovative designs that took the AK-74 in a different direction. Although visually similar to the AK-74, the AN-94 was a dramatically altered design. It featured three selector settings allowing semi-automatic, fully-automatic and burst fire, the latter an unusual feature last seen on the likes of the M16A2 and FAMAS F1. This selector does away with the standard Kalashnikov design of placing it on the right side of the receiver and is instead located behind and above the trigger guard.

The fully-automatic cyclic rate is some 600 rounds per minute whilst the 2-round burst setting cyclic rate is an astounding 1,800 rounds per minute. This burst feature takes advantage of the so-called 'blowback shifted pulse' action of the AN-94 by effectively slowing the action of the receiver, allowing the first and second rounds to be fired before the weapon begins to recoil.

Matched with the high rate of fire, this meant that the AN-94 produced a very tight grouping using the burst mechanism. In fully-automatic fire too, the first 2 rounds are fired at the higher cyclic rate before following rounds are fired at the lower 600 RPM. The AN-94 was also considered a reliable design, easily surpassing a stated 10,000 round Mean-Time-Between-Failures requirement. A later variant, the AN-94N added a rail on the receiver for mounting optics.

So why did the AN-94 not become the replacement for all AK-74Ms within Russian service? It was announced as far back as 1994 that it would be adopted by both Army and the Interior Ministry, but the cost of producing this complicated weapon has negated against widespread adoption. It is also heavier than the most recent AK-74M at almost half a kilogram more than the AK-74M loaded with a 30-round magazine. Its improved accuracy over its competitor has also been called into question by Western observers without significant training for the end user to make the most of the burst feature.

A number of AN-94s served with Interior Ministry troops in the Second Chechen War and the weapon is still apparently in use (one researcher noted at least one example seen in Crimea in 2014). Sadly, it is highly unlikely that further adoption of the design will be seen.

## AK-12

The AK-12 is one of the latest variants in the AK family and has been announced as the replacement for the AK-74M for Russian infantry. Initially based on the AK-200 design, the version the Russian Army adopted in 2018 was based on the later, and simpler, AK-400 which had been developed to prototype stage in 2016 and offered in both 5.54 × 39mm and 7.62 × 39mm. The AK-12 however, is a 5.45 × 39mm design.

A spokesperson from Kalashnikov Concern noted:

The AK-12 assault carbine also has a new ergonomic fire selector control . . . a person can operate the mechanical controls of the assault rifle with one hand. A soldier can still do everything he needs to do with the weapon: move the safety, pull back the bolt and replace the magazine even if wounded or when using his other hand.

Intriguingly, the apparently better performing Degtyarev A-545 in 5.45 × 39mm and its bigger brother, the A-762 in 7.62 × 39mm, were chosen for Russian special operations forces. The Kalashnikov platforms are apparently a simpler design more suitable for widespread adoption. Amusingly, (and perhaps unfairly as the AK-12 seems to be a fine rifle) the Russian deputy prime minister compared the AK-12 to 'economy class' and the A-545 as 'business class'.

The AK-12 has also been tested as part of the Russian Future Soldier concept, the Ratnik-2, and some sources report that only units fielding Ratnik will be equipped with the AK-12 with the rest of the Army still issuing the AK-74M. Like most stories of small arms procurements in Russia, it is difficult to discern the truth with the AK-12. According to its manufacturers, full-scale production will begin in 2019.

Along with the AK-12, the AK-15 in 7.62 × 39mm has also been adopted. Why the Russian Army has adopted two different calibres is unclear but likely due to large ammunition stocks of the 7.62 × 39mm still being held. Supposition sees the

The replacement for the AK-74M in Russian Army Service, the AK-12 in 5.45 × 39mm. Note additional rails, adjustable side folding stock, and a 2-round burst capability.
*(Kalashnikov Group/Kalashnikov Media)*

AK-12 going to front-line units, whilst the AK-15 will arm support troops. Both rifles feature a pair of Picatinny-type rails for the attachment of optics and lights. A suppressor is offered as standard with the AK-12 and a compact version, the AK-12K, is also available. The AK-12 also offers a number of magazine options including a 60-round extended magazine and compatibility with the 96-round drum magazine of the new RPK-16 light machine gun.

The AK-12 features the unusual 2-round burst setting along with fully and semi-automatic. The 2-round burst setting has been seen on the AN-94 and seemingly offers a greater chance of getting a burst on target although Western armies still train for similar results from an aimed pair of semi-automatic shots which will be more accurate.

### AK-15

The 7.62 × 39mm AK-15 was adopted by the Russian Army in 2018. The AK-15 visually resembles an AK-74M but with a SOPMOD style collapsible stock and Picatinny rails above the receiver and forearm. Notably it is chambered for the M43 7.62 × 39mm round. A shortened carbine version called the AK-15K is also available.

### AK-74M

The latest 5.45 × 39mm AK-74 variant is a modernised design based heavily on the original. It is not actually a new weapon but a series of upgrades to existing AK-74s and its folding stock variant, the AKS-74. A receiver rail has been added to aid the addition of optics as has a new side folding stock with multiple stock

One of the two replacements for the AK-74M in Russian Army service, the 7.62 × 39mm AK-15, this version with a sound suppressor. *(Kalashnikov Group/Kalashnikov Media)*

length positions, similar to the SOPMOD or early Vltor designs. Again confusingly, the upgraded AK-74M will still apparently remain in use despite the adoption of the AK-12 and AK-15.

Izhmash, now Kalashnikov Concern, provided an excellent overview of all types of AK-74 and is worth reproducing here to understand the development of the AK-74M:

**AK-74**: Kalashnikov assault rifle, caliber 5.45mm. In 1967, pursuant to the Resolution of the CPSU Central Committee and the USSR Council of Ministers, a competition was organized to design an assault rifle fit to use the new 5.45mm cartridge. The AK-74 was designed by A.D. Kryakushin's group under the designer supervision of M.T. Kalashnikov. Based on the competition results, this assault rifle was included in the inventory in 1974 as part of the 5.45-mm small arms complex. The cartridge used in the AK-74 weighs 1.5 times less as compared with the 7.62mm cartridge. The soldier can carry 1.5 times more cartridges without increasing the weight of the portable reserve ammunition. In addition, the bullet speed of the 5.45mm caliber is higher.

**AK-74N**: Kalashnikov assault rifle with night sight NSPU, caliber 5.45mm. This model was included in the inventory in 1974.

**AK-74N1**: Kalashnikov assault rifle with a night sight mount, caliber 5.45mm. This model was included in the inventory in 1974.

**AK-74N3**: Kalashnikov assault rifle with night sight 1PN51, caliber 5.45mm. This sight is smaller in size than NSPU: it is twice as short, which considerably improves operating properties, especially its carrying. This model was included in the inventory in 1974.

**AKS-74**: Kalashnikov assault rifle with a folding stock, caliber 5.45mm. This model was included in the inventory in 1974 for landing forces.

**AKS-74N**: Kalashnikov assault rifle with a folding stock and night sight NSPU, caliber 5.45mm. This model was included in the inventory in 1974.

**AKS-74U**: shortened Kalashnikov assault rifle with a folding stock, caliber 5.45mm. It was designed by S.N. Furman's group under the designer supervision of M.T. Kalashnikov. Its shortened barrel makes this assault rifle

The modernized 5.45 × 39mm AK-74M is the current Russian service rifle but is being replaced by the AK-12 and AK-15. (*Kalashnikov Group/Kalashnikov Media*)

easier to handle and lighter in weight. This model was included in the inventory in 1979.

**AK-74M**: modernized Kalashnikov assault rifle, caliber 5.45mm. This model was designed under the supervision of chief designer N.A. Bezborodov and M.T. Kalashnikov, under the technical development plan of the Central Artillery and Missile Department, and included in the inventory in 1991. The AK-74M is based on all four AK-74 modifications. It has a folding plastic stock, which is similar to the stationary model in shape, and a lateral base for mounting an optical or night sight.

**AK-74MP**: modernized Kalashnikov assault rifle with optical sight 1P29, caliber 5.45mm.

## AK-103

The 7.62 × 39mm AK-103, essentially a modernised and rechambered AK-74M, was introduced in 1993 as a next generation export model, part of the original 'Hundred Series' by Kalashnikov Concern (including the AK-101 in 5.56 × 45mm and the AK-105 in 5.45 × 39mm). They are made to a very high standard, with stocks and foregrips constructed of black plastic to reduce weight. The AK-103 features an AK-74 style flash suppressor, side rails for optics and can accept RPK magazines. Again, from Izhmash/Kalashnikov Concern:

> All assault rifles of the '100' series feature a mount for night and optical sights, and a more durable folding plastic stock. They are more convenient for carrying and firing. Like the AK-74M, these assault rifles distinguished by their faultless performance in more difficult operation conditions (lower or higher temperatures, in muddy environment, etc.); optimum technical dispersion when using salvo fire in unstable stances; long service life; easy maintenance and repair (disassembly, assembly, cleaning, lubrication, etc.).

The AK-103 is currently in service with the armies of Venezuela, Pakistan, Iran, Saudi Arabia and Namibia (who also issue the 5.54 × 45mm AK-105). As noted previously, Pakistan, Saudi Arabia and Venezuela are establishing joint ventures to produce the AK-103 and other Kalashnikov Concern small arms domestically.

The AK-105, the 5.45 × 39mm carbine variant of the AK-103 (itself an updated and rechambered AK-74), has been purchased in limited numbers by the Russian Army to supplement the 5.45 × 39mm AKS-74U. (*Kalashnikov Group/Kalashnikov Media*)

India has also procured AK-103s and is looking at a similar agreement on licenced production.

## AK-200

The AK-100 or 'Hundred Series' was recently renamed the 'Two Hundred Series' denoting upgraded or modernised versions of the 'Hundred Series' platforms. The Russians have recently adopted the AK-200 and AK-205 carbine variant in $5.45 \times 39$mm for their National Guard units, replacing the AK-74 and AK-74M. The AK-200 features a collapsible M4 style stock, which folds to the side, and multiple Picatinny rails mounted on the foregrip and atop the receiver.

## WAC-47

The WAC-47 is an American commercial design for the Ukrainian military who have professed both a political and logistical desire to align with NATO in terms of small arms. Ukrainian troops deployed under the NATO ISAF mission to Afghanistan were forced to borrow $5.56 \times 45$mm G36s from Lithuanian troops as resupply of $7.62 \times 39$mm was fraught with difficulties.

Looking something like the Knight Armaments Company design, the SR-47, originally developed for US special operations forces during the initial stages of the Afghan War to allow them to use AK magazines and $7.62 \times 39$mm ammunition in an M4 style platform, the WAC-47 is the first step toward interoperability. Although issued with a barrel and upper for the $7.62 \times 39$mm round, of which Ukraine has large stocks, the WAC-47 can be relatively simply adapted to fire the $5.56 \times 45$mm which Ukraine aims to adopt by 2020. A Ukrainian spokesperson explained:

> One just needs to unfasten the rifle's barrel receiver off the platform in a couple of moves and then mount a necessary caliber, a 5.56 NATO barrel in our case. And that's it, a piece of cake. It can be done immediately in action, without any tools in one's hands.

Bizarrely however, the $7.62 \times 39$mm design doesn't accept AK magazines and instead a proprietary magazine is issued with the weapon. This is likely due to the magazine-well being designed to be adaptable to $5.56 \times 45$mm STANAG magazines.

The first WAC-47s were delivered in late 2017 with the aim of '*the first batch of WAC-47 modification will go into trial operation in the combat units of Ukrainian army, during this time all information on using the rifle in the field will be collected. Gathering feedback from Ukrainian soldiers will enhance necessary changes before mass production starts,*' according to the manufacturer.

## Steyr AUG

Another ground-breaking bullpup design from the 1970s, it was originally developed by the famed Austrian gunmaker to replace the $7.62 \times 51$mm Stg.58, another variant of the Belgian FAL. Adopted in 1977 and first in service the following year by the Austrian army as the Stg.77, it was commercially known as the AUG or *Armee Universal Gewehr*.

The AUG was adopted by a range of nations including Ireland, Luxembourg, Malaysia, Oman, Saudi Arabia, Tunisia and Uruguay. It was also adopted by Australia and New Zealand to replace their M16s and FALs. Ironically the Falkland Island Defense Force adopted the AUG in preference to the British L85A1 – rumour suggests that whilst both weapons performed similarly in accuracy testing, the reliability of the AUG and the fact that the price from Steyr was half of that of the L85A1 were the deciding factors.

The AUG was one of the first assault rifles to feature an integral fixed power optic and was an early forerunner to the current trend for modular weapons with a range of barrel lengths offered to convert the weapon to different roles, such as a carbine or light support weapon (for which 42-round magazines were provided). It was also unusual in that it had no external fire selector and instead relied upon a two-stage trigger – pressing the trigger to the half-way point resulted in semi-automatic fire, whilst depressing it fully caused the weapon to fire on full automatic.

The initial Australian version, the F88 (named after its year of adoption) also featured the standard integral 1.5 power optic although it proved somewhat problematic. Former Master Sniper at the Sniper Cell of the Australian School of Infantry, Nathan Vinson, recalled to the author:

> I first used the F88 back in 1992 when our company went overseas to New Zealand for a few weeks of training. Initially the weapon seemed okay as it was slightly lighter than the SLR but did not have the punch. The sighting system in the first models was very poor as they used the doughnut optic system, which meant that anything in the circle was capable of being hit by your fall of shoot.
>
> This was great if the target was within 100 meters (i.e. the jungle) but once your range was extended past 100 meters your chances of accurate fire was limited. To compensate, users of the weapon came up with different ways to increase accuracy by adjusting the scope to engage targets more accurately. One method was called the 'cupping' method which meant the firer adjusted his scope so that you used the bottom of the inner circle to provide a point of aim. It was not until a number of years later that different sights were brought into the system and our soldiers' accuracy started to improve.

Both Steyr and Thales Lithgow, the domestic manufacturer of the AUG in Australia, soon developed a new variant that replaced the integral optic with a Picatinny rail allowing any type of optic to be mounted. In Australian Army service this version was known as the F88SA1 and was typically paired with a Canadian Elcan C79 optic. The SA2 variant was adopted whilst the Australians were deployed to Afghanistan which included the addition of further Picatinny rails.

In 2017, the introduction of the latest iteration of the F88 was begun. Known as the EF88 or the F90 for export sales, the weapon was a rather dramatic redesign and upgrade to the SA2. Key amongst these changes are a free-floating fluted barrel to increase accuracy and reduce heat build-up from extended firing, more

An Australian soldier examines the trial version of the 5.56 × 45mm EF88 fitted with Trijicon ACOG and sound suppressor. (*Commonwealth of Australia, Cpl Nick Wiseman*)

rails, a more ergonomic stock that also improves the balance of the weapon and a decrease in weight by up to 500 grams dependent on variant.

A spokesperson from Thales Australia noted:

> The big winners from our customer's point of view were the rifle's weight and the grenade launcher. We did something really interesting with this and it's a key feature. The in-service F88SA2 had a grenade launcher that needed to be attached by an armourer. By contrast, the F90 [EF88] includes a side-loading 40mm grenade launcher that attaches quickly on a rail so any soldier can do it in a couple of seconds. The launcher's trigger goes through the rifle's trigger-guard and is placed just in front of the rifle's trigger. This means the soldier does not have to move his hands or change the grip to fire the grenade, which is so much easier. The grenade launcher itself is equipped with a lightweight robust quadrant sight that ensures rapid target acquisition, can be used at night, and is compatible with night vision goggles.

The EF88 has seen action in both Afghanistan and Iraq to much praise by Australian infantrymen with the commander of one recent Iraq deployment saying: '*The EF88 has proven itself as an extremely reliable, accurate and versatile weapon which has gained the praise of not only Australian personnel but also our New Zealand counterparts and Coalition partners.*'

### Beretta AR70/90

Italy was one of the last NATO nations to transition to a 5.56 × 45mm platform in 1990, replacing their version of the 7.62 × 51mm M14, the BM-59 manufactured by Beretta. The AR70/90 was an upgraded version of the AR70 and carbine length SC70 that had been in service with Italian SOF since the 1970s.

The AR70/90 features plastic furniture to reduce weight, like the M16 series, whilst offering a detachable carrying handle that uncovers non-Picatinny, but NATO standard optics mounts when removed (a standard Picatinny rail was later fitted, examples of which could be seen in service with the Italian ISAF contingent in Afghanistan). Like many older designs, it features the once fashionable 3-round burst in addition to semi and full automatic and the ability to launch rifle grenades like the French FAMAS.

Italy recently donated some 5,000 examples of the AR70/90 to the Albanian Army to supplement their 2014 acquired Colt M4s that are replacing various domestically produced AKM variants. Whilst not a huge export success, a number of other nations such as Malaysia, Mexico, Morocco, Nigeria and Zimbabwe maintain stocks of the AR70/90.

### Beretta ARX160

The largely polymer ARX160 replaced the AR70/90 in 2010 in service with the Italian Army as part of its Soldato Futuro programme (the upgraded ARX160A2 came into service several years later). It is a thoroughly modern design that fully embraces the concept of modularity by offering a quick-change barrel allowing a 12-inch carbine or 16-inch rifle chrome-lined barrel to be selected. Additionally, it

An Italian Airborne soldier takes part in a NATO exercise in 2012 carrying the 5.56 × 45mm Beretta AR70/90 with Aimpoint. The ageing AR70/90 are being replaced by the ARX160 series. (*US Army, Spc. Jordan Fuller*)

offers a rapid change ejection port to suit both left- and right-handed shooters and an adjustable gas regulator for use with a sound suppressor.

Increasing the modularity, the lower receiver, barrel and bolt can be reasonably simply replaced with variants in other calibres such as 7.62 × 39mm, 5.45 × 39mm and even 6.8 × 43mm. It comes standard with a SCAR-style side folding stock which offers multiple stock positions and Picatinny rails on both the receiver and forearm. A 7.62 × 51mm variant, the ARX200, has been adopted by the Italians as both a DMR and battle rifle.

A 2018 agreement to licence-manufacture Beretta small arms in Qatar indicates that the Qataris may well be adopting the ARX family to replace their issue M16A2 and Colt carbines. The ARX160 has been exported to numerous Middle Eastern and European SOF units and may still be in the running against the CZ 805 as the new issue rifle for the Egyptian Army (in 7.62 × 39mm to take advantage of ammunition stocks). It has also been seen in the hands of Peshmerga irregulars trained by the Italian military in northern Iraq.

## TAR-21 Tavor

The Tavor was developed by Israeli Weapon Industries (IWI) as a potential replacement for the various M4 carbines issued by the IDF. The M4, along with older Colt carbines, has long been in service with the Israeli Defense Forces (IDF). Today the M4 is largely relegated to issue to reservists and some special operations units.

The 5.56 × 45mm Beretta ARX160A2 fitted with EOTech optic carried by Albanian in Afghanistan 2013. (*US Army, Staff Sgt. Shane Hamann*)

The now standard issue bullpup Tavor 5.56 × 45mm design was field tested by IDF units for a number of years before adoption in 2003, although fielding only began to occur in 2006 and it has never fully replaced the M16/M4 in IDF service. Early production models were prone to stoppages from fine sand fouling the working parts, but a number of fixes implemented by IWI have solved the issue.

Largely constructed from polymer to reduce weight, the weapon is fully ambi-dextrous with ejection ports on both sides and a switchable charging handle and utilises STANAG 30-round magazines to take advantage of the huge numbers of M16 pattern magazines in Israeli inventory. The designers also cleverly mirrored the placement of the selector and magazine release on the M16/M4 to ease shooter transition to the new bullpup.

It is unique in that it has no separate upper and lower receiver and cleaning and stripping the weapon is done via a hinged butt-plate. This aids immensely in reducing the amount of dust that can enter the system. Additionally, it features a domestically-produced red dot optic called the ITL MARS (Multi-purpose Aiming Reflex Sight) that incorporates a visible laser projector, although the Meprolight Reflex optic is also commonly encountered.

The standard issue Tavor with 18-inch barrel is complemented by the CTAR-21 carbine variant with 15-inch barrel and the 14-inch barrel MTAR or Micro Tavor (now known as the X-95), both of which are in front-line service with the IDF. The GTAR variant features an M203 launcher under-barrel replacing both M203 equipped Galils and M16s. The X-95 has been selected as the new standard issue Tavor variant by the IDF and began to be issued in 2013 to army units, along with a new Meprolight M5 holographic sight.

The X-95 is favoured as most infantry combat experienced by the IDF is within largely urban zones making the compact X-95 a solid choice. Longer range targets are engaged by the designated marksman variant, the STAR-21, or by section machine guns. IWI marketing material explained somewhat excitedly:

> The SCAR, M4 and G36 feel like elephant guns in comparison. The TAVOR was designed to kick down doors, swing around in hallways, [and] shoot from cars while driving and 'bring it' to any close quarter battle (CQB) situation.

The Tavor has now seen extensive combat service and is popular thanks to its reliability which is on par with the AK series. An Israeli report noted:

> It has been functioning without a hitch and in a superb way for over a year. A team on the Givati Regiment's reconnaissance unit that used the Micro-Tavor gave very favourable assessments about the weapon, as did the battalion commanders in the regiment.

Example of the Israeli 5.56 × 45mm Micro Tavor with 13-inch barrel and Meprolight M21 optic now known as the X95 carbine in use with IDF soldiers in 2014.

*(Creative Commons, Shay Wagner, IDF Spokesperson's Unit)*

## M16A4

The M16A4, a descendant of the original M16 and M16A1, was the US Marine Corps' standard 5.56 × 45mm service rifle during much of the Iraq and Afghanistan wars. Although the USMC has now officially adopted the M4A1 as their general issue service rifle, the M16A4 still serves with non-infantry combat arms units. As the new M27 is adopted by the infantry, excess M4A1s will replace these M16A4s. The M16A4 was the final iteration of the M16 platform. It essentially added a flat top receiver and Picatinny rails (including replaceable hand-guards) to the standard M16A2. It retained, for instance, the same selector as the M16A2 with the 3-round burst option. A solid and dependable weapon, it exhibited great accuracy when paired with the Marine issue Trijicon ACOG.

The M16A4 has been issued to both the Iraqi Army and the Afghan National Army (which also has earlier stocks of M16A2s and Canadian C7s). Ironically, Marines (and US Army soldiers issued the M16A2 at the time) consistently voiced a preference for the carbine variant, the M4 and M4A1, whilst operating in Iraq as the full-length M16 rifles were considered too long for urban operations or whilst dismounting from vehicles. As we noted earlier, the shorter carbine barrels have a significant impact on range and terminal effectiveness, particularly before the introduction of the M855A1 and Mk 318 ammunition.

## M4 and M4A1

The M4 and M4A1 are the standard against which all other assault rifles are compared. It is the issue rifle of the majority of the US Army and Marine Corps and is widely employed by militaries across the world. The key difference between base models of both weapons is the selector. On the M4 there is a 3-round burst option which on the M4A1 has been replaced by a full auto setting. The M4A1 was originally intended for SOF and was again modified with a heavier barrel in 2002 that was more resistant to heat build-up caused by extended firing.

First adopted in 1994 (although there were examples already in use by SOF units like the US Army Rangers), it was considered as something of a PDW to issue to officers, radio operators and the like in lieu of the heavier and more cumbersome M16A2. It proved popular, particularly thanks to its compactness and use by SOF (as we have seen, rightly or wrongly, SOF use drives adoption by conventional forces).

The 5.56 × 45mm M16A4 issued to the US Marine Corps for most of the War on Terror. Infantry units are now replacing it with a mix of M27s and M4A1s. (*US Army*)

In the late 1990s, a revolutionary upgrade for the M4A1 was announced for US SOF units. Known as the SOPMOD or Special Operations Peculiar Modification, it included a number of different optic types including reflex sights and ACOGs, along with infrared illuminators, replacement hand-guards featuring Picatinny rails and a vertical forward grip manufactured by Knights Armaments. The vertical forward grip was already a feature on weapons like the Steyr AUG but has since become a standard accessory for nearly all types of assault rifles from the L85A2/A3 to the Russian AK series. Versions such as the Grip Pod even included a collapsible lightweight bipod that extends from the base of the handgrip.

By the time of the Iraq invasion, elements of the SOPMOD package were being issued to infantrymen and their M4s were often seen sporting flat top receivers mounting optics and forward rails for the PEQ-4 infrared illuminator. The US Army's M4 carbine modification programme later saw the M68 Aimpoint red dot sight become standard for most M4s and M4A1s in service.

Today the Army is modifying all in-service M4s to M4A1 standard, including the addition of the heavier SOCOM Profile Barrel and an ambidextrous selector. An Army spokesperson noted in 2015 that the upgrade to M4A1 standard '*allows us to fire a better suppressing fire. At some point, a barrel is going to bend. It could be solid steel, but as soon as you reach a certain heat point it's going to do some damage to the barrel.*' As M16A2s are retired, the newly refurbished M4s will take their place.

The abortive M4A1+ programme, which offered a free-floating barrel and an improved trigger amongst other enhancements, was cancelled in 2016 amid fiscal politicking, but the following year saw the Product Improvement Program (PIP) announced which would incorporate many of the proposed changes – even the public statements from Army spokespersons were similar on the improvements: '*The heavier barrel is more durable and has greater capacity to maintain accuracy and zero while withstanding the heat produced by high volumes of fire. New and upgraded M4A1s will also receive ambidextrous fire controls.*'

The PIP enhancements are being made to existing stocks within the Army and to all new M4A1s produced by the likes of Colt and Fabrique Nationale (the patent on the M4 and M4A1 expired in 2009 allowing other manufacturers such as FN to produce the weapon for the US Army). Despite these many improvements, the M4 series has been plagued by accusations of poor reliability and accuracy along with questions about the terminal performance of the 5.56 × 45mm. One US veteran explained to the author:

> M4 is plenty accurate, [although] scopes help. My fav was the old school ACOG made by Trijicon that had the crosshairs rather than the red triangle. Reliability in an environment like Afghanistan or Iraq where everything is constantly covered in dust and sand wasn't great. Never had any issues stateside [however].

The same soldier added that in terms of terminal effectiveness:

> My only problem with the 5.56 is it is so small and high velocity it just punches right through people. Stopping power can be an issue. I remember

one instance where we had to shoot an Afghan hound that was attacking our canine working dog. I swear it took almost 10 rounds of 5.56 from an M4 to finally kill that dog.

It is worth noting that this was with the earlier M855 round rather than the current M855A1 which seems to improve the consistency of terminal effectiveness.

A series of environmental tests was launched in 2006 aimed to address criticisms of the M4's reliability in dusty, sandy environments like parts of Iraq and Afghanistan. The results did not go particularly well for the M4 – it reportedly suffered a stoppage every 68 rounds. The experimental XM-8 surprisingly placed first in the testing with 472 rounds between stoppages. The SCAR-L followed with some 265 rounds between stoppages and finally the 416 which was rated at one stoppage for every 257 rounds. Additionally, a number of the M4 barrels failed at the 6,000-round mark, well below the prescribed 10,000 benchmark. These results must however be compared to the results of 2,600 individual surveys conducted by the US Army of service members in 2006 who had recently returned from Iraq or Afghanistan tours. The Soldier Perspectives on Small Arms in Combat survey found that:

> Over 50 per cent of soldiers utilizing the M4 and M16 reported that they never experienced a stoppage while in theater (this finding includes stoppages

A US Marine loads a practice 40mm round into the M203 grenade launcher fitted to his 5.56 × 45mm M4A1 carbine. It is equipped with Trijicon ACOG optic, PEQ-15 infrared illuminator and KAC sound suppressor which have been trialed to great success within the Corps. (*USMC, Lance Cpl. Alexis C. Schneider*)

during an entire deployment and is therefore not limited to firefights and includes training).

Indeed, 89 per cent of respondents were 'fully satisfied' with the M4, the highest of any of the weapons systems included in the survey; 19 per cent of M4 users reported suffering a stoppage in combat, but the overwhelming majority of these were of minor consequence and were able to be quickly cleared. These figures influence the survey's findings that 80 per cent were satisfied with the reliability of the M4 platform in combat conditions.

The M4 and M4A1 have survived numerous attempts to replace them, most recently the Individual Carbine Competition in 2013, however even today allied armies issued with other rifles seem to prefer an M4 based platform. Again, Nathan Vinson explained his feelings within the Australian Army which issue the Steyr AUG derived F88 and now EF88:

I first joined the Army in 1989 and for the first two years in the battalion I was the forward scout, which meant I carried an M16 [A1], the grandfather of the M4. When the M4 came into use I was easily able to adapt and only required a short conversion course. Every infantryman would prefer to carry the M4. One it looks mean, two it was light and easy to clean, three you were able to carry more magazines in your gear (the Steyr magazine is very bulky) and four we were able to request ammunition and replacement parts from our major coalition partners i.e. the US military.

## HS Produkt VHS-1/VHS-2

Another of the new generation of bullpups, the 5.56 × 45mm VHS-1, is a domestically produced Croatian assault rifle, the design of which dates back to a bullpup AK derivative developed in the 1990s. Whilst the weapon was first unveiled in 2003, a small batch of the VHS-1 was combat trialed by Croatian Army deployed to Afghanistan with ISAF in 2007 and the weapon was issued to the wider Croatian Army from 2009 in two variants, the VHS-D with standard length 20-inch barrel and the VHS-K carbine with a 16-inch barrel.

Heavily influenced by the FAMAS in both looks and by some of its features, the VHS-1 allows the extractor to be switched to accommodate left-handed shooters and uniquely has sights for both an underslung grenade launcher and for rifle grenades. It also features a selector contained within the trigger guard like the FAMAS, but this controls all firing modes.

An upgraded version, the VHS-2, was launched in 2013 featuring additional Picatinny rails on the hand-guard, an adjustable stock and an upper receiver rail that replaces the FAMAS style carrying handle. Perhaps most importantly, the selector has been replaced by a more traditional M16 style selector above the pistol grip, easing transition training. It also alleviates a common complaint about the VHS-1 by deflecting empty casings forward of the shooter rather than straight past their face which made the VHS-1 somewhat uncomfortable to shoot.

Examples of the VHS-1 have been seen in the hands of Syrian insurgents and Kurdish irregulars, likely sourced from a purchase by the Iraqi military (the

Croatian Army infantryman instructs an American soldier in the use of the 5.56 × 45mm VHS-2 bullpup. (*US Army, Spc. Hubert D. Delany III*)

VHS-2 was also purchased by Iraqi SOF in 2015). The US Department of Defense also made a purchase of 500 examples which may have been provided to the Kurdish Peshmerga.

## Future Trends

As we have discussed previously, the monetary cost and logistical impact of moving to a new general service calibre within any sizeable military is staggering. Until a new calibre appears that offers a significantly revolutionary step up from the 5.56 × 45mm, NATO and Western nations will continue to make small evolutionary improvements to the ammunition. The M885A1 is a good case in point, however how much further the 5.56 × 45mm can be improved upon is open to question due to the physical limitations of the casing itself.

If the US Army alone decides to purchase a new general issue assault rifle, and it looks increasingly likely they will once a new calibre is decided, they will require some 1.1 million examples. This should put both the logistical and cost implications into stark relief for the reader. And remember that once that new rifle is placed into service, those 1.1 million end users will need retraining on the new platform – something which incurs its own extensive costs, hence why an M4/M16 pattern rifle, at least in terms of user controls, is preferable.

In comparison it is rather simple for a special operations unit to adopt or trial a new rifle or carbine. They can, and do, simply contact the manufacturer for samples, run them through their paces (including live combat trials) and, if they

A Norwegian Army soldier carrying the retractable stock 7.62 × 51mm AG-3F2 variant during pre-deployment training for Afghanistan 2008. The AG-3 series was replaced by the 5.56 × 45mm HK416N. (*US Army, Spc. Kalie Frantz*)

meet the grade, make a purchase using their own discretionary budgets that operate outside of normal military procurement systems.

US Army Lieutenant General John Murray, deputy chief of staff for Army modernisation noted:

> We have been pushed on the M27, which the Marine Corps has adopted, that is also a 5.56mm which doesn't penetrate [current generation Russian trauma plates], so we are going to go down a path next generation squad weapon automatic rifle first to be closely followed, I'm hopeful, with either a rifle or a carbine that will fire something other than a 5.56mm. That is what we see as a replacement for the M4 in the future.

Murray added: '*It probably won't be a 7.62mm; it will probably be something in between – case-telescoping round, probably polymer cased to reduce weight.*'

Textron Systems, which has been working with the US Army on the LSAT programme for many years in an effort to lighten the weight of both $5.56 \times 45$mm and $7.62 \times 51$mm ammunition, has applied their knowledge to develop their 6.5mm Intermediate Case Telescoped Carbine (ICTC). The carbine fires from a closed bolt using a gas piston operating system and weighs a reported 3.75 kilograms. Textron say that the plastic cased 125-grain 6.5mm CT ammunition fired by the ICTC is 35 per cent lighter than $7.62 \times 51$mm in traditional brass cases like the M80. They also claim a 30 per cent 'lethality' increase over the older cartridge, although this appears to be based on the pure mathematics of the 6.5mm CT retaining greater velocity at extended ranges. How this will affect fragmentation of the round is unknown, as a bullet design has yet to be publicly released.

Statistics made available by Textron in 2017 indicate that despite the advances made with the 6.5mm CT, the basic weapon designed to fire it weighs 40 grams more than an M4A1 and has a reduced magazine capacity of 20 rounds because of the shape of the CT ammunition. Along with its calibre, the new Textron carbine does have the advantage of being a piston-driven design which should reduce fouling. Where the weight saving with the 6.5mm CT is more evident is with machine guns and SAWs, a topic we will cover in following chapters.

The Next Generation Squad Weapon and its NGSW-R (Rifle) component is supposed to enhance range and penetration of Russian body armour, whilst hopefully reducing ammunition weight and increasing terminal effectiveness, if we have learnt anything from the LSAT programme. Key though, and the driver behind the Pentagon's support for the programme, seems to be that ability to defeat enemy body armour.

In the author's view, this will make or break the NGSC. Programmes like the SPIW, ACR and OICW all tried to tackle the difficult issue of increasing hit probability, mainly through an over reliance on technology. Whilst all provided important lessons, they were all ultimately cancelled. NGSW does not specifically address the key concerns of those clamouring for a new calibre, but does so by default. It may have the greatest chance of success purely based on the relatively narrow scope of the programme – defeat those armour plates consistently out to 1,200 metres.

The author still believes that without some very good optics and a solid commitment to continual training, the technical advances will be all for nothing. Theoretically the soldier may be able to hit an enemy at 1,200 metres and pierce his body armour with the NGSC, he has the technology, but does he have the skill? As noted previously, combat shooting is nothing like range shooting and hitting those briefly glimpsed targets within the standard range of a current assault rifle, arguably 300 metres in real terms, is a difficult task.

As we have noted, even the best trained soldier cannot hit his target if he cannot see it and identify it as a hostile combatant. Thomas Ehrhart explained:

> When using magnified optics such as the ACOG or a low power variable optic, the lower recoil results in less sight movement during the firing cycle, which allows soldiers to observe the impact of their rounds and rapidly make corrections if necessary. Additionally, the primary benefit of magnification is the ability to positively identify threats or civilians. I have tested and been part of looking at variable power optics (1 to 6 ×) for combat effectiveness and durability. While no decision has been made that I am aware of, I foresee us moving to a low power variable in the next few years.

Along with optics, sound suppressors can provide an enormous advantage to the infantryman in both disguising the report of a soldier's weapon, making him harder to locate, and by enabling verbal communication within the squad or section. It also saves soldiers' hearing. Will suppressors become more widely issued to the infantryman? Certainly, all the signs indicate that at least in the US military this may be the case. SOCOM has recently issued an order to SIG Sauer for their new MCX based SURG (Suppressed Upper Receiver Groups) uppers which replace the standard M4A1 with an integrally suppressed version. The USMC continues their testing with overall positive results and certainly one or more M27s in each Marine squad will be equipped with a suppressor in the near future. An Army spokesperson noted sagely: '*Suppression gives you that ability to make that guy more survivable by not being as easily identifiable on the battlefield.*'

The Canadians too have been quietly working with Colt Canada developing a next generation infantry small arm under the auspices of the Soldier Integrated Precision Effects Systems (SIPES) programme. The weapon, which resembles the OICW platform,

> includes a firing mechanism to shoot lightweight cased telescoped ammunition, a secondary effects module for increased firepower and a NATO standard power and data rail to integrate accessories like electro-optical sights and position sensors.
>
> In order to support the multi-role nature of the weapon, the prototype's secondary effects module features the ability to install either a 3-round 40mm grenade launcher, or a 12-gauge shotgun. When optimized, the integrated weapon prototype could weigh less than a C7 equipped with a M203 grenade launcher, reducing the burden on soldiers.

The 5.56 × 45mm Colt Canada C7A2 with Elcan C79 (M145) optic is the standard issue assault rifle of the Canadian military. (*Kelly Stumpf, Colt Canada*)

The advent of the new general issue US calibre (likely in 2022 if not further delayed as is the all too predictable case in many large small arms procurement programmes) will create a new two-tier effect on infantry small arms. Along with the US and its wealthy foreign export markets, the United Kingdom, Australia and some NATO countries will look to adopt a new platform in the 2025–2030 date range, if not sooner, using either reworked variants of their current assault rifle rechambered for the new round or an entirely new weapon, most likely the eventual Next Generation Squad Carbine. The US Army has confirmed that both the USMC and the British are involved in the development.

US Brigadier General Brian Cummings:

> For the next-generation, we wanted to make one end-all solution. With the M4, when you look at it, it's got all these things hanging on top of it. We keep evolving by putting on things. The next-generation is going to be kind of like what we did with the pistol, with the modular handgun system. It'll be one complete system, with weapon, magazine, ammo and fire control on it and we will cut down on the load and integration issues associated with it.

Chief of the US Army, General Mark Milley was famously quoted in 2017 as saying that: '*Our next individual and squad combat weapon will come in with a 10 × improvement over any existing current system in the world.*' A very tall order indeed.

## Breaking News

As this book was going to press a number of important procurement decisions became public. Portugal has inked a deal with Belgium's Fabrique Nationale to replace almost all of their infantry weapons with FN designs. The elderly Portuguese G3 variants will be replaced by the SCAR-L in 5.56 × 45mm. The 7.62 × 51mm SCAR-L has been adopted as a designated marksman platform. Both 5.56 × 45mm and 7.62 × 51mm Minimis will replace existing MG4 and MG3 platforms.

The SCAR series beat out the HK416 and HK417, likely based on delivery timeframes as Heckler and Koch appear very busy fulfilling the French Army HK416F order. Interestingly, rumour indicates that the French trials team actually preferred the SCAR-L but Fabrique Nationale fell afoul of the complicated French procurement rules and was judged to be non-compliant on technicalities.

The latest iteration of the L85, the 5.56 × 45mm L85A3, is currently being issued to British troops rotating through Afghanistan. Upgraded as part of the 'Equipped to Fight Improvement' programme, A2 TES rifles were upgraded with a new receiver and additional rails, as well as a coat of paint. The L85A2 is equipped with the current issue Elcan Specter OS 4 × optic and Shield CQS Close Quarter Battlesight. (*Open Government License v3.0*)

The Indian government have incredibly finally made some procurement decisions and have placed orders for the 7.62 × 51mm SIG 716 and the 7.62 × 39mm AK-203 (an export version of the AK-12 which will be produced in India under a joint venture) and are inching ever closer to finalising a deal for the 5.56 × 45mm Caracal CAR816, an AR style platform manufactured in the UAE.

The Estonian Defence Force have also completed their procurement process for both a new standard assault rifle and designated marksman rifle. Lewis Machine & Tool (more commonly referred to as LMT) beat competitors from Heckler and Koch and SIG-Sauer with variants of their 5.56 × 45mm CQBPS (Close Quarter Battle Piston System) platform (itself the basis of the MARS-L adopted by NZDF) and their 7.62 × 51mm CQBMWS (Close Quarter Battle Modular Weapon System), based on the MARS-H.

SIG-Sauer lodged not one but two formal disputes allegedly relating to the integrity of the LMT designs in drop tests but both complaints were dismissed. Price appears to have been the deciding factor on the decision to adopt LMT (their bid was almost half that of H&K for example).

Finally, the German System Sturmgewehr Bundeswehr programme to identify a replacement for the G36 has been delayed as both the HK433 and the Haenel MK556 failed 'individual mandatory requirements' according to the German Ministry of Defense. With the programme delayed, the G36 will remain in service for the foreseeable future.

## CHAPTER FOUR

# BATTLE AND DESIGNATED MARKSMAN RIFLES

### Overview

In this chapter we will discuss rifles chambered for rounds larger than the standard 5.56 × 56mm and 7.62 × 39mm. These can be reasonably neatly divided into two types: firstly, battle rifles – typically 7.62 × 51mm selective fire rifles and designated marksmen rifles or DMRs and secondly, those designed for use by a platoon or squad level marksman to provide accurate fires beyond the range of 5.56 × 45mm weapons.

The term battle rifle is really a misnomer as the only difference between an assault rifle and a battle rifle is calibre. If an assault rifle is not chambered for an intermediate calibre, it is a battle rifle – except if it's chambered for something else, like the Russian 9 × 39mm. Battle rifle or assault rifle? Or sub machine gun? Is the 6.5mm CT really an intermediate cartridge? Semantics aside, we will

A US Army designated marksman scanning for insurgents in Afghanistan 2004. He carries a scoped semi-automatic 7.62 × 51mm M14 with aftermarket bipod. (*US Army, Staff Sgt. Bradley Rhen*)

The granddaddy of battle rifles – the 7.62 × 51mm Fabrique Nationale FAL. (*USMC*)

continue with the chunky definition of the battle rifle being a 7.62 × 51mm semi or selective fire rifle that isn't designed as a specific sniper or marksman rifle.

Thankfully the definition of a DMR is simpler. According to US Army doctrine, the designated marksman is described as follows:

> The designated marksman acts as a member of the squad under the direction of the squad leader or as designated by the platoon leader. Although normally functioning as a rifleman within one of the fire teams in a rifle squad, the designated marksman is armed with a modified M4, 5.56-mm rifle. He is employed at the direction of the squad leader or reorganised with the other squads' designated marksmen into a platoon sniper section. He is trained to eliminate high-payoff enemy personnel targets (such as enemy automatic rifle teams, antitank teams, and snipers) with precision fires.

The concept of the DMR really began with the Russians who recognised the utility of issuing a scoped 7.62 × 54mm SVD to every infantry platoon in the 1960s. Some units even received the SVD at squad level (particularly during tours of Afghanistan in the 1980s). The idea was almost exactly as defined above by the US Army, except the Russian marksman received little to no training on the actual tactical employment of his weapon.

Modern DMs go through an abbreviated version of sniper school in most Western armies although during times when the manpower crunch was being felt, like at the height of the Iraqi insurgency, the DMR or Squad Designated Marksman (SDM) was simply issued to the best shot in the squad. The DMR really came into being in Western militaries during the early years of the Afghan conflict, with units deployed to areas such as the mountainous east of Afghanistan experiencing firefights at ranges that defeated their 5.56 × 45mm weapons.

The US Army Mk 14 Enhanced Battle Rifle in 7.62 × 51mm. (*US Army*)

The average insurgent armed with an AK was also at a disadvantage in such contacts and thus relied on medium machine guns like the PK series and the ubiquitous RPG.

School-trained snipers were at a premium, so it was decided to reissue some 5,000 elderly 7.62 × 51mm semi-automatic M14s to infantry units within the US Army to tackle these longer-range encounters. Incredibly, these first M14s were initially issued with only one magazine per weapon and with no mounting options for an optic. In Iraq too, extended ranges encountered particularly in the west and north of the country saw DMRs being issued to deploying units.

Special operations forces had been developing and fielding such weapons for years and were having great success with the Knights Armament SR-25, a scoped AR-10 derivitave. It would later be issued to infantry units as the Mk 11 and M110 marksman rifles. SOF had also been experimenting with 5.56 × 45mm M4A1s with longer 16-inch barrels and optics as another form of light marksman rifle.

The USMC followed this path when initially developing their M16 based SDM-R or Squad Designated Marksman Rifle for their Squad Advanced Marksman. Others, such as the British Army in Afghanistan, first used 7.62 × 51mm bolt-action L96A1 sniper rifles as their platoon marksman rifle before adopting the vastly more fit for purpose LMT-designed 7.62 × 51mm semi-automatic L129A1. Along with being able to deliver longer range fires, typically between 300 and 600 metres, the designated marksman also provided the unit commander

A detail view of the British Army 7.62 × 51mm LMT L129A1 (officially known as the 'Sharpshooter Assault Rifle') with × 6 ACOG and RMR close-quarters sight. (*Open Government License v3.0, Stuart Hill*)

A US Army designated marksman operating in Hawijah, Iraq 2006, with his SR-25 based 7.62 × 51mm Mk 11 Mod0 DMR, the forerunner to the M110 SASS. (*US Army, Spc. Linsay Burnett*)

US Army designated marksmen provide overwatch for an Iraqi Police traffic control point, Iraq 2005. Both are armed with the M16 based 5.56 × 45mm Squad Designated Marksmen- Rifle (SDM-R). (*US Army, Sgt. Matthew Acosta*)

| | Calibre | Magazine | Weight Unloaded | Length |
|---|---|---|---|---|
| HK417 | 7.62 × 51mm | 20 | 4.45kg | 985/905mm (with 16in barrel) |
| FAL | 7.62 × 51mm | 20 | 4.45kg | 1,090mm |
| M14 | 7.62 × 51mm | 20 | 5.1kg | 1,120mm |
| M110 | 7.62 × 51mm | 20 | 4.9kg | 1,200mm |
| G28 | 7.62 × 51mm | 20 | 5.8kg | 1,085/965mm |
| SVD | 7.62 × 54mm | 10 | 4.7kg | 1,230mm |
| Mk 17 | 7.62 × 51mm | 20 | 3.59kg | 960/711mm |
| G3A3 | 7.62 × 51mm | 20 | 4.7kg | 1,025/840mm |
| MTP-76 | 7.62 × 51mm | 20 | 4.1kg | 920mm |
| L129A1/A2 | 7.62 × 51mm | 20 | 4.5kg | 990/900mm |

with a useful sensor, as the marksman could evaluate situations and PID individuals through his optics. He can also search for concealed insurgent spotters and IED trigger-men, along with providing a valuable overwatch function for his squad or section.

Battle rifles, on the other hand, are a less commonly encountered type, although some militaries are returning to 7.62 × 51mm variants due to the overmatch controversy or due to the terrain types found in their geographical area. (Turkey for instance recently adopted the domestically produced 7.62 × 51mm MTP-76 as their issue rifle which makes some sense when you consider the terrain Turkish infantrymen will encounter.) Counterintuitively, these rifles often do not feature magnified optics but instead red dot or holographic sights, limiting their precision use at longer ranges.

## Calibres and Ammunition

As noted, most DMRs and battle rifles are chambered for the 7.62 × 51mm. The Russian SVD (which is also arguably a sniper rifle although it is slowly being replaced by the bolt action SV-98 and SV-98M) is of course chambered for the excellent 7.62 × 54mm. As the aim (pun intended) of the DMR is to engage targets beyond the capabilities of 5.56 × 45mm (or 5.45 × 39mm), a 7.62mm round makes perfect sense. Recoil is considerable, however DMRs are typically only fired semi-automatically in aimed fire against point targets and employ bipods, reducing the impact on accuracy.

Most nations use 'match' grade ammunition for their marksmen, but until recently this simply meant hand selected ammunition chosen by the factory. Enhanced accuracy and specialist sniper loadings are now more commonly used in DMRs. The recently adopted US Army M80A1 Enhanced Penetration Round is one such example. Its 130-grain bullet has proven exceptional in terms of barrier blindness, armour penetration and terminal effects. It does increase wear on barrels, however this is a small price to pay for the capabilities of the M80A1.

A Bundeswehr marksman patrols the streets of Mazar-e Sharif, Afghanistan 2011 armed with the 7.62 × 51mm Heckler and Koch G3A3ZF which served as DMR until the procurement of the HK417 based G27 and G28. (*US Navy, Mass Communication Specialist 2nd Class Jonathan David Chandler*)

The previous issue 7.62 × 51mm round, the M80, was heavier at 147 grain and used a lead core rather than the copper plug of the M80A1, along with a hardened steel penetrator that is responsible for the improvement in armour penetration and barrier blindness. The M118LR 175 grain is also available but is typically used by snipers employing the M24 and M40 series and the current issue M2010 sniper rifle. The M118LR, developed from the earlier M852 Open Tip Match (which was ground-breaking in that it featured an open-tip design that facilitates expansion whilst still being Hague compliant) maintains its velocity over longer ranges, making it ideal as a sniper round.

Other rounds, like the 175-grain Mk 316 Mod0, were developed for SOF sniping applications whilst the Mk 319 Mod0 is a 130-grain Open Tip Match projectile designed for use in SOF battle rifles like the Mk 17 SCAR and DMRs. The Mk 316 programme was launched due to 'accuracy inconsistencies' with the issue M118LR and saw a new casing and new bullet along with modified propellant. These kind of specialist rounds can be justified for SOF use, but they are typically cost prohibitive for general issue to infantry DMRs.

The latest US 7.62 × 51mm load is the XM1158 Advanced Armor Piercing (ADVAP), specifically designed to deal with defeating light armour and body armour plates. An 82-grain 5.56 × 45mm version has also been developed. The

An Estonian scout sniper in Helmand Province, Afghanistan 2013, checking his scoped 7.62 × 51mm M14. (*USMC, Staff Sgt. Ezekiel R. Kitandwe*)

XM11158 is under consideration for adoption by the US Army. A spokesperson explained that the round was based on the M80A1 now in service:

> In the last decade, many improvements have been made in small caliber ammunition resulting in the improved general propose round, the M80A1 7.62mm Enhance Performance Round. The XM1158 retains the improvements fielded in the M80A1 7.62mm EPR with the addition of enhanced hard-target effects resulting from its tungsten carbide penetrator.

One new calibre has emerged in recent years which may eventually be seen in the hands of infantry DMRs. The 6.5mm Creedmoor has been slated for adoption by SOCOM under the 'Precision Intermediate Caliber Effort'. Platforms including the FN Mk 17 SCAR-H, the current issue M110 DMR and the newly issued M110A1 CSASS have all been trialled with the 6.5mm Creedmoor. The 6.5mm Creedmoor offered increased range by up to 40 per cent and less susceptibility to wind (by up to 30 per cent) whilst exhibiting significantly less felt recoil than the 7.62 × 51mm. As importantly, the 6.5 Creedmoor only requires a barrel change from the 7.62 × 51mm parent rifle. What could this mean for conventional infantry forces?

As we have seen, where SOF leads, the larger army tends to follow – if slowly. Innovations adopted by the US military then influence partner and allied nations and military small arms procurements in general. Although there is currently no express requirement for a 6.5mm Creedmoor replacement for the US Army and

US Marines provide overwatch during a training exercise with a sound suppressed 7.62 × 51mm M110 SASS. Note the worn Beretta M9s carried by both Marines. (*US Navy, Lt. Jennifer Franco*)

A Lithuanian mechanized infantry soldier provides security with his semi-automatic 7.62 × 51mm Fabrique Nationale SCAR-H PR (Precision Rifle). (*US Army, Staff Sgt. Michael Behlin*)

USMC designated marksman rifle stocks, its performance with SOCOM units will be carefully monitored.

Tom Ehrhart agreed with the 6.5mm Creedmoor as a viable calibre for infantry DMRs:

> Personally, I think the 6.5mm Creedmoor cartridge would give us consistent hit and precision in excess of 1,000m and that it should be a semi-auto capability located in the platoon weapons squad. The platoon leader is normally the person directing our DMRs currently and by placing the capability in the weapons squad it would mean the standard rifle squad didn't have to worry about another system or additional training.

The 6.5mm Creedmoor would seem to be an excellent choice to eventually replace the 7.62 × 51mm in DMRs and sniper spotter's rifles. SOCOM have tested both the .260 Remington and the 6.5mm Creedmoor extensively and have decided to progress with the latter, although performance and reliability in both Mk 17 SCARs and M110s has been equally impressive. The fact that existing

US Marines patrolling through a Helmand village, Afghanistan 2012. The squad designated marksman to the left carries the 5.56 × 45mm M16A4 based Squad Advanced Marksman-Rifle (SAM-R) with GripPod bipod. (*USMC, Sgt. Jacob Harrer*)

weapons can be relatively easily rechambered is another key advantage, reducing procurement and retraining costs.

## Current Trends

Many nations simply modified their standard assault rifle to serve as a DMR. The Swedish are a good example, taking the issue Bofors 5.56 × 45mm AK5A, modifying the stock and adding a four-power SUSAT optic (the same model once issued with British L85A1s), although they have more recently begun using their older G3 variant, the AK4, with modifications from Spuhr until a suitable dedicated DMR can be identified (in-line with their on-going programme to replace their 5.56 × 45mm AK5C assault rifle).

As noted earlier, the USMC issued the 5.56 × 45mm SDM-R, an accurized and scoped M16 platform, and the Mk 12 SPR or Special Purpose Rifle which were both later replaced by a 7.62 × 51mm M14 variant, the M39 Enhanced Marksmen Rifle. The British also initially used a 5.56 × 45mm platform, the much maligned L86A2 Light Support Weapon (LSW), as a field expedient DMR, although how many times it actually saw action is open to question.

The first true 7.62 × 51mm DMRs were the SR25 series adopted as the Mk 11 and later M110 as the standard issue DMR for both the US Army and Marine Corps. The Canadian Army purchased a small batch of suppressor-equipped ArmaLite AR10 (T) platforms to serve as spotters' weapons in Afghanistan, however their DMR requirements are currently met by an accurized 5.56 × 45mm C7 known by the designation C7CT produced by Colt Canada (formerly Diemaco). A new

A Marine SDM in Helmand Province, Afghanistan 2013 takes aim with his 5.56 × 45mm SAM-R fitted with sound suppressor. (*USMC, Sgt. Bobby J. Yarbrough*)

platform – christened the SASW or Semi-Automatic Sniper Weapon System – is due in service within 2018, although it is unclear if the SASW will be issued only to sniper teams or to the wider infantry community as a dedicated DMR.

New Zealand adopted their first DMR in 2011 to be issued at a rate of one per section. Termed the DMW or Designated Marksman Weapon, it is based on an LMT MWS308 design with issued Leupold six-power optic. Afghanistan seems to have been the impetus, with a spokesperson explaining that the NZDF *'have identified a need to be able to conduct precision engagements at ranges greater than can be achieved with the current in-service weapon'*. The spokesperson may have been somewhat exaggerating when he next claimed that the then issue Steyr AUG IW was *'not powerful enough to identify accurately adversaries and ineffective at ranges greater than 200 metres'*!

The German Bundeswehr used a 7.62 × 51mm G3 variant in Afghanistan, some with rails whilst others employed by the German OMLT based at Kunduz in 2009 were straight G3s equipped with the classic Hensoldt 4-power optics. During the Cold War, the Bundeswehr had in fact issued one 7.62 × 51mm G3 SG/1 per squad although the practice had ceased in the 1990s. After the (largely politically motivated) debacle with the G36 described in the previous chapter, the Bundeswehr purchased additional HK417s in the guise of the G28 for troops deployed to Afghanistan. From 2010 a billet within each German infantry squad was created for a designated marksman.

A New Zealand soldier carrying the recently issued 7.62 × 51mm Designated Marksman Weapon, based on the LMT MWS308. (*US Air Force, Master Sgt. Barry Loo*)

A close look at a typical 7.62 × 51mm Heckler and Koch G3A3ZF used by the Bundeswehr in Afghanistan. Note this rifle has a vertical foregrip fitted.
*(US Navy, Mass Communication Specialist 2nd Class Jonathan David Chandler)*

The British Army currently fields the 7.62 × 51mm LMT L129A1 and L129A2 as their marksman rifle. The weapon has performed more than adequately in Afghanistan where the rifle was deemed very popular with the troops. A study noted: '*The weapon has proved itself to be not only popular but very effective (anecdotal reports from operations backed up with quantifiable data through experimentation).*'

Now that the British Army has largely exited Afghanistan, the L129A1's future is always in some question, although it is currently part of the TO&E of each dismounted infantry section and looks set to stay that way. As of the time of writing, the Army even has ordered a further 397 examples in the wake of the impending withdrawal of the Minimi LMG from infantry sections (a controversial move we will cover in Chapter 8).

After trials as part of the 'Platoon Combat Experiment' that was designed to assess the needs of infantry soldiers in the near future, the issued six-power ACOG sight calibrated for 5.56 × 45mm was replaced with a modified version better suited for the 7.62 × 51mm calibre – worryingly the issue was not presumably identified during combat operations in Helmand.

As is traditional with any army, the lessons of combat are soon forgotten. The L129A1 is in danger of being dropped from mechanised units as its role could supposedly be met by the co-axial mounted 7.62 × 51mm machine gun of the Warrior infantry fighting vehicle. Exactly how the Warrior's co-ax will provide the same level of precision, let alone manoeuvrability of the L129A1, is unknown.

A British Army marksman armed with the 7.62 × 51mm LMT L129A1 supports a GPMG gunner in a security position in Helmand Province, Afghanistan 2010.

(*Open Government License v3.0, Corporal Barry Lloyd*)

As noted previously, in 2017 the US Army launched a short-lived effort to procure a 7.62 × 51mm general-issue battle rifle, spurred on by comments at a Congressional hearing that the issue M855A1 round is not able to penetrate Russian trauma plates. The Interim Service Combat Rifle (ICSR) requirement soon petered out as we have seen many such programmes do. Instead, the requirement to penetrate Russian body armour plates would be met by the introduction of a 7.62 × 51mm G28E based SDMR which one US Army Lieutenant General John Murray noted perhaps a little over-enthusiastically: '*That gives us the ability to penetrate the most advanced body armor in the world. We are accelerating the Squad Designated Marksman Rifle to 2018; we will start fielding that in 2018.*'

The 7.62 × 51mm Heckler and Koch G28 with Schmidt & Bender variable power scope and Aimpoint Micro T1, laser light module and bipod. (*Heckler and Koch*)

An Army spokesperson further explained:

The Army's current rifle technology is most effective below the 300-meter range; however, soldiers are fully capable of fighting beyond that threshold. The new rifle addresses the 300 to 600 meters range gap outlined in the 2015 US Army Small Arms Capabilities Based Assessment.

Confusingly, the G28E SDMR selected is similar to the Army's new Compact Semi-Automatic Sniper System, or CSASS, also based on the G28E.

The introduction of the SDMR will be matched with another new 7.62 × 51mm load. Murray asserted that the current M80A1 fired from the SDMR *'will still penetrate that body armor, but you can't get that extended range that is possible with the next generation round'*. It is uncertain if Murray, in charge of Army modernisation, was referring to the new XM1158 Advanced Armor Piercing (ADVAP) round or another design from the Next Generation Squad Automatic Rifle (NGSAR) programme. As we have discussed earlier, the XM1158 looks to be able to penetrate body armour plates at extended ranges and will likely be issued with the new SDMR platform.

In terms of battle rifles, Turkey against all expectations recently adopted a 7.62 × 51mm rifle, the MTP-76, as its general issue individual weapon. They had previously signed an agreement in around 2011 to licence-produce a 5.56 × 45mm

A Guatemalan Navy sniper trains with the Israeli 5.56 × 45mm STAR-21 Tavor DMR.
*(US Navy, Mass Communication Specialist 2nd Paul D. Williams)*

HK416 variant domestically, but apparently that deal fell through. The new weapon is based on German technology and appears visually to resemble the 417 but with an apparent weight reduction of 0.3 of a kilogram.

Other nations continue with 5.56 × 45mm DMR platforms. The IDF have been using the 5.56 × 45mm bullpup CTAR with a four-power ACOG as their DMR although the STAR-21 is also issued as a bipod-equipped marksman rifle. The Poles are following somewhat in the footsteps of the USMC in adopting a 5.56 × 45mm variant of the common issue assault rifle as their DMR – in the Polish case the Grot fitted with a CKW Bazalt day/night sight.

With reference to the Marine Corps, their newest DMR is the M27 based M38, issued at a rate of one per squad. Equipped with a Knights Armaments suppressor and Leupold variable magnification Mk 4 optic (the same as was originally issued with their Mk 12 SDM-Rs), the M38 is otherwise a stock M27. The former Gunnery Sergeant in charge of the Marine Corps' small arms modernisation programme noted however that he soon expected all Marine infantrymen to be able to act as designated marksmen: *'What I expect is that with the issuance of the M27 to all Marines in every squad, the ongoing mass employment of suppressors, and the development of variable power optics, every Marine in the squad will have the M38 capability in his own rifle.'*

## Individual Weapon Summaries

### Mk 14

The Mk 14 Mod0 was the first of the modernised M14s to be produced. Although originally designed for SOF, a variant was soon introduced into US Army units in 2007. The original Mk 14 saw the M14's barrel reduced by 4 inches to make it handier for SOF use. The Army version, known as the Enhanced Battle Rifle (EBR) or EBR 14, added a new full-length 22-inch barrel but otherwise was reasonably similar to the original.

In 2009 the Army added a second EBR to each infantry squad deployed to Afghanistan from stocks maintained in-country. Each rifle was equipped with the versatile Leupold 3.5-10 power scope. After some 6200 examples were fielded, the rifle is to be replaced by the new Heckler and Koch G28 based SDM-R.

### M39

The M39 was the second M14 based platform to be adopted by the USMC. The first was a modified M14 with a McMillan aftermarket stock and bipod and a stainless-steel match barrel to increase accuracy. They were hand built by the USMC Rifle Team, initially for EOD detachments and later for Marine reconnaissance teams before being issued to Marine infantry. This DMR was replaced by the M39 in 2008. The M39, issued at a rate of one per platoon, was heavily based on the Mk 14 using the Sage International adjustable stock.

### M38

The M38 is the latest Marine Corps issue squad designated marksman rifle. Essentially it is a 5.56 × 45mm M27 IAR fitted with a Leupold Mk 4 2.5–8 × 36mm

A US Army designated marksman in Spin Boldak, Afghanistan 2012 providing patrol overwatch with his Mk 14 (or M14 EBR-RI; Enhanced Battle Rifle-Rock Island) built from M14s on Sage stocks. *(US Army, Staff Sgt. Brendan Mackie)*

A US Marine scout sniper firing the 7.62 × 51mm M39 Enhanced Marksman Rifle (EMR) which replaced the M14 based Designated Marksman Rifle and is now being replaced by the M38. *(USMC, Cpl Timothy Childers)*

The new 5.56 × 45mm M38 Squad Designated Marksmanship Rifle adopted by the USMC based on the M27 IAR, itself based on the HK416A5. (*USMC, Lance Cpl Michaela R. Gregory*)

variable magnification scope. One will be issued to each infantry squad leaving the squad leader the discretion to assign it to his or her best shot.

## SR-25/M110 SASS

As previously indicated, much of the pioneering work on DMR platforms was the result of Knights Armament and their $7.62 \times 51$mm SR-25 platform. The SR-25 was popular amongst American and Australian SOF units before the outbreak of hostilities in Afghanistan and was found to be a near perfect platform for longer range operations in that theatre.

The SR-25 was adopted as the Mk 11 Mod0 and served with SOF units in both Iraq and Afghanistan. It was issued by the USMC as the Mk 11 Mod2 to serve as a spotter's weapon for sniper pairs and as a primary weapon on certain sniping missions such as in urban environments. A modified variant was the winner of the US Army's Semi-Automatic Sniper System (SASS) requirement and was adopted army-wide in 2007.

Although initially issued to sniper teams in 2008, by 2010 the rifle was trickling down to infantry units which sometimes supplemented their EBRs with the M110. In 2011 the Marine Corps adopted the rifle for their scout snipers whilst maintaining their M39s for infantry SDMRs.

US Army snipers protecting a Shura at the district center of Spin Boldak, Afghanistan 2013. The spotter in the foreground aims a $7.62 \times 51$mm Mk 14 EBR whilst his sniper partner uses the sound-suppressed $7.62 \times 51$mm M110 SASS. (*US Army, Staff Sgt. Shane Hamann*)

## HK417

A 7.62 × 51mm variant of the HK416, the HK417 builds on the success of the piston-driven 416 and was introduced by Heckler and Koch in 2005. It was immediately procured by a number of Western SOF units in a number of barrel-length variants including a 12-inch barrel battle rifle. The more standard DMR version featured a 16-inch (now increased to 16.5) with hand-guard mounted rails and an adjustable stock.

In the case of conventional forces, the weapon was issued to Australian infantry battalions as part of an operational purchase for Afghanistan after its successful implementation by their own SOF. The 417s were used to supplement and later replace the worn stock of SR-25s that had been in use. Both sniper observers and designated marksman in infantry platoons were issued the new 417s.

The rifle is now used by the Croatian, Danes, Norwegians and Portuguese as their issue DMR and is currently being trialled against the SIG716 G2 and LMT CQBMWS as the new designated marksman rifle for Estonian forces. The German Bundeswehr issue two variants to their infantry – the selective fire G27 which is employed as both a DMR and automatic rifle and the G28 as their standard marksman rifle. The G28 in German service is fitted with a Schmidt & Bender variable power optic with an Aimpoint T2 red dot sight mounted atop the scope to allow shooters to engage close range targets. It is finished in H&K's distinctive RAL8000 flat earth colour.

An Australian infantry marksman in Uruzgan Province, Afghanistan 2011 carrying the 7.62 × 51mm HK417 with Trijicon ACOG × 6 optic and Ruggedized Miniature Reflex sight.
(*Commonwealth of Australia, PO Damian Pawlenko*)

A German Bundeswehr marksman on exercise in 2015 with the newly issued semi-automatic 7.62 × 51mm Heckler and Koch G28 mounting a Schmidt & Bender variable power scope and Aimpoint Micro T1 red dot sight. The Bundeswehr notes: 'The G28 is employed against targets such as enemy snipers and particularly dangerous individuals, but also against technical targets as the optics of weapon systems on combat vehicles.' (*NATO, Alessio Ventura*)

The latest acquisition of the G28 series is by the US Army which is seemingly adopting two separate versions, one as their new SDM-R and the other as the replacement for the M110, the M110A1 CSASS or Compact Semi-Automatic Sniper System. We will only discuss the SDM-R variant, the official replacement for the EBR, in this chapter. The SDM-R is equipped with the SIG Tango 6 variable magnification optic, an unusual choice that perhaps underlines SIG Sauer's increasing place within US military small arms acquisition. It will initially be used with the M80A1 until the introduction of the XM1158. General Murray noted:

> We are accelerating the SDMR, or the Squad Designated Marksman Rifle, to '18, so we will start fielding that in '18. We had hoped to accelerate the ADVAP round, the Advanced Armor Piercing to '18 as well to line-up with that, but we'll wind up about a year off, so we will develop that ammo, field it in '19. You can still fire 7.62 and you can still penetrate, you just can't get quite the range you will with the next generation round.

An Army spokesperson explained that the SDM-R is the official replacement for the EBR and will be organically issued:

> That is exactly what it is designed to do, replace the EBR 14 because it was based on an operational needs statement, there were never any fielded for

A 13-inch barrel 7.62 × 51mm Heckler and Koch HK417A2 battle rifle. *(Heckler and Koch)*

home-station training. You fell in those weapon systems in theater … The basis of issue for SDM-R … is one per squad in the infantry, engineer and scout formations. Right now, we are roughly sitting at 6,000 rifles.

The optic that will be issued with the new SDM-R is not confirmed although the same spokesperson noted: *'What we are looking at would be in the realm of a 1–6 variable-power illuminated reticle. The concept would be if I am doing anything under 50 meters or even 100 meters, I am on one power.'*

### MPT-76 National Infantry Rifle

A domestically designed and produced 7.62 × 51mm battle rifle, the MPT-76 replaced the licenced-built G3 in Turkish service in 2014. A specific DMR variant and a 12-inch barrel carbine has also been announced. The MPT-76 is visually similar to a hybrid of the MK17 SCAR and the HK417. It appears that the DMR variant – the KNT-76 – has proven too expensive and thus the standard MPT-76 is being issued with a bipod, Bushnell variable magnification optic (although Schmidt & Bender optics have also been seen) and a domestically-produced infrared laser illuminator.

## Future Trends

Although 5.56 × 45mm DMRs are still being developed and issued, take the M38 as a recent example, the DMR and battle rifle market is 7.62 × 51mm dominant. Even the Russians are developing 7.62 × 51mm battle rifles. The AK-308 launched in mid-2018 appears to be a new variant of the AK-200 series (a renaming of the old AK-100 series) and may have been produced in part for on-going trials for the Pakistani Army. The weapon looks like a souped-up AK-12 with rails on the receiver and foregrip and an M4-style collapsible stock.

Israeli Weapon Industries has announced a 7.62 × 51mm variant of their excellent bullpup called the Tavor 7, featuring a variable gas regulator to facilitate the use of suppressors. It is another thoroughly modern design and offers a very compact option as a battle rifle. The ARX200 from Beretta is another recent design which looks promising with the Italian Army set to issue one ARX200 per squad.

The ARX200 is being adopted as both a battle rifle and as a DMR with a 16-inch barrel. Both feature a free-floating barrel for increased accuracy, and both offer full and semi-automatic fire. Like the previous ARX160 assault rifle, it can be easily converted to fire other calibres including 5.56 × 45mm and 7.62 × 39mm. Perhaps

A Canadian Army sniper zeroes his 7.62 × 51mm ArmaLite AR10 (T) spotter's rifle, procured as a stop-gap measure for Afghanistan. (*Canadian Forces, Corporal Nathan Moulton*)

Estonian Scouts armed with the 7.62 × 51mm G3 variant, the AK4. The AK4, Galil ARM and M14 DMRs in service are due to be replaced with a new assault rifle and DMR – the competition is currently between the LMT MLCPS/CQBMWS (the latter similar to the DMR procured by New Zealand) HK416/HK417 and SIG Sauer's MCX/SIG716. (*US Army, Specialist Jason Johnston*)

most importantly, an adaptor is available allowing the use of SR-25/M110 magazines in the 7.62 × 51mm version.

The DMR variant will use a Steiner Optics Intelligent Combat Sight which offers a six-power optic matched with a laser rangefinder, inclinometer to measure the angle of elevation (particularly important when operating in mountainous regions) and a ballistic computer which will calculate bullet drop, drift and trajectory – all in one compact package. The ARX200 may also feature an 'Intelligent Rail' system which would provide power for the ICS and any other accessories like weapon lights and infrared lasers.

After Italy, Argentina is looking increasingly likely to replace the Argentine Army's venerable FN FAL variants with the ARX200, particularly as they are already licence producing a range of Beretta small arms.

Will we see a new calibre emerge for DMRs in the longer term? In the same way as the immediate future of the assault rifle is dependent on the outcomes of the US NGSW programme, the future direction of the DMR, at least in terms of ammunition, will be defined by the NGSW-DM or Next Generation Squad Weapon-Designated Marksman, another sub-programme of the NGSW. A 6.5mm CT round would make sense for a DMR, particularly if used with a longer barrel, suitable optics and bipod. It can already exceed the range of most, if not all, 7.62 × 51mm loadings and if the round enters full production as the new US assault rifle calibre, a DMR version cannot be far away.

In 2018, following the SOCOM decision to adopt the 6.5mm Creedmoor as an intermediate sniper round, an announcement was made confirming that the Mk 20 SSP (the SCAR sniper support platform) would be rechambered for the 6.5mm Creedmoor. Although this is currently for SOF use only, and thus strictly speaking outside the scope of this book, it is nonetheless an interesting development that may indicate the future direction if the 6.5mm CT is not adopted.

## Breaking News

Estonia announced in May 2019 the adoption of a 7.62 × 51mm LMT MWS variant as their new designated marksman rifle.

## CHAPTER FIVE

# COMBAT SHOTGUNS

### Overview

Shotguns have had a storied if minor combat history in the last century. Adopted initially by British and later American troops during the trench warfare phase of the First World War, the shotgun also saw use with the USMC during the 'Banana Wars' and followed them into the Second World War during the island-hopping campaign against the Japanese in the Pacific.

Post-war, the shotgun saw action during counter-insurgency operations in Malaya and later Vietnam where it was prized by some as the ideal shoulder weapon for the lead scout or 'point-man'. The theory was that the spread of buck-shot increased the chances of striking a briefly-glimpsed target in heavily vegetated terrain.

After Vietnam, the combat shotgun was relegated to two specific purposes within most Western armies: crowd control (what we would now call 'less than lethal' applications) and ballistic breaching. In the 1980s, the US Army conducted

A US Marine ballistically breaches a door with his 12-gauge Mossberg M590A1 shotgun during street fighting in Iraq. (*USMC, Lance Cpl Matthew Hutchison*)

A US Army soldier maintains security with his 12-gauge Mossberg M590A1 shotgun, Iraq 2004.
(*US Army, Staff Sgt. Joseph Roberts*)

the short-lived CAWS or Close Assault Weapon System programme as part of the larger OICW programme to develop a new type of improved shotgun ammunition which would increase hit probability and a new weapon to fire it. Emerging from the CAWS programme were a number of new and innovative shotgun designs including the AAI and Heckler and Koch CAWS, the Atchisson AA-12 and the Pancor Jackhammer. All were designed to offer selective fire and used a range of fletchette shotshells. Ultimately the programme was cancelled and none of the weapons reached production for the US military.

Fully automatic shotguns, whilst sounding devastating in theory, have one major disadvantage – the weight of the ammunition required to keep the shotgun in action. The late Colonel Charlie Beckwith, founder of the US Army's Delta Force, was once quoted as exclaiming: '*I certainly wouldn't want an automatic shotgun – I'd have to have four boys along just to carry the ammunition!*'

Until recently, the CAWS programme was the last time shotguns were considered as a primary combat weapon and during the 1990s they became a tool to launch less than lethal munitions such as CS gas and bean-bag rounds against rioting civilians, or to blow locks off doors in a breaching capacity.

The Joint Service Combat Shotgun Program which followed in the late 1990s eventually saw the procurement of a new semi-automatic shotgun, the M1014 Joint Services Combat Shotgun, a version of the Benelli M4, become the standard issue for US forces. The requirement spelled out the weapon's intended uses, '*the execution of security/interior guard operations, rear area security operations, guarding prisoners of war, raids, ambushes, military operations in urban terrain, and selected special operations*'. Due to budgetary considerations, the US Army stayed with their varied collection of Winchester 1200, Mossberg M500 and Remington M870 pump action shotguns rather than transitioning to the new M1014.

Operations in Iraq and Afghanistan changed thinking around the shotgun to a degree. A USMC report on the utility of shotguns during the Global War on Terror argued: '*Currently, the shotgun's roles can be divided into three general roles: 1. Offensive Weapon, 2. Breacher, 3. Less-Lethal Munitions delivery system.*'

A US Army NCO fires a Marine issue 12-gauge Benelli M1014 semi-automatic shotgun, Iraq 2008. (*US Army, 1st Sgt. Joseph Gray*)

The M26 MASS (Modular Accessory Shotgun System) blows a lock clear from the door.
*(US Army, Sgt. Micah Merrill)*

The British Army in Afghanistan noted that the shotgun still retained a combat role:

> When operating in close country, both in the rural and urban environments, commanders should consider the carriage of shotguns where the SIED [Suicide IED] and SVBIED [Suicide Vehicle Borne IED] threat is present. Shotguns allow the rapid application of a short range effect with adequate stopping power, but a reduced risk of collateral damage than that posed by use of the GPMG.

US Army Captain Jeremy Phillips agreed in his study of combat shotgun employment focusing on Iraq:

> A less common use for shotguns is as a secondary weapon for crew-served gunners on high mobility multi-wheeled vehicles (HMMWVs) or mine-resistant ambush-protected vehicles (MRAPs). The limitations of the shotgun as a long-distance weapon are what make this such a good choice for gunners to carry in the turret.

The British used urgent operational requirement funding to issue the L128A1, a Benelli M4 semi-automatic shotgun, in 2009. According to the British Army, the objective was to '*apply a quick rapid rate of fire over a large area using a variety of*

A pair of British Army 12-gauge L128A1 Benelli semi-automatic shotguns on Operation Herrick XIII, Afghanistan 2011. *(Phil Boshier)*

*ammunition'* and was procured specifically for patrolling the heavily irrigated 'Green Zone' in Helmand Province. Heavy vegetation which blocked lines of sight and the need to clear compounds saw an initial surge of enthusiasm for the shotgun which tapered off as many preferred to lose the extra weight of the shotgun and its ammunition in favour of their L85A2 and pistol. By all accounts, only a small number of insurgents were ever engaged with the shotgun.

Still, the combat shotgun was primarily employed as a breaching tool. A USMC after action report on operations in Fallujah stated: *'Ballistic breaching was used mostly on exposed pad locks. Both M16A4s and shotguns were used. The M16A4s were employed because there was not enough shotgun ammunition for the amount of locks that had to be breached.'*

Today the shotgun is commonly only employed for breaching and for less than lethal munitions. The latter includes force protection of installations and vehicle convoys, along with riot control. Most shotguns employed by infantrymen are pump-action designs as these function more reliably with so-called 'low impulse' rounds like the specialist Hatton breaching round or with the M1012 rubber slug. Some semi-automatic shotguns will not reliably cycle such rounds, whereas the pump action allows the shooter to manually cycle and eject rounds.

The 12-gauge M26 MASS (Modular Accessory Shotgun System) in action on the range.
(*US Air Force, Spc. Michael Germundson*)

US Marines practising ballistic breaching with 12-gauge Mossberg M590A1 shotguns.
(*USMC, Sgt. Kassie L. McDole*)

## Calibres and Ammunition

Only one calibre exists within the military when it comes to shotguns – the venerable 12 gauge. Other calibres are either considered too light for military use – such as the 20 gauge – or produce too much recoil to use without extensive training, like the 10 gauge. Kalashnikov Concern in Russia do produce both .410 and 20-gauge variants of their semi-automatic Saiga-12 and the truly fearsome Russian KS-23, a pump action design from the 1970s that used a barrel made from a ZPU 23mm anti-aircraft cannon, firing a 23 × 75mm or 6.27 gauge shell!

The range of shotgun shells available is impressive, largely thanks to their wide-spread law enforcement use. Typical offensive military shotgun loads include 00 (or double-ought) buckshot for anti-personnel use which contains nine .33 pellets and solid slugs that carry a single large projectile ideal for penetrating cars and

| | Calibre | Action | Magazine | Weight Unloaded | Length |
|---|---|---|---|---|---|
| Mossberg M590A1 | 12GA | Pump | 6+1 | 3.4kg | 1,003mm |
| Remington M870 Mk 1 | 12GA | Pump | 5+1/8+1 | 3.6kg | 971mm |
| M1014/L128A1 | 12GA | Semi | 5+1 | 3.8kg | 1,010/889mm |
| M26 MASS | 12GA | Bolt | 5/10 | 1.2kg | 488mm |
| Saiga-12 | 12GA | Semi | 8 | 3.8kg | 1,145mm |

A US Marine loads shells into his 12-guage Benelli M1014 semi-automatic shotgun. In most shotguns, the shells are held in a tubular fixed magazine under the barrel. (*USMC, Cpl. Khalil Ross*)

Loading a 12-gauge Mossberg M590A1. (*US Navy, Mass Communication Specialist 2nd Class Michael T. Eckelbecker*)

thus very suitable for use at vehicle checkpoints. Solid slugs were also employed in Iraq for breaching due to the scarcity of specifically designed breaching ammunition. Slugs also increase the offensive range of the shotgun, but the trade-off is obviously the single projectile versus the spread of nine pellets which made them so useful in the jungles of the Pacific.

Next, we have less than lethal ordnance. In current military use, these rounds include the M1012 and M1013 fin-stabilised rubber slugs, Ferret CS rounds and a number of grenades that can be launched using a grenade launcher cup such as the XM104 Non-Lethal Bursting Hand Grenade which '*produces a shower of high velocity rubber pellets that sting and disorient potential targets*'.

The M1012 is for point targets (i.e. for shooting individuals) whilst the M1013 is for area targets: '*The area target cartridge round gives the soldier a capability to stun/deter two to three people without penetrating the body by delivering a strong blow to the body.*' The M1012, which fires a fin stabilised rubber slug, has an effective range of 30 metres, whilst the area-effect M1013 has a maximum range of 18 metres as it employs rubber pellets. Another more recent development is the XM1116 which fires a paint marking bean-bag out to 75 metres.

The USMC are investigating a new form of less than lethal round – the human electro-muscular incapacitation, or HEMI, round which would provide a Taser-like shock out to 100 metres. Such a round already exists in the form of the Taser XREP but is limited to a range of just 30 metres making it more suited for law enforcement applications. It will be interesting to see what develops from the USMC HEMI programme.

US Marine breaching a door during training with 12-gauge Benelli M1014 semi-automatic shotgun using an M1030 breaching round. (*US Army, Staff Sgt. Armando R. Limon*)

The M1030 is the US military's primary breaching round. Some UK forces employ breaching ammunition manufactured by Hatton who provide specialist breaching loads for many SOF units. Buckshot (and as noted earlier slugs) can be employed for breaching, but this brings a much-increased chance of wounding to both any occupants in the target premises and to fellow soldiers. British infantry in Iraq and Afghanistan were issued both slug and buckshot, but not any specialist breaching rounds. These rounds are frangible, typically made from powdered metal in a wax binding which destroy locks and hinges, usually disintegrating as they strike. They are by far the safest method of ballistic breaching as they reduce or eliminate overpenetration or ricochets.

## Current Trends

Very little is occurring in the world of combat shotguns as most militaries are content with their issue weapons, typically Remington, Winchester or Mossberg pump-action models that can withstand decades of abuse. Apart from the M26 MASS there has been little innovation outside of a handful of shotguns designed primarily for SOF use.

These include a number of systems like the US Crye Six12 – a bullpup shotgun using a revolver-type action that can be fired standalone or under the barrel of an M4 or HK416 family carbine; the Israeli Tavor TS12 – another bullpup design notable for its novel feed mechanism: three 5-round tubes which rotate into place as each is emptied; and the American designed Fostech Origin-12, a selective fire shotgun which can be suppressed and can use a 30-round drum magazine which it can apparently empty in 8 seconds!

The Russians continue to produce numerous variants of the magazine-fed Saiga-12 and Molot Vepr-12 (based on the RPK light machine gun chassis) including compact versions and side-folding stock variants, but these are essentially rather straightforward semi-automatic shotguns with AK operating features to ease transition. The Chinese adopted the gas-operated QBS-09 in 2009, a 12-gauge semi-automatic that outwardly resembles a Benelli design and includes a manual gas regulator to allow 'low impulse' ammunition to be employed.

The British Army's much heralded L128A1, its version of the semi-automatic Benelli M4, has been officially struck from the infantry TO&E after its adoption as a UOR during the latter years of Operation Herrick in Afghanistan. The exact whereabouts of these weapons today is unknown. UK Special Forces still maintain

Russian 12-gauge semi-automatic Saiga-12K. (*Kalashnikov Group/Kalashnikov Media*)

A US Army soldier clearing a building with his 12-gauge Mossberg M590A1 shotgun, Iraq 2003. (*US Army, Spc. Ben Brody*)

The newly issue 12-gauge Benelli M3 dual pump/semi-auto shotgun issued to the New Zealand Army. (*Commonwealth of New Zealand*)

stocks of Remington 870 variants for use as breaching shotguns, and some are equipped with folding stocks, EOTech sights and lasers for specialist roles, but the wider Army has apparently retired shotguns from official use (although rumours suggest they may again be in the market for replacements – which, if true, would be another example of the waste inherent in military procurement!).

The Dutch are looking to add to their stocks of their current issue Mossberg M590A1. They currently employ two variants of the M590A1 – one with collapsible stock and a shortened breaching version. The New Zealand Army has recently purchased Benelli M3s whilst the Australian Army has rather surprisingly issued a 2018 contract for the development of a modular shotgun system to local firm Defendtex. The company currently produces the modular MAUL (Multi-shot Accessory Underbarrel Launcher) semi-automatic shotgun (originally designed by the now defunct Metal Storm) which can be operated as a standalone or underbarrel and weighs less than a kilogram! It is not known whether this is for SOF or will eventually replace the issue Remington M870s in service.

## Individual Weapon Summaries

### M26
First deployed in Afghanistan in 2004 in front-line trials, the M26 MASS or Modular Accessory Shotgun System) is a straight pull-bolt action shotgun designed for breaching. It's intended for use in an underbarrel mount on the M4 series carbines but can be configured as a standalone platform. Its original version was

The M26 MASS (Modular Accessory Shotgun System) mounted under a 5.56 × 45mm Colt M4 carbine. The bolt-action on the M26 is clearly visible. (*US Army*)

based on a traditional pump action, however in trials this was found to be difficult to operate and was replaced by a side-mounted folding cocking handle which operates like a straight pull-bolt action rifle to eject and chamber the following round.

Magazine fed from 5- or 10-round magazines, the M26 is an ungainly but apparently reliable breaching shotgun and has been employed extensively by the US Army in both Afghanistan and Iraq. It can be used as a standalone shotgun with the addition of an M4 style stock and can fire all less than lethal rounds in US inventory.

A US Army spokesperson explained about its adoption in 2012:

> Right now, if a soldier wants to use a shotgun, he uses a shotgun and slings his rifle, and when he uses his rifle, he has to sling the shotgun and then get out the rifle. With the M26, it's an all-in-one piece. It has a door breaching attachment which goes flush against a door lock and allows the 12 gauge shell to blow the lock off a door and the soldier to room clear without changing weapons.

### Benelli M4 (L128A1/M1014)

The Benelli M4 was the winner of the US Joint Service Combat Shotgun Program and adopted by all US services apart from the Army, who continued to issue a mix of Mossberg and Remington shotguns and who are now issuing the M26 MASS as their issue shotgun. The Benelli has seen service with numerous European special operations units and with the British Army as the L128A1 (equipped with an EOTech holographic sight and folding vertical grip).

The down side to the M4 design is that 'low impulse' rounds must be manually cycled. The Benelli M3 used by New Zealand and Estonia is a dual pump and semi-automatic shotgun in the same fashion as the iconic Franchi SPAS-12, allowing the shooter to decide which system to use with particular types of rounds.

A US Marine engages a target with a 12-gauge Benelli M1014 semi-automatic shotgun during training. *(USMC, Lance Cpl. Ashley Phillips)*

## Mossberg 500 Series

The Mossberg M500/M500A2 and later M590 and M590A1 variants have equipped both the US Army and Marine Corps for many years and were heavily employed in street fighting in Iraq. US Army Brigade Combat Teams, for instance, were issued some 178 Mossberg 500s. They are still being employed by the USMC to such an extent (due to the high cost associated with the M1014) that the Corps issued a 'Military Enhancement Kit' (MEK) for their M500s in 2017. The MEK offers three new stocks that users can swap out dependent on task – a stock-less pistol grip, a lightweight rigid stock and an M4 style collapsible stock. The MEK also includes a saw-tooth breaching stand-off device and a Picatinny rail-equipped replacement forearm. A Marine spokesperson noted:

> When you're breaching or conducting methods of entry, having the ability to secure the weapon on your body without it becoming cumbersome is important. Having a shorter barrel and a pistol grip removes all of the extra space that is not necessary for ballistic breaching. So when you stow it, you can stow it much more rapidly.

The 12-gauge Mossberg M590A1 shotgun. *(US Army)*

As noted, they were also much cheaper than the much longer M1014:

> By using the MEK with currently-fielded M500A2 shotguns, the Marine Corps only had to buy the kits. Also, modifying the shotgun in local armories will save time and shipping costs, and units will retain their shotguns on-hand, as opposed to sending them in to a depot for maintenance.

### Remington M870

Since the 1950s, the Remington M870 has been the most widely employed pump action shotgun by the world's militaries. It is a simple but reliable design – the AK of shotguns. It has been produced in every configuration imaginable, from pistol-grip breaching shotguns to under, over and side folding stocked variants.

Australian Army infantrymen training with 12-gauge Remington M870 breaching shotguns.
(*Commonwealth of Australia, LCPL Kyle Genner*)

The latest military variant is the MCS or Modular Combat Shotgun. The MCS was later mirrored by the Mossberg MEK in that it features three different stock configurations that can be user modified. The first is the pistol-grip breacher with 10-inch barrel and 4-shell capacity. The next is a 14-inch barrel, 6-shell capacity version with a rigid, pistol grip stock. The final version extends the barrel to a full 18 inches and holds 7 rounds. The breacher variant can also be mounted under the barrel of an M4 series carbine.

## Future Trends

It's unlikely that we will see some of the new innovative shotguns such as the Origin-12 or Tavor TS12 in the hands of infantrymen any time soon. The existing issue weapons do the job required of them and are solid and reliable shotguns that can be easily maintained. Shotguns will never become a primary weapon for the infantryman, except in extremely limited circumstances such as the British experience in southern Afghanistan, and even then most soldiers still carried their L85A2 along with the shotgun.

Further development of less than lethal rounds like the HEMI will guarantee a future as the preferred force protection/public order tool and for ballistic breaching the shotgun cannot be beaten. There may be one area that the humble shotgun can offer a unique capability – countering low flying UAVs or unmanned aerial vehicles. Specialist handheld counter-UAV platforms are being issued in increasing numbers to Marine, Army and SOF units in Syria, such as the Dronebuster, but the simple shotgun may provide an in-extremis capability, particularly for the low flying commercial drones employed by Syrian and Iraqi insurgents. With the increasing threat of so-called 'drone swarm' attacks we may even see units issued with no. 8 birdshot or similar to increase the chance of knocking down these aerial menaces.

The Military Enhancement Kit (MEK) options for the US Marine issue 12-gauge Mossberg M500A2 shotgun. (*USMC, Alan Matthews*)

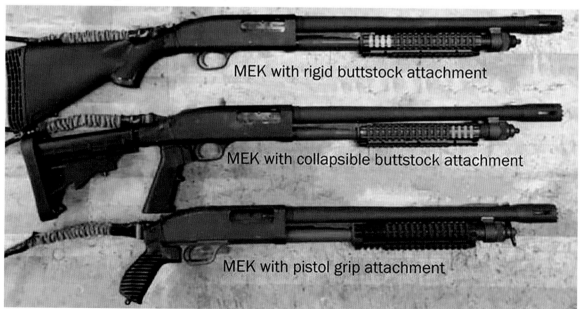

# CHAPTER SIX

# SNIPER AND ANTI-MATERIEL RIFLES

## Overview

Sniper rifles have perhaps been the most effective infantry weapon employed during the Global War on Terror. They allow soldiers to apply precision lethality at extended ranges and, perhaps more importantly, act as an important sensor for the infantry platoon commander. The sniper's rifle optics and his spotter's scope can identify threats, examine vulnerable points for IEDs, and discern between friend and foe far more reliably than the Mk1 human eyeball. They can also gauge what became known as 'combat indicators' – signs of an impending ambush as civilians flee or take cover in buildings, allowing the snipers an early warning to their comrades on the ground.

Indeed, in Afghanistan the British Army noted that snipers were also the perfect complement for anti-tank teams using the Javelin missile to target insurgent positions:

> Snipers and Javelin together make a powerful combination, the snipers acting as spotters for the Javelin and enhancing the selection of targets. The sniper spotting scope ( × 40) is one of the best daytime sights available and its employment by trained observers eases a difficult and often complex problem of directing fires against multiple and well concealed enemy firing positions.

They are a tremendous discretionary weapon system, particularly in a counter-insurgency environment. One insurgent can be engaged and killed while sheltering among a crowd of villagers, an IED 'trigger-man' can be neutralised without harm to the farmer standing next to him and insurgents attempting to flank friendly positions can be killed without fear of collateral damage to any nearby civilian infrastructure. Indeed, the US Army Sniper School states: 'Where precision fire is concerned, the sniper exists as the premiere and undisputed answer to the use of deadly force with the least chance of collateral damage and use of excessive force.'

The classic US Army sniper rifle, the 7.62 × 51mm M24. Now replaced by the M2010. (*US Army*)

A Bundeswehr sniper firing his 7.62 × 51mm G28 semi-automatic sniper rifle.
(*US Army, Markus Rauchenberger*)

The British Army's after action report on Operation Herrick noted that on one of the last Herrick deployments to Afghanistan, '*96% of recorded Enemy Killed in Action (EKIA) were delivered by precision fires, and 90% of all direct fire EKIA was achieved by snipers or sharpshooters*'. This is an incredibly impressive result that highlights the vital importance of snipers (and designated marksmen) in the small arms mix. On one 2009 tour alone, a sniper pair accounted for seventy-five insurgents in forty days.

Noted a serving British Army infantry platoon commander to the author:

Accurate sniper fire was always a battle winner for me. The ratio of rounds to kills from section weapons was staggering – that's why I preferred sharp-shooters and snipers rather that heavy weight [fire], this minimised civilian casualties. Only on HERRICK 6 and 10 did I see mortars used and that was the 81mm – they never lasted long. We never used mortars on HERRICK 15

British Army bolt-action 7.62 × 51m L96A1 which was replaced by the L115A3. (*Accuracy International*)

due to their blast radius and you could see certainly in the areas that I was in as the Herricks went on they were used less.

In eastern Afghanistan, the sniper gave US forces so-called 'ridge-to-ridge' capability. As we have discussed previously, in places like the infamous Korengal Valley, US forces would be engaged from neighboring mountains with PKM medium machine guns, SVD marksman rifles and even 12.7mm and 14.5mm heavy machine guns. Whilst many of these targets were neutralized by mortar, artillery or from the air, snipers gave the troops the capability to hit back whilst they were under fire. In Iraq too, snipers proved their worth in both the teeming urban mazes of Ramadi and Fallujah, to the open desert of al-Qaim on the Syrian border. Importantly, they provided an overwatch function, watching over infantry patrols or monitoring trouble spots for IEDs and those who laid the IEDs.

After the later capture of much of Iraq by the Islamic State, Coalition Forces brought their snipers with them to provide similar overwatch and force protection for their training teams working with the Iraqi military to recapture key cities. In one memorable case, a Canadian SOF sniper from their Tier One unit, Joint Task Force 2, engaged and killed an insurgent at the incredible range of 3,540 metres, a number confirmed by Canadian Special Operations Command (and currently the longest range recorded sniper shot in history).

A Belgian Army sniper aims his 7.62 × 51mm Accuracy International Artic Warfare in pre-deployment training for Afghanistan 2012. (*US Army, Spc. Tristan Bolden*)

British Army snipers in Nad-e Ali District, Helmand Province, Afghanistan 2007. The sniper on the left is armed with the .338 Lapua Magnum L115A3. (*ISAF, Corporal John Scott Rafoss*)

Infantry snipers also made their fair share of long-range shots in both Iraq and Afghanistan. Famously Sergeant Craig Harrison of the Household Cavalry killed an Afghan insurgent machine-gunner at 2,475 metres in 2009. He explained in media interviews:

> They came forward carrying a PKM, set it up and opened fire ... Conditions were perfect, no wind, clear visibility. I rested the bipod of my weapon on a compound wall and aimed for the gunner firing the machine gun. The driver of my Jackal spotted for me, providing all the information needed for the shot, which was at the extreme range of the weapon.

Another British sniper, this time from the Coldstream Guards, set another kind of record when he engaged and killed a suicide bomber, detonating his vest which killed five other insurgents in the blast! In the 'ridge-to-ridge' battle along the

The Accuracy International .50BMG AX50. Earlier versions (the AW50F) are in service with the British and Australian armies. (*Accuracy International*)

border with Pakistan, US Army Sergeant Nicholas Ranstad engaged and killed an insurgent at 2,092 metres using his .50-calibre M107 anti-materiel rifle.

Engagement ranges in Iraq tended to be shorter as Coalition Forces were fighting against what was primarily an urban insurgency. Still, long-distance shots were recorded – a USMC scout-sniper team in 2004 providing overwatch for a dismounted patrol engaged an insurgent machine gun team at 1,600 metres, firing repeatedly through the brick wall the insurgents were using for cover with their .50 M107. Another Marine sniper killed a suicide car bomber at 640 metres as the vehicle barreled toward a Coalition Forces convoy.

At other times the employment of snipers undoubtedly saved civilian lives:

The sniper engaged the RPG gunner with his M14 sniper rifle and continued firing single rounds at the figure until he incapacitated him with a wound to the arm. The situation on Market Street below sorted itself out. With the sound of [the sniper's] first shot, the crowd immediately dispersed, leaving only insurgents and American soldiers in the Market Street area.

Both conflicts demonstrated the need for heavier calibre sniper rifles. Whilst the .50 Barrett M107 and similar platforms provided unbeatable barrier penetration, they were also heavy and cumbersome. Much preferred were the .300 Winchester Magnum and .338 Lapua Magnum – both provided an increase in range over the standard 7.62 × 51mm, were more resistant to the effects of wind and provided consistent terminal effects.

Today, the .338 Lapua Magnum has generally been accepted as the ideal calibre for bolt-action sniper rifles operating in rural or semi-rural environments; 7.62 × 51mm still reigns supreme in semi-automatic platforms, particularly in

A British Army sniper firing his .50BMG Accuracy International AW50F (L121A1 in British service) from a Viking BVS10 armoured carrier during a contact with insurgents in Helmand Province, Afghanistan 2010. (*Open Government License v3.0, Corporal Barry Lloyd*)

An Australian Army sniper wearing a Ghillie Suit firing the .338 Lapua Magnum straight bolt Blazer R93 Tactical II. (*Commonwealth of Australia*)

A Canadian Army sniper practises with his sound suppressed .338 Lapua Magnum C14 Timberwolf MRSWS, the standard issue sniper rifle for Canadian Forces.
(*Canadian Forces, Master Corporal Andrew Davis*)

|  | Calibre | Action | Magazine | Weight Unloaded | Length |
|---|---|---|---|---|---|
| L115A3 | .338LM | Bolt | 5 | 6.9kg | 1,230mm |
| L96A1 | 7.62 × 51mm | Bolt | 10 | 6.5kg | 1,180mm |
| M40A5 | 7.62 × 51mm | Bolt | 5 | 6kg | 1,035mm |
| M2010 | .300WM | Bolt | 5 | 8kg | 1,122mm |
| SVD | 7.62 × 54mm | Semi | 10 | 4.3kg | 1,225mm |
| M110 | 7.62 × 51mm | Semi | 20 | 4.8kg | 1,118mm |
| Type 88 | 5.8 × 42mm | Semi | 10 | 3.8kg | 920mm |
| C14 | .338LM | Bolt | 5 | 7.1kg | 1,200mm |
| M107A1 | .50BMG | Semi | 10 | 16kg | 1,447mm |
| Type 99 | 12.7 × 108mm | Semi | 5 | 12kg | 1,480mm |
| OSV-96 | 12.7 × 107mm | Semi | 5 | 12.9kg | 1,746mm |

urban terrain or situations which may see the sniper have to use the rifle in close range self-defence.

## Calibres and Ammunition

The 'rule of thumb' effective range of sniper calibres generally breaks down into a number of range bands. In the first, up to 800 metres, is the 7.62 × 51mm or 7.62 × 54mm. In the second, out to 1,200 metres, is the .300 Winchester Magnum. The third, out to 1,500 metres, is the domain of the .338 Lapua Magnum. Beyond this, out to 2,000 meters and sometimes beyond, is the .50 calibre.

The US Army and Marine Corps have maintained the 7.62 × 51mm as their principal sniping round since the retirement of the .30-06 M1D in the early 1960s. As noted in the introduction however, the longer engagement ranges in parts of Afghanistan pushed them toward a new calibre. The .300 Winchester Magnum was introduced for the Army M2010 with a new .300 Winchester Magnum load, the 220-grain Mk 248, which increased the effective range of the round out to 1,500 metres replacing the 190-grain M118LR. The M2010 (an extensive conversion of existing M24 actions) and its new round replaced the 7.62 × 51mm M24A2 from 2011 with the first rifles destined for snipers deployed to Afghanistan.

The Marines eventually followed suit with their .300 Winchester Magnum Mk 13 Mod7 replacing the 7.62 × 51mm M40A6. The Mk 13 had been extensively employed by Navy SEALs and later Marine SOF since the 1990s. A Marine spokesperson commented at the time: '*The .300 Winchester Magnum round will perform better than the current 7.62 NATO ammo in flight, increasing the Marine sniper's first round probability of hit.*'

Other calibres are being developed and issued, but principally within the SOF world. SOCOM have announced that the .300 Norma Magnum is the selected choice for their Advanced Sniper Rifle (ASR) requirement along with the 7.62 × 51mm and .338 Norma Magnum. The .300 Norma Magnum is a flatter shooting round with less felt recoil than the .338 Lapua Magnum, whilst offering

A Swedish sniper firing his PSG-90, the Swedish version of the 7.62 × 51mm Accuracy International Artic Warfare. The Swedes issue a 4.81mm tungsten carbide sabot sniper round designed to penetrate body armour. (*US Army, Specialist Gertrud Zach*)

Peruvian Marine snipers firing the semi-automatic Israeli 7.62 × 51mm Galil Galatz sniper rifle. (*USMC*)

a significant velocity and range improvement over the standard .300 Winchester Magnum. Calibres like the .300 and .338 Norma Magnum will take years to trickle down to infantry snipers, if ever. Note the 50 plus years it took for the USMC to adopt a new calibre.

The Russians have maintained the 7.62 × 54mm as their standard sniping round from the SVD and bolt-action SV-98M firing the 152-grain 7N14 Match round which was designed to increase the armour penetration of the older 7N1. For longer range engagements, the OSV-96 anti- materiel rifle (AMR) is used. This fires the 12.7 × 107mm round which is ballistically similar to the .50BMG. Again, the Russians place great importance on armour penetration and the OSV-96 is provided with the B-32 armour-piercing incendiary round.

Finally, we must mention the most curious sniper ammunition yet developed. Russia's Instrument Design Bureau has designed the intriguing bullpup ShAK-12 or ASh-12.7 heavy sniper rifle (also known as the '*Vychlop*' or 'Exhaust') chambered for the massive 12.7 × 55mm round. Incredibly the weapon is selective fire, fed from a 10- or 20-round magazine. Not surprisingly it was designed for use with a suppressor and is compatible with specially developed 12.7 × 55mm subsonic ammunition. It is apparently capable of engaging lightly armoured targets out to 600 metres. According to noted firearms authority Max Popenker, the standard subsonic load is the whopping 910-grain STs-130PT produced from solid bronze. A specialist armour-piercing round is also available at 1170 grains.

A Canadian Army soldier firing a Ukrainian issue 7.62 × 54mm SVD Dragunov, the standard sniper weapon for most of the Cold War and still used by a number of armies along with appearing in the hands of insurgents. (*Canadian Forces*)

## Current Trends

Along with assault rifles, the buzzword for sniper rifles is modularity. SOCOM's ASR requirement for a bolt-action rifle capable of being switched between three different calibres depending on task is a good example. They had previously run a competitive tender for a similar platform under the Precision Sniper Rifle (PSR) programme, which was awarded to Remington for their Mk 21 variant of the commercial Remington Modular Sniper Rifle. However, the procurement agreement was cancelled when the quality of the delivered rifles did not meet SOCOM's specification.

Multi-calibre sniper rifles are likely to eventually be deployed by infantry snipers, although with the addition of multiple, often expensive, specialist calibres to the logistics chain, this will likely take some time. Nonetheless, the idea of a sniper being able to choose the appropriate calibre (and barrel length) for a task is an attractive one. Surprisingly, one military that is heading down the multi-calibre route is the Venezuelan Army which is producing a new domestically-designed multi-calibre bolt-action platform, the Catatumbo, apparently in both .338 Lapua Magnum and .50BMG.

Most armies are reasonably content with their mix of 7.62 × 51mm, .338 Lapua Magnum and .50BMG platforms. In Afghanistan, the British Army found that the .338 Lapua Magnum L115A3 quickly became the weapon of choice for its snipers, largely due to its vastly increased effective range, along with the terminal effects of the heavy .338 Lapua Magnum.

In their own evaluations of the small arms employed during Operation Herrick, they discovered that the older 7.62 × 51mm L96A1 still had its place however, particularly whilst operating within the Green Zone, as its lighter weight was appreciated. As the heavy vegetation within this region bordering the Helmand River

US Army snipers firing the 7.62 × 51mm M110 (foreground) and .300 Winchester Magnum M2010 (background) during training in Djibouti 2016. (*US Air Force, Master Sgt. Barry Loo*)

Accuracy International base model .338 Lapua Magnum AW338 which became the L115A3.
(*Accuracy International*)

drastically reduced engagement ranges, the lighter L96A1 was considered an ideal compromise of weight, lethality and range. The L115A3 was particularly prized for engaging targets ensconced within defensive positions or firing from behind walls or within buildings:

> L129A1 and sniper rifles were excellent at targeting the TB [Taliban] at range, we operated both L96 and .338 sniper rifles in the teams. They would very often pick-off and target TB resupply routes up to the firing points in sustained contacts with great effect, we also through ISTAR [Intelligence, Surveillance and Reconnaissance] assets targeted with snipers the firing holes the TB used in compounds.

The Australians are maintaining a typical mix of all three calibres in the form of the 7.62 × 51mm SR-98 (similar to the British L96A1) and HK417, the .338 Lapua Magnum Blaser 93 Tactical 2 and the .50BMG Barrett M82 and AW50F. The New Zealanders adopted the .338 Lapua Magnum Barrett MRAD (Multi-Role Adaptive Design) in 2017 to supplement and eventually replace their 7.62 × 51mm Accuracy International Arctic Warfare platforms. A spokesperson noted the preference for the .338 Lapua Magnum as being driven by the increased terminal effectiveness of the round: '*Our snipers need to be able to fire once and achieve their mission.*'

The Indian Army had added a new sniper platform to their lengthy foray into replacing the main small arms of their infantry and reservist units. They currently deploy the Russian SVD but are now looking for a platform with an increased range out to 1,000 metres employing a variable magnification optic. If their quest for a new assault rifle is any indication, their snipers sadly may be waiting some time for a new weapon.

The French are also looking for a replacement for their 7.62 × 51mm FR-F2 bolt-action rifles. In Afghanistan and Mali, the HK417 has served as an interim sniping rifle. The Fusil de Précision Semi-Automatique tender released in 2018 calls for a semi-automatic 7.62 × 51mm platform. With the French Army adopting the HK416F as their standard assault rifle, the Heckler and Koch G28 variant of the HK417 is hotly tipped.

Poland is in the process of upgrading its fleet of Sako 7.62 × 51mm TRG-22 bolt-action rifles including a new trigger, an ambidextrous safety and the addition

An exhausted-looking Australian Army sniper team providing overwatch in Uruzgan Province, Afghanistan 2008. The sniper is armed with the 7.62 × 51mm SR-25 whilst his spotter carries an F88SA1 mounting an M203 grenade launcher. (*Commonwealth of Australia*)

A French sniper engages targets at the 2018 Europe Best Sniper Team Competition with a 7.62 × 51mm HK417A2. (*US Army, SPC Emily Houdershieldt*)

of Picatinny rails to facilitate the mounting of clip-on thermal and night vision sights. They have also recently purchased a quantity of .338 Lapua Magnum TRG M10s with side-folding stocks.

China is one of the few nations to favour the bullpup configuration for their sniper rifle with the 5.8 × 42mm Type 88, although the Russians did develop a bullpup variant of their SVD in the form of the OTs-03 that saw service in Chechnya. The Type 88 is also unusual amongst sniper rifles in that it offers both semi and full automatic fire. It features a proprietary rail for mounting optics and Western style back-up iron sights that fold down out of the way when not required.

Bullpup anti-materiel rifle designs are far more common. The Steyr HS (unfortunately most well-known for its use by Iranian-supported insurgents in southern Iraq but issued to the armies of Turkey and Albania amongst others) being an obvious example. The advantage of the bullpup design makes much sense for AMRs as their normally unwieldy length can be reduced.

As noted in a previous chapter, the US Army is purchasing a new semi-automatic sniper rifle to replace their Knights M110, at least until the outcome of the Next Generation Squad Weapon programme is known. The Heckler and Koch G28-based 7.62 × 51mm M110A1 CSASS (Compact Semi-Automatic Sniper

An Italian sniper armed with a bolt-action .338 Lapua Magnum Sako, Afghanistan 2010. (*ISAF, SSG Romain Beaulinette*)

A US Marine sniper tries out the French issue .50BMG PGM Hecate II under the eye of a French sniper. (*USMC, Cpl. Michael Petersheim*)

KAC 7.62 × 51mm M110 SASS (Semi-Automatic Sniper System) which will be replaced in US Army service by the Heckler and Koch G28E CSASS (Compact Semi-Automatic Sniper System). (*US Army*)

System) will be equipped with a Schmidt & Bender PMII Ultra Short Scope and OSS suppressor as standard. It also features high-end Geissele M-Lok rails, a company that initially only supplied their goods to the special mission units of the US military.

A spokesperson explained: '*The rifle is easier to shoot and has less recoil, all while shooting the same round as the M110. The CSASS has increased accuracy, which equates to higher hit percentages at longer ranges.*' Additionally, it is 600mm shorter and 1.3 kilograms lighter than the M110. The USMC have shown interest in and tested the CSASS for their scout-sniper teams as a supplement or replacement for the M110.

# Individual Weapon Summaries

## Barrett M82 & M107

The M82 (or M107 in US service) is the daddy of all .50-calibre anti-materiel rifles. Developed in the 1980s, the USMC bought 125 examples of the rifle to equip their scout snipers during Operation Desert Storm in 1991. The M82 saw limited service with Army SOF units until 2002 when it was officially standardized within the US Army as the M107 and issued to all sniper teams. Since that time, and partly thanks to Hollywood, the Barrett now defines the .50 sniper rifle category. It is the most widely adopted AMR on the planet with the Australians, British, Brazilians, Danes, Germans (as the G82), New Zealanders, Norwegians, and the Mexican Army along with dozens of others. A number of variants have been offered (including the bolt-action bullpup design M95 which was originally going to be adopted by the US Army) and a number of firms even produce sound suppressors for the weapon.

.50BMG semi-automatic Barrett M82A1/M107 with sound suppressor. (*Barrett Firearms*)

A US Army sniper pair training with the .50BMG Barrett M107 anti-materiel rifle. (*US Army, Spc. Andrew McNeil*)

## Accuracy International Precision Model and Arctic Warfare Magnum (L115A3, G28)

If the Barrett is the world's most used AMR, the Accuracy International (AI) AWM and its numerous variants are quite likely the most popular bolt-action sniper rifle. Originally designing 7.62 × 51mm rifles for British and American SOF, they subsequently won the 1985 contract to replace the British Army's ageing L42A1 Enfield with their PM (Precision Model) which was type classified the L96A1.

Whilst the L96A1 was popular with British snipers (it was nicknamed the 'Green Meanie' thanks to the greenish hue of its stock), it was supplemented in UKSF service with a .338 Lapua Magnum version termed the L115A1. Looking for a replacement for the L96A1, the British Army eventually adopted the slightly modified L115A3 in 2007 with the first example appearing in Afghanistan the following year. The L96A1 continued in-service as a platoon marksman weapon until the 2010 procurement of the semi-automatic LMT L129A1.

Accuracy International have ceased production of the original PM and AWM builds and now offer a new, modernized range of platforms based around the AX which is available in a number of calibres. Their rifles can be found in armies around the globe including Australia, Ireland, Italy, Netherlands, New Zealand, Spain, Sweden and Turkey (even Russian SOF use variants as witnessed in Syria).

The AWM is known as the G22 in Bundeswehr service, in a .300 Winchester Magnum variant. It has recently begun being replaced by a new platform, the

A Bundeswehr sniper firing his .300 Winchester Magnum G22 bolt-action sniper rifle. The G22 is scheduled to be replaced by the .338 Lapua Magnum G29 (the Haenel RS9).

(*US Army, Markus Rauchenberger*)

British Army bolt-action .338 Lapua Magnum L115A3 with issued sound suppressor.
(*Open Government License v3.0*)

Haenel RS9 (Rifle System 9), designated the G29 in German service. The procurement programme began in 2014 for a new .338 Lapua Magnum rifle, with the RS9 announced as the winner in 2016 with an initial purchase of 115 platforms. The Bundeswehr note: '*Compared to the G22, the larger caliber of the G29 ensures a more stable trajectory and increased projectile energy, making it particularly suitable for use in extreme weather conditions such as mountains, on the coast or at sea.*'

The new folding stock G29 is equipped with a Steiner variable power optic and an aluminum B&T suppressor that cuts muzzle report to a very respectable 31dB. Weighing in at 7.54 kilograms unloaded, the G29 features a 10-round magazine and is rated as effective against point targets out to 1,500 metres.

A US Army officer fires the new .338 Lapua Magnum bolt-action G29 (the Haenel RS9) adopted by the Bundeswehr. (*US Army, Specialist Dee Crawford*)

Barrett bolt-action MRAD (Multi-Role Adaptive Design) available in a range of calibres including 7.62 × 51mm, the .300 Winchester Magnum and .338 Lapua Magnum. (*Barrett Firearms, Nathan Lux*)

### Barrett MRAD (Multi-Role Adaptive Design)

The MRAD was initially developed to compete in the American PSR programme that was won (and eventually lost!) by Remington. The key to the MRAD was its modularity (there's that term again). It could be reasonably effortlessly switched between the 7.62 × 51mm, the .300 Winchester Magnum and the .338 Lapua Magnum (kits are also now produced for the 6.5mm Creedmoor).

Purchased by the New Zealand Army in 2017 to replace their AI Artic Warfare models in 7.62 × 51mm, the Norwegian Army has also adopted the .338 Lapua Magnum Barrett MRAD using the excellent Schmidt Bender 3-20 × 50 PMII optic.

### Mk 13 Mod7

Formerly only employed by US SOF, including the Navy SEALs and MARSOC, the Mk 13 was announced in mid-2018 as the replacement for the venerable M40A7 in Marine Corps service. It features an AICS stock produced by Accuracy International.

US Marine scout snipers training with the newly issued .300 Winchester Magnum Mk 13 Mod7. The Mk 13 replaced their 7.62 × 51mm M40A6/7s in 2018. (*USMC, Cpl. Jon Sosner*)

A clear detail shot of the USMC's .300 Winchester Magnum Mk 13 Mod7 based on a rifle used by US Navy SEAL Teams. (*USMC, Kristen Murphy*)

Some have questioned the move to the .300 Winchester Magnum rather than the more internationally common .338 Lapua Magnum, but concerns about the length of current ranges used by the Corps' four sniping schools (limited to 1,000 metres) and a professed interest in the results of SOCOM's Advanced Sniper Rifle programme meant that the interim solution would be the .300 WM.

### C14 MRSWS (Medium Range Sniper Weapon System)

The .338 Lapua Magnum C14 Timberwolf is the standard sniper platform of the Canadian Army and replaced the McMillan stocked C3A1, itself based on the classic Parker M82 in 7.62 × 51mm. The C14 was acquired from 2005 as the Army noted the need to replace their ageing C3A1 and the general NATO move toward .338 Lapua Magnum.

McMillan again provided the issue stock for the C14 based on the USMC M40A3. Canada's experiences in Kandahar Province, Afghanistan proved the need for a larger calibre sniper platform to deal with the extended ranges being encountered. A small number of C14s have also been procured by the UK Ministry of Defence destined for Special Forces.

### McMillan TAC-50 LRSWS (Long Range Sniper Weapon System)

Along with the AI AW50F, the other major competitor to the Barrett M82 series is the McMillan TAC-50. As well as being selected as the Navy SEALs preferred AMR, the McMillan has the distinction of being the weapon system that delivered two of the longest sniper shots on record. Both the previously mentioned JTF2 contact and a 2002 shot in Afghanistan, at an astounding 2,430 metres, were delivered from the C15, the Canadian Army issue AMR (adopted in 2000) built by McMillan and known commercially as the TAC-50.

A pair of Canadian Army .338 Lapua Magnum C14 Timberwolf MRSWS (Medium Range Sniper Weapon System) sniper rifles. (*US Army, Sgt. Aaron Ellerman*)

### M40 Series

The 7.62 × 51mm bolt-action M40 in a number of constantly upgraded variants has been the issue sniper rifle for the Marine Corps since 1966, based on the civilian short-action Remington 700. During the war in Afghanistan there were public calls for its replacement with a heavier calibre, with media outlets publishing quotes from scout snipers claiming they were outgunned by the Taliban. Unfortunately, the short action chosen back in 1966 means that unlike the Army's M24, the rifle cannot be simply upgraded to .300 Winchester Magnum.

The USMC finally announced that the Corps would be receiving a new sniper rifle in 2019: the Mk 13 Mod7 that has seen much service with Navy SEAL Teams and other SOCOM units. The new rifle, chambered for the .300 Winchester Magnum, is being procured to supplement rather than replace the current generation M40A6 and A7 rifles currently in use across the Corps.

### M24/M2010

The M24 series is the US Army equivalent of the M40 series, again built from the civilian .308 (7.62 × 51mm) Remington 700, but remarkably presciently the Army chose the long action version, allowing the longer .300 Winchester Magnum to be chambered should they ever decide to switch calibres. In 2009, such an upgrade was begun, thanks in large part to the experiences of snipers in eastern Afghanistan. The resultant weapon had a new free-floating 24-inch barrel and a new

A US Marine scout sniper firing his 7.62 × 51mm M40A5 bolt-action sniper rifle fitted with sound suppressor. (*USMC, Cpl. Timothy Childers*)

A close up view of the action of the new .300 Winchester Magnum Mk 13 Mod7 adopted by the USMC. (*USMC, Cpl. Timothy Valero*)

The .300 Winchester Magnum M2010 of the US Army. (*US Army*)

skeletonized chassis with folding stock. The first examples reached Afghanistan in 2011 and has proved popular, particularly when mated with the improved Mk 248 ammunition.

## Future Trends

Whilst US SOCOM looks set to adopt the 6.5mm Creedmoor as their Precision Intermediate Caliber choice for gas operated semi-automatic platforms, most Western armies will remain with the 7.62 × 51mm for the foreseeable future. Russia and Russian supplied states will also stay with the 7.62 × 54mm which makes for an excellent long-distance round, although the issue of new semi-automatic .338s to their SOF is likely.

Canada is one country that has had a gestating sniper requirement for a number of years. They are in the market for two different platforms under their Sniper System Project. One is for a multi-calibre weapon following the modularity trend, the other for the Semi-Automatic Sniper Weapon (SASW), a semi-automatic spotter's rifle (that can be used by snipers if the terrain and task dictate).

A spokesperson noted:

> The purpose of the weapon is to provide our snipers with a lighter weapon that can be used to deliver a high volume of precise fire at a shorter range (such as in built-up areas), and for quick engagement on fleeting targets or for sniper team protection. The SASW is expected to receive the C20 designation (small arms weapons are numbered sequentially as they come into service). The SASW is a new capability as we do not have a semi-automatic precision rifle with scope and suppressor in service within the Canadian Army.

The Russians, never ones to shirk from innovation, are incorporating sniping into their Future Soldier programme known as Ratnik-2 and are testing a variety of sniper platforms to be integrated into the system including the SVDM

7.62 × 54mm bolt-action SV-98M sniper rifle that is replacing the SVD in Russian Army service. (*Kalashnikov Group/Kalashnikov Media*)

КАЛАШНИКОВ
MEDIA

7.62 × 54mm semi-automatic SVDS (Dragunov) with folding stock. (*Kalashnikov Group/Kalashnikov Media*)

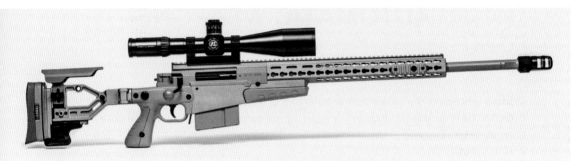

The latest Accuracy International .338 Lapua Magnum sniper rifle, the AXMC338 which is entering Belgian Army service. (*Accuracy International*)

7.62 × 54mm, the 9 × 39mm VSSM and the 12.7 × 97mm ASVKM. Kalashnikov Concern continue to innovate and have developed the Chukavin SVCh range of semi-automatic sniper rifles including a .338 Lapua Magnum variant that weighs just 6.3 kilograms which addresses one of the key challenges with previous semi-automatic weapons in this calibre.

In terms of anti-materiel rifles, Barrett have developed a 25 × 59mm version of their M82 design to give infantrymen a tool to tackle light armoured vehicles or to engage IEDs at a safe stand-off distance, but to date none have been publicly procured. The Austrian Steyr IWS 2000, chambered in the proprietary 15.2 × 169mm, is still under development and is aimed at a similar role. The ultimate in handheld destruction is the Chinese QLZ87B which, whilst being more of a grenade launcher, does feature a magnified optic and has an alleged range of 600 metres (surprisingly for a four-shot capacity grenade launcher, it only weighs 9.1 kilograms).

# CHAPTER SEVEN

# LIGHT MACHINE GUNS, LIGHT SUPPORT WEAPONS AND SQUAD AUTOMATIC WEAPONS

## Overview

During much of the twentieth century, the light or medium machine gun was an integral part of every infantry squad or section. German doctrine in the Second World War basically built their squads around the MG34 and later MG42 $7.92 \times 57$ medium machine gun. The riflemen were to protect the machine gun team and ferry ammunition for what was the principal casualty (and suppression) inflicting weapon.

Much has been written about the superiority of the MG34/42 series but the weapon family, and the doctrine, had its disadvantages. For one, it somewhat discouraged manoeuvre; for another the weapon's awe-inspiring rate of fire meant that keeping it fed was a full-time job. The rate of fire also meant that barrel changes were far more regular than comparative allied weapons. In a defensive role, the MG34/42 was unsurpassed. On the offensive, however, it lost many of its benefits. This is not to say the German weapon didn't have a disproportionate impact – it certainly did. Many British infantry memoirs note the distinctive sound of the MG42, so it certainly had a direct psychological impact, which as we have seen, is one part of the suppression equation.

The British light machine gun of the Second World War and into Korea (and even later when it was rechambered for $7.62 \times 51$mm) was the iconic Bren. Again, much commentary has been directed at its 30-round magazine and thus its suitability to suppress a target. It was also considered a very accurate weapon, probably too accurate for its intended role as machine guns should deliver a beaten zone of fire to suppress area targets. Riflemen should be engaging the point targets (individuals). It's worthwhile keeping this comment in mind when we discuss the British L86A1/A2 light support weapon (LSW), and to a lesser extent the USMC M27, in a moment.

Post-war, most armies developed and employed $7.62 \times 51$mm machine guns patterned to some degree on the German weapon. Some were essentially the MG42 like the Bundeswehr's MG3. Others, like the US M60, directly included elements from the MG42 (and the FG42 automatic rifle which was far more influential than is typically credited). The Russians moved in a different direction. Instead of a belt-fed medium machine gun, they took the AK47 and added a longer barrel, a folding bipod and designed extended 40-round magazines and 75-round drums. This was a far lighter and more portable weapon than its contemporaries, with reasonable accuracy (thanks to both the barrel length and the M43 round) and could be fired and maintained by a single soldier rather than manned by a two-man team like the M60 or MG3.

By all accounts, including a number of people who have been on the receiving end in recent years, the RPK does what it is intended to do – provide consistent, accurate, suppressive fire for the infantry squad out to 300 to 400 metres. The Russians also designed a true medium machine gun, the $7.62 \times 54$mm PK (and later PKM and PKP), although until relatively recently this was held in the infantry company's machine gun platoon.

By the 1980s, NATO was finally catching up and looked to replace in the infantry squad the M60, L7A2 GPMG and similar weapons with a man-portable light machine gun more in keeping with the RPK. The result was the Belgian $5.56 \times 45$mm Minimi which was adopted as the M249 SAW or squad automatic weapon by the US. The British embarked on the disastrous Small Arms for the 1980s programme which resulted in the L86A1 LSW. The trend throughout the 1980s and 1990s was for $7.62 \times 51$mm weapons to be held at company level, whilst a SAW or LSW was issued to each fire team.

The 1991 war in Kuwait saw little comment on the effectiveness of the SAW or LSW as it was predominantly an armoured affair with infantry firefights few and far between (although the notorious L85A1 or SA80 reinforced its poor reputation

A joint British Army and Afghan National Army (ANA) patrol is contacted by insurgents in Helmand Province, Afghanistan 2009. Note the British $5.56 \times 45$mm Minimi Para LMG (L110A2) and the ANA $7.62 \times 54$mm PK in the foreground. (*Open Government License v3.0, Dave Husbands*)

US Marines train Iraqi Army personnel in the use of the 'Al Quds' domestically produced 7.62 × 39mm RPK. The Iraqi Army fields both the 'Al Quds' which cannot feed from the Russian 75 round drum and a Romanian RPK copy. *(USMC, Lance Cpl. Jeremiah Murphy)*

during the conflict). It was not until the war in Afghanistan that significant issues were raised around the LSW, and later about the effectiveness of 5.56 × 45mm light machine guns outside of urban combat. The British rushed an order through for the Minimi, inexplicably ordering the short barrel Para version (despite their own Special Forces using the standard full-length barrel), whilst the Americans and their ISAF allies began to push their 7.62 × 51mm machine guns down to section and squad level. The British followed suit with the unofficial readoption of the GPMG at section level during the break-in battles in Helmand in 2006, as much as for the extra penetrative power of the 7.62 × 51mm as for the increased range.

In Iraq, there were few complaints about the SAW until the conflict had dragged on for a number of years and the SAWs were literally wearing out from multiple deployments affecting reliability. Although many American M249s experienced stoppages simply due to their age and well-worn working parts, other reliability issues were rare: *'We were told horror stories about 249s cooking off, or being a runaway gun. We received training on breaking the links to stop the weapon from cycling. I never saw it, and I never talked to anyone who saw it. I suspect it may have happened early on and the suspicion of a weapon firing from the open-bolt position kept*

The much-maligned British Army 5.56 × 45mm L86A2 light support weapon seen here with the recently adopted Elcan Specter optic and Shield CQB sight. The L86A2 was finally officially withdrawn from service in late 2018. (*Canadian Forces, Corporal Doug Burke*)

US Army soldiers returning fire in southern Baghdad, Iraq 2007. Note the 5.56 × 45mm M249 Para SAW with EOTech optic. His colleague fires a 5.56 × 45mm M4 with Trijicon ACOG.
(*US Air Force, Master Sgt. Jonathan Doti*)

*the stories going,*' explained Ron Dahlgren, a US Army veteran of both Iraq and Afghanistan.

Because of their size, the SAWs were far from ideal for house clearing. This is from a USMC lessons learned document on the battle of Fallujah:

> The assault element must contain no SAWs if that is possible. A SAW gunner must never clear rooms ... The support element will supplement the assault by falling in the stack and peeling off to clear rooms. A SAW gunner should be included in this section in order to provide massive firepower in the house if contact is made ... The support section will fall in the stack behind the assault element to assist in any way.

One American veteran of Iraq and Afghanistan from the 504th Parachute Infantry Regiment of the 82nd Airborne Division told the author: '*In CQB situations, [the] M249 is usually used as last man in to watch behind or to set up security outside the building. You don't want that many rounds flying around an enclosed area. You want accurate, controlled, well thought out shots.*' He added though that for suppressive fire, he felt that the SAW was a definite asset:

> M249 is essential to any infantry squad. Accuracy was spot on, reliability similar to M4. Definitely a suppressive fire weapon, it keeps heads down and allows us to maneuver undetected without having to reveal the presence of a larger weapons system such as an M240B or a M2 .50 cal.

A British soldier manning the 5.56 × 45mm L110A1 Minimi Para LMG in Helmand Province, Afghanistan 2007. Note that this is the earlier A1 which did not have the Picatinny rail on the receiver (the A2). *(ISAF, Corporal John Scott Rafoss)*

The British L110A2/A3 Minimi (known commonly as the LMG) is a curious case. In testing, as we will discuss in a moment, the weapon proves to be inaccurate at anything beyond 200 to 250 metres, however it is still popular with the infantrymen who have used it in combat. Some of this is undoubtedly psychological with the weapon providing an immediate morale boost upon contact: *'You could argue that the sound that it made was quite warming when in contact,'* conceded a serving British Army Helmand veteran to the author. Another mentioned, *'it was a great noise-maker'*.

The veteran also understood the Minimi's limitation:

As a tool for suppression the LMG was great, it gave a good rate of fire and aided with the ACOG sight was accurate to some degree. Other than a suppression weapon, the LMG was out of its depth. Accuracy was always talked about, but on Herrick and the environments we operated in, contacts would be short to medium range, where accuracy wasn't an issue. If we were engaged at longer range I would have doubts about the accuracy of the system.

\* \* \*

Combat experience has changed much of the thinking around the role of the machine gun and the nature of suppressive fire. The ineffectiveness of 5.56 × 45mm machine guns at ranges beyond several hundred metres, coupled with the successful introduction of the designated marksman rifle to service targets beyond the range of infantry assault rifles, has seen a dramatic move toward what one British officer called *'suppression through precision'*.

We will cover this idea in some depth later in the chapter but put simply this supports much of the operational research conducted since the Second World War which indicates that suppression is not solely about volume of fire. Accuracy is at least as important if not more so. As another Afghan veteran mentioned to the author: *'blazing away in the general direction doesn't really cut it'*.

The USMC has withdrawn the majority of their M249 SAWs from front-line service after just such a change in their thinking about the role of the weapon in combat. It has been replaced by the M27 IAR or Infantry Automatic Rifle (IAR), a variant of the 5.56 × 45mm HK416. Although some argue darkly that the M27 is simply a back-door way for the Corps to eventually replace their M4s with HK416s, the concept seems to be working in combat.

The genesis of the idea of the IAR dates back to a training exercise at Twenty-nine Palms, California. A senior Marine officer was observing Marine riflemen clearing a trench-line and queried why the M249 SAW wasn't used during the close quarter battle phase of the clearance. The reply was that the SAW was too heavy and unwieldy for such actions and it fired from an open bolt. The latter

A Spanish Marine tries his hand at the USMC issue 5.56 × 45mm M27 IAR based on the HK416. (*USMC*)

point is an interesting one and goes to the old Marine adage of never initiating an ambush with an open-bolt weapon like the SAW as there is a greater chance of a misfeed and stoppage.

From this humble beginning, the Infantry Automatic Rifle programme was born. The USMC trialled a number of weapons including the Colt 6940 IAR, based on the basic M4A1 platform but including what Colt described as a *'unique heat sink system [that] significantly reduces risk of cook-offs during extended periods of firing'* mounted under the barrel. This also aids in prolonging barrel life (as an aside, the Colt 6940 IAR has now been adopted by the Mexican Marines equipped with 100 round Beta C-Mags).

The other principal competitor was a variant of the Mk 16 SCAR-Light known as the HAMR (Heat Adaptive Modular Rifle) from Fabrique Nationale, a unique design which fires from both the open and closed bolt positions. For semi-automatic fire, the closed bolt action is used. For fully automatic bursts, the weapon is set to the open bolt position which allows the action to cool and reduces the chances of a cook-off or similar failure in high volume firing.

A thermal actuator mounted internally monitors the heat build-up and, as Fabrique Nationale explains, *'automatically transitions into open-bolt operation in semi-automatic or fully-automatic before reaching cook-off temperature for a chambered cartridge'*. The author suspects that this innovative system may well feature in the US Army's NGSAR programme.

Heckler and Koch's entry into the IAR programme, a variant of their proven HK416A5, famously won the competition largely thanks to its accuracy and reliability due to its piston operation which generates much less internal heat and reduces the amount of carbon build-up. By 2010, the first examples were in field trials topped with 3.5 power Trijicon ACOGs which the Marines refer to as the Squad Day Optic (SDO). For CQB shooting, the SDO scope is fitted with the Trijicon Ruggedized Miniature Reflex (RMR).

Marine riflemen have made first round hits with this combination of optic and weapon beyond 600 metres using the M855A1 in Afghanistan. USMC training dictates close range targets are engaged with short bursts whilst longer range suppression is conducted by aimed single shots. Much of the reasoning behind the IAR concept also fell to the very admirable objective of lightening the load of the infantryman. LMGs of whatever type incur significant weight penalties on the user. If research can show that accuracy trumps volume of fire, as the Marine Corps (and now the British Army, as we will see in a moment) seem to be saying, can the heavier LMG or SAW be replaced with such a rifle?

Part of the criticism of the M27 has been its limited 30-round magazine, particularly when viewed through the traditional prism of volume of fire equating to suppression. Interestingly, some Marines have been issued 60-round D-60 Magpul drum magazines as part of a trial programme. One Marine who served in Afghanistan with one of the first battalions to be issued the M27 noted that gunners carried twice the normal 210-round load carried by riflemen.

The British Army announced in 2018 that with a 'heavy heart', the L110A2/A3 Minimi LMG is being withdrawn from service. Note that the L86A2 is also being

An Australian infantryman in Uruzgan Province, Afghanistan 2008, armed with the 5.56 × 45mm F89 light support weapon. Note the MAG58 flash suppressor unique to Australian variants, the Elcan M145 optic and the 50-round soft pouch with AUSCAM pattern cover. He also carries a spare barrel on his day pack. (*Commonwealth of Australia*)

withdrawn but to no such soliloquy. The commander of the British Army's Infantry Trials and Development Unit (ITDU) argued that: *'We want to reduce the burden and there are better ways to provide suppression through precision.'*

According to a British Army report detailing the results from a three-year series of weapons trials known as the 'Platoon Combat Experiment' or PCE, with the aim of 'the optimum mix of weapons at platoon level', the Minimi did not fare well: *'In the first year of PCE it was found that 70 per cent of rounds fired from the LMG not only missed the target but missed by such a distance that they had no suppressive effect. This meant that over the course of a 72-hour series of battle runs each LMG gunner carried more than 20 kg of ammunition that did nothing more than make a noise.'* Rather damning stuff.

Even the Minimi's relevance in urban combat was called into question by the ITDU study:

The final year of PCE was focussed upon short range, close terrain fighting against moving targets. It was expected that the LMG would then come into its own, compensating for its inherent inaccuracy through its ability to fire bursts. However, the cumbersome size of the weapon is such that by the time the weapon is brought into the aim any fleeting target has already gone.

A US Marine fires a Singaporean 5.56 × 45mm Ultimax 100 Mark 3 LMG; it is fed from either 100-round drums or 30-round magazines as seen here. The weapon is known for its light recoil as its design ensures the bolt group does not impact with the back-plate of the receiver. It is employed by a small number of nations including Brunei, Peru and the Philippines. (*USMC, Sgt. Kowshon Ye*)

It must also be remembered that British Army Minimi stocks, like those of both the US Army and Marine Corps, are now feeling their age after heavy use in numerous overseas deployments. Although not explicitly stated by either the British Army or the USMC in their reasonings, this may well be another factor in the removal of the LMG/SAW from combat troops.

| | Calibre | Magazine | Weight Unloaded | Length |
|---|---|---|---|---|
| L110A2 | 5.56 × 45mm | 200/belt | 7.1kg | 908/762mm |
| L86A2 | 5.56 × 45mm | 30 | 6.1kg | 900mm |
| Mk 3 Maximi | 7.62 × 51mm | 100/200/belt | 8.8kg | 1,026/950mm |
| M249 | 5.56 × 45mm | 200/belt | 6.85kg | 1,004mm |
| Mk 46 | 5.56 × 45mm | 100/200/belt | 5.7kg | 908mm |
| MG4 | 5.56 × 45mm | 200/belt | 7.5kg | 1,005/810mm |
| Type 95 | 5.8 × 42mm | 30/75 | 3.95kg | 838mm |
| Negev | 5.56 × 45mm | 30/150/200 | 7.6kg | 1,002/780mm |
| Negev NG-7 | 7.62 × 51mm | 100/200 | 7.95kg | 1,100mm |
| RPK-74 | 5.45 × 39mm | 30/45 | 4.7kg | 1,065mm |
| RPK-16 | 5.45 × 39mm | 30/45/90 | 4.5kg | 1,080/830mm |

Czech Republic infantrymen during a NATO exercise in 2018. The soldier in the centre carries a 7.62 × 51mm FN Minimi 7.62 Mk 3 which replaced the 7.62 × 54mm vz.59. The other soldiers carry the 5.56 × 45mm CZ805A1 Bren assault rifle. (*Canadian Forces, eFP BG ROTO 10 LATVIA*)

The 5.56 × 45mm Negev in IDF hands in 2002 seen here with standard 200-round box magazine. The Negev is slowly being replaced by its 7.62 × 51mm variant, the Negev NG-7. (*Creative Commons, IDF*)

## Calibres and Ammunition

The vast majority of LMGs and LSWs are chambered for the 5.56 × 45mm – this makes much sense thanks to interoperability with the assault rifle carried by the rest of the section/squad. Newer high pressure 5.56 × 45mm loadings however have not been adopted without some challenges being overcome. The improved M855A1 for example, which we have previously detailed, has caused some durability issues with the USMC's M27 IARs.

This is not unexpected with such high-pressure ammunition with its exposed steel tip, and wear on the actions and barrels will typically be increased. For some time it appeared that the Mk 318 SOST, which had long been championed by both SOCOM and the Marines, would win out, however the M855A1 was formally adopted by the USMC for use in the M27 in December 2017.

A Marine Corps spokesperson explained: '*The M855A1 provides improved performance over the current M855, 5.56mm round in a lead-free form factor, and provides improved steel penetration, hard- and soft-target terminal effects, with more consistent terminal effects than the M855 at ranges out to 600 meters.*'

Despite the increased wear through the M27, the Marines stated that the M855A1 was still '*operationally suitable*' with the M27.

The future direction for LMGs and LSWs ammunition will be largely dependent on the Assault Machine Gun (AMG) and NGSW-AR programme. As the 6.5mm Creedmoor gains adherents within the US Army and SOCOM (with one spokesperson explaining that the 6.5mm Creedmoor will '*stay supersonic longer, have less wind drift and better terminal performance than 7.62mm ammunition*'), it may

5.56 × 45mm Caseless Telescoped ammunition (bottom); Cased Telescope (CT) (top) developed for the LSAT programme. (*US Army*)

also be being evaluated as a possible contender for the NGSW-AR. More likely, however, is an as yet unannounced 6.8mm chambering. It will be a non-traditional round in some form: *'The requirement is going to drive us to a new type of ammunition. It's going to have to be lighter. You can't just go out and get a brass type, which pushes us to a polymer or some type of steel or something I don't even know about yet,'* explained an Army spokesperson. A cased telescope (CT) round is the obvious contender but other options are being examined.

Much of the development in CT technology dates to an older programme – Lightweight Small Arms Technology or LSAT, now effectively replaced by the NGSW-AR programme – which saw both 5.56 × 45mm and 7.62 × 51mm CT rounds developed. A Textron AAI LSAT LMG prototype was tested extensively and looked to be the successor to the M249 until the ascendency of the NGSW-AR programme which builds upon its learnings.

The LSAT LMG offered a weight saving of over 40 per cent in terms of the 5.56 × 45mm CT ammunition. A spokesperson explained that the cased telescoped ammunition *'uses a strong plastic case instead of a traditional brass case'*. The LSAT LMG itself was also 3.75 kilograms lighter than the standard issue M249 SAW.

A US Army report was glowing about the LSAT LMG:

> Squads employing the LSAT CT Light Machine Gun had increases in lethality during short and long range engagements, improvements in speed of engagement and shot placement. Soldiers attributed better mobility to the machine gun's reduced size and weight in comparison to the current M249. Weight and recoil reduction provide more precise fires on the objective particularly when AR gunners are firing from standing and kneeling positions. Automatic Riflemen were able to move quicker because of the lighter weight, with a positive impact on key AR missions.

## Current Trends

As highlighted earlier, the biggest change in the field of LMGs has been the shift toward accuracy over volume in terms of suppression. This is not necessarily a new concept however: 'Accuracy versus rate of fire is also what the Australian Army has been practising for a long time. We were preaching the concept when I was a Recon Platoon Sergeant back in early 2000s mainly to conserve ammunition and ensure the target was engaged accurately,' explained veteran Nathan Vinson to the author.

The question of short versus longer barrels has also been a continuing question, particularly with relation to the British choice to go with the Para barrel for their Minimis. The author has pondered for years what the results would look like if the initial purchase of Minimis had come instead fitted with the full length 18 inch barrel (or even the longer Australian version) versus the Para length (13 inch). It seems so did the ITDU:

> In the belief that this inaccuracy was caused by the short barrel of the 'Para Minimi' we conducted the second year of PCE using the longer barrelled

The US 5.56 × 45mm M249 Para PIP squad automatic weapon. Note fabric pouch rather than hard plastic box, additional rails, collapsible stock and angled foregrip. (*US Army*)

version. We looked at would an increase in barrel length make the weapon more effective. However, once we analysed the data it transpired that the weapon was no more accurate even with the longer barrel.

William F. Owen commented to the author:

The story of how the Minimi got into British Army service is pretty farcical. Regardless of who did what and why they ended up with a 5.56mm weapon with 13-inch barrel that really added nothing but weight to the section. It can't punch CRISAT at 400m! Now it's not useless, but there are far better choices for the accumulated weight versus the effect on the target. Even opting for the 18 inch barrel or a 20 inch would have added a bit of whack.

The latest news on the British Army decision on the Minimi is that it is in the process of being retired and that three 7.62 × 51mm L7A2 GPMGs will be issued to each infantry platoon. It is not currently clear if these will be held by the support company and issued as necessary or if the GPMGs will be organic to the infantry platoons. The L86A2 has not received the A3 upgrade and is also being retired. British infantry sections for the foreseeable future will be equipped with one L129A2 marksman rifle, two underslung grenade launchers and one GPMG based on the above information. The other members of the section will carry the standard L85A3.

The French Army are aiming to replace their stocks of 5.56 × 45mm Minimis with either a mix of 5.56 × 45mm and 7.62 × 51mm calibre platforms or solely with a 7.62 × 51mm weapon. Two hundred or so Maximi 7.62 × 51mm LMGs were purchased for service in Afghanistan as an urgent operational requirement,

The original issue 5.56 × 45mm L110A1 Minimi Para LMG with SUSAT fixed power optic in 2006. *(Open Government License v3.0, Harland Quarrington)*

which seems to indicate that the Belgian weapon may be in the running with a better than fair chance in the 7.62 × 51mm requirement.

In 2005, the Bundeswehr adopted the 5.56 × 45mm MG4 to replace the ageing but reliable MG3 in 7.62 × 51mm, a direct descendant of the wartime MG42. The lack of any 7.62 × 51mm weapons in the German infantry squad saw a return of refurbished and scoped G3s as DMRs and the MG3 take the place of the MG4, although the 5.56 × 45mm weapon was considered a reliable and effective light machine gun at shorter ranges. The MG4 was supplemented in Afghanistan by a number of bipod-equipped G36s with drum magazines, although these were apparently not the LMG36 with heavier barrel offered by Heckler and Koch.

A superb close up of the Canadian issue 5.56 × 45 C9A2 LMG with Elcan M145 optic. Note the low infrared signature coating. *(Kelly Stumpf, Colt Canada)*

The Germans also adopted the HK417 in a variant known as the G27 which according to the German Army is *'a heavy fully automatic assault rifle and complements the armament of the infantry squad. Equipped with a riflescope with fourfold magnification and a reflex sight, it can still be effective beyond the reach of the G36 due to the larger caliber.'*

Bear in mind that the Bundeswehr has also adopted the HK417 (in semi-auto only) as their DMR in the form of the G28E2. The G27 has been deployed in Afghanistan and in use since 2011 in a similar manner to the USMC's M27 – as a light automatic rifle and as a defacto DMR. The intent seems to have been to again increase the number of 7.62 × 51mm platforms in the squad and the G27 appeared to have largely replaced both the G3 and the MG4 in Afghanistan. Part of the reason seems to have been the penetrative qualities of the 7.62 × 51mm but even it struggled firing through mud brick Afghan compound walls.

India may be finally adopting a new LMG after several years of extended, and confusing, procurement challenges. The design selected will be a commercial off-the-shelf offering to speed deployment of the weapon. With the licencing deal with IWI, the Negev seems to be the preferred option, but as with all Indian small arms procurements, only time will tell (maybe!).

The current in-service 5.56 × 45mm INSAS weighs in at 6.23 kilograms and features a fixed barrel (and rather bizarrely a grenade launcher attachment). The new Indian LMG needs to be lighter weight and to have increased range out to 1,000 metres (one Indian account rather generously states that the current INSAS has an effective range of 700 metres which may be just a slight overestimate!). To reach those sort of distances a 7.62 × 51mm design is more likely and luckily IWI produce exactly the weapon, the Negev NG-7, although it weighs in at a kilogram more than the INSAS.

The Russian Army is adopting the new 5.45 × 39mm RPK-16 based on the AK-12 assault rifle from 2018. The RPK-16 features a quick-change barrel, facilitating extended suppressive fire and fires from a closed bolt. Two barrel lengths are available, with the shorter 14.5-inch designed for urban combat and the standard 19.6-inch for more open battlefields. For portage of the weapon in tight spaces like the back of an APC, it is sensibly equipped with a side folding stock.

The replacement for the Russian RPK-74, the 5.45 × 39mm RPK-16, shown here with compact barrel. (*Kalashnikov Group/Kalashnikov Media*)

The biggest shake-up in the field of LMGs is not surprisingly the American NGSW-AR programme which has set ambitious goals:

It will combine the firepower and range of a machine gun with the precision and ergonomics of a rifle, yielding capability improvements in accuracy, range, and lethality. The weapon will be lightweight and fire lightweight ammunition, improving soldier mobility, survivability, and firing accuracy.

The programme requires a whopping 20 per cent minimum reduction in ammunition weight.

## Individual Weapon Summaries
### Minimi (M249, Mk 46, F89, L110A2/A3)
We have covered the Minimi in some detail already. Suffice to say, despite its retirement from the British Army and 'quasi retirement' from the US Marine Corps, the weapon is still popular and widely employed by many armies around the world.

The Serbian Army is one of the latest to acquire the 5.56 × 45mm Minimi as a replacement for its domestically-produced 7.62 × 39mm Zastava M72 based on the Russian RPK and the Zastava 7.62 × 51mm M77. The Danes have also adopted the Minimi in limited numbers based on their experiences in Afghanistan, but it

The Canadian Minimi variant, the 5.56 × 45mm C9A2. The Canadian Army notes: 'The C9A2 is an upgrade from the C9 and C9A1 LMGs. This upgrade provides low infrared signature, a foldable and extendable 4-position butt, a cover with a longer rail mount and adjustable rear sight assembly [and] a short barrel assembly with folding handle.' (USMC)

The 5.56 × 45mm Colt Canada LSW which was issued to Danish troops in Afghanistan with the notoriously unreliable Beta C-Mag. (*Kelly Stumpf, Colt Canada*)

appears to have been eclipsed in infantry sections by the new 7.62 × 51mm M60E6 which we will detail in the next chapter.

Danish troops previously carried a Colt LSW (essentially a heavy-barrel M16 with bipod) known as the M/04 issued with 100-round Beta C-Mags that were unreliable at best. So common were stoppages with the C-Mags that the LSW was often replaced in the field by a standard assault rifle, meaning that Danish sections were typically operating with one 7.62 × 51mm MG62 (another descendant of the MG42) and the rest with rifles – a second MG62 might be carried if available but these were obviously at a premium.

The Minimi is also in service with Australia (as the F89), Belgium (M2 and M3 Para), Canada (as the C9A2), France, Italy, Japan (where it is produced under licence), Malaysia, Netherlands, Norway, Slovenia and Turkey, amongst many others.

The Australian Army still issues its version of the 5.56 × 45mm Minimi as the F89 Light Support Weapon, however, on recent tours to Afghanistan, the F89 has been largely replaced by its up-gunned cousin as noted by Nathan Vinson:

> The F89 was not taken on deployment post 2012, at least not with the infantry. It was replaced by the time of my [2012] tour by the Maximi which is the 7.62mm variant of the F89. The reason for the change was similar to the Brits, the F89 just did not have the range or penetration power required for open warfare experienced in Afghanistan and Iraq. I do not think there were any infantry soldiers on the selection panel when they decided to remove 7.62mm MGs [MAG58s] from the infantry sections for, as you know, they have now been brought back into service with the infantry battalions as of 2012.

Vinson additionally commented about the Australian Army experience when the F89 was issued with a longer 22-inch barrel:

> One of the main issues with the F89 is in later years [was] they replaced the open sites with a scope [ELCAN C79 or Wildcat] which was a disaster for engaging targets over 300 meters as there was no way of adjusting the sights.

An ANA soldier firing the US-supplied 5.56 × 45mm M249 PIP with full-length barrel and rigid plastic stock. Picatinny rails have been added and a vertical foregrip mounted. (*ISAF*)

Secondly, the round tended to tumble after 400 meters and thus reduced accuracy and penetration. It basically did not have the punch we in the infantry required to engage and kill the enemy.

The Mk 3 Minimi, or Maximi as it is referred to by Australian soldiers, has been filling the gap in a number of armies. Even the British purchased a small number for operations in Afghanistan, although these all appeared to have been issued to Special Forces. Along with the Australians, the 7.62 × 51mm Mk 48 variant (the FN Mk 3) has been purchased by the Czech Republic where it is replacing their 7.62 × 54mm vz.59 medium machine guns.

The Mk 48 variant was first developed at the behest of American SOF who wanted both a lighter medium machine gun and a SAW with more range, although it was first conceived in 2003 as a replacement for the M60E4 then being operated by the Navy SEALS. Proving popular, limited numbers were eventually issued to regular infantry units operating in Afghanistan as a supplement to their M240G medium machine guns (the Mk 48 being 30 per cent lighter than the standard 240G).

The issue of the Mk 48 also led to the field expedient innovation of a new feeding system, nicknamed the 'Iron Man' as the soldier who invented the Predator-style ammunition backpack explained:

The ammunition sacks that came with it [the Mk 48] made it too cumbersome and heavy to carry over long, dismounted patrols and especially when climbing mountains. Initially, we came up with using 50-round belts and just reloading constantly, which led to lulls of fire and inefficiency.

We wondered why there wasn't some type of dismounted CROWS (Common Remote Operating Weapons Station) that fed our machine guns instead of a minigun as portrayed in the movie. So, I decided to try it using the feed chute assembly off of the vehicle CROWS. We glued a piece of wood from an ammo crate inside the ammo cans to create the decreased space necessary so the rounds would not fall in on each other. My Mk 48 gunners who also had input to the design and evaluation, took it to the range and tested it, and even with its initial shortcomings, it was much better than the current TTP (tactics, techniques and procedures) we employed. On Feb. 26, 2011, our prototype 'Ironman' pack even saw its first combat use … when our squad was ambushed by up to fifty fighters in a river valley, and it worked great!'

A refined version of the *'Iron Man'* backpack is now in limited issue to squad machine gunners in the US Army.

The 7.62 × 51mm Mk 48 based Fabrique Nationale Minimi 7.62 or Maximi as it is commonly known in Australian service. This Maximi mounts an EOTech optic, note also the 1-in-5 tracer in the belts. The Maximi was introduced into service in Afghanistan and is retained alongside the F89 and MAG58 by Australian forces. (*Commonwealth of Australia, Sgt. W. Guthrie*)

## L86A2 LSW

The much maligned LSW is known far more commonly within the British Army as the 'Crow Cannon'. 'Crows' is the nickname for junior soldiers who have yet to prove themselves with their section and thus are often relegated to carrying this most hated of weapon systems.

For a number of years it was regularly dusted off to serve as a poor man's DMR and to act as a de-facto Minimi, particularly in Iraq, when the LMG was in short supply. Both the L85A1 rifle and the LSW were elements of the grandiosely named Small Arms for the 1980s programme. For its original role, it was a poorly conceived and constructed weapon that should never have seen service. Entire books have been written on the debacle of the SA80 series of small arms and the interested reader is directed to Steve Raw's *The Last Enfield – SA80: The Reluctant Rifle* and Matthew Ford's *Weapon of Choice: Small Arms and the Culture of Military Innovation* to further understand the programme that spawned these weapons.

The LSW was intended originally to replace the 7.62 × 51mm L7A2 GPMG at section level, a change that never took place due to the poor reliability, regular parts breakages and limited 30-round magazine of the long-barrel LSW. Like the L85A1, it was praised for its accuracy and indeed a number of studies have proven its effectiveness in this department out to an astonishing 800 metres when deployed from the bipod, however the weapon soon lost the confidence of the soldiers assigned it. Indeed, as a DMR with the right optics provided, it could do the job, however its length and its poor reputation meant that it was never fully adopted for this role.

In fact, in the early years of Operation Herrick in Afghanistan, a marksman was appointed in each infantry platoon to provide a designated marksman ability. He was armed with the bolt-action 7.62 × 51mm L96A1, a sniper rifle that had largely been replaced by the .338 Lapua Magnum L115A3. The L96A1 was hardly ideal for the role as the platoons often found themselves fighting in close quarters and a good argument could be made that the LSW would have been a better selection.

When the Minimi was purchased as an Urgent Operational Requirement for Afghanistan in 2001, the LSW was relegated to the bench, with section machine

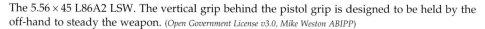

The 5.56 × 45 L86A2 LSW. The vertical grip behind the pistol grip is designed to be held by the off-hand to steady the weapon. (*Open Government License v3.0, Mike Weston ABIPP*)

gunners overwhelmingly showing a preference for the Belgian LMG. Of course, the Minimi, as we discussed earlier, has had something of an interesting history itself with UK forces, but never suffered the derision reserved for the LSW.

Even after the Heckler and Koch upgrade programme which saw the L85A2 slowly begin to regain the confidence of its users, the upgraded L86A2 was still a rare sight on the battlefield. British infantry sections in Afghanistan instead carried multiple Minimis and often a GPMG on patrol. L85A2s were occasionally encountered at static security positions, but most remained in the arms room.

The improvements to the L85A2 further led to the downfall of the LSW. A recent British Army study at the Infantry Trials Unit spelled out the deficiencies with the L86A2. According to respected operational researcher Jim Storr:

> For years there has been a belief that the long barrel and bipod of the LSW provided it with superior accuracy to the SA80. Indeed, some of the initial work in the first year of PCE supported this. However, work conducted by ITDU and the Royal Marines has shown that the SA80 with a down grip/ bipod is just as accurate as the LSW in most situations and indeed at certain ranges is more accurate. Furthermore, in snap and unsupported shooting scenarios and the close confines of urban fighting the LSW is much slower to bring to bear.

Where the L86A2 shone was in its accuracy, particularly versus the short-barrelled Minimi:

> L86 magazine fed SA80 Light Support Weapon (LSW), with its bipod, is extremely good at suppressing targets out to 500m or more and, in conjunction with L85 rifles, keeping them suppressed. That is principally because it is accurate enough for almost every shot fired to contribute to suppression.
>
> The L110 (Minimi) Light Machine Gun (LMG) performs far worse in such trials. At best, only the first shot of a short burst passes close enough to suppress. However, subsequent shots in that burst go anything up to 6m wide of the mark at battlefield ranges. Since perhaps 3 to 5 rounds in 3 to 5 seconds are required to suppress, a typical LMG gunner will rarely achieve suppression. He would have to fire 3 to 5 bursts in as many seconds to do so. Furthermore, since only the first round typically passes near enough, he would have to fire a burst every 3 seconds or so to keep the target suppressed. That takes much more ammunition than a mixture of SA80 Rifle and LSW alone.

### Negev

The Negev series of machine guns are an Israeli design with the base 5.56 × 45mm model developed as a replacement for the unpopular 5.56 × 45mm Galil ARM automatic rifle and the 7.62 × 51mm MAG58 at the squad level. Adopted by the IDF in 1997, the 5.56 × 45mm Negev version was replaced by the 7.62 × 51mm NG-7 variant beginning in 2014.

The weapon is available in both a standard and compact version (18-inch versus 13-inch barrel). Both feature chrome-lined barrels and a side folding stock. The Negev offers an adjustable gas regulator which allows the reliable use of Galil and

A great detail view of the Israeli 5.56 × 45mm Negev LMG. Note the unusual placement of the additional Picatinny rail on the barrel, likely for a weapon light or infrared illuminator.
(*Creative Commons, Zachi Evenor*)

M16 pattern magazines, although the latter requires an adapter. The Georgian Army for instance also uses the 5.56 × 45mm Negev although with STANAG rifle magazines to supplement their 7.62 × 54mm PKMs.

## Ameli

The Ameli is a 5.56 × 45mm light machine gun designed by CETME, often with a British SUSAT optic mounted on the receiver. It serves as the Spanish infantry squad automatic weapon at the rate of one per fire team. The Ameli (in Spanish the *Ametralladora ligera* or 'light machine gun') is unusual in that it visually resembles the MG42 but in the lighter calibre of 5.56 × 45mm. For an LMG, it has one major failing in that it does not accept box magazines and instead is fed from disintegrating link belts like a medium machine gun. The Ameli has also been criticised for the poor quality of its build components which has led to a reputation for unreliability. Spanish soldiers serving in both Iraq and Afghanistan stated a preference for their 7.62 × 51mm MG42/59, principally for its reliability.

## M27

As with the Minimi, we have already discussed the M27 to some significant level of detail. A friend of the author, noted firearms authority Miles Vining, was kind enough to allow reproduction of his thoughts on the experience of his Marine unit in Helmand Province using the M27 for the first time, previously published in the excellent *Small Arms Defense Journal* (www.sadefensejournal.com):

> Of the engagements involving 1/9 Marines, the M27 proved to be worthy and reliable. Most took place beyond a hundred or more meters and against small numbers of insurgents. The need to establish superior firepower was often not necessary. But this did not mean the M27 gunners brought any less ammunition on patrols. While the combat load for Marine riflemen with M16A4s is a standard six magazines in pouches and one in the rifle, M27 gunners loaded twice or more.
>
> Replacing a belt fed, quick-change barrel, light machine gun with a magazine fed, fixed barrel automatic rifle reflects the changing nature of the

Full automatic fire from the USMC's 5.56 × 45mm M27 IAR, this example mounting a Harris bipod and Trijicon ACOG, the Corps' standard combat optic. (*USMC, Sgt. Justin A. Bopp*)

Close-up of the USMC 5.56 × 45mm M27 IAR on the firing line. (*USMC, Lance Cpl. Luke Hoogendam*)

American military. This has already been experienced by many countries such as the UK with the L86 LSW, Russia with the RPK and China with the QBZ series.

Similar to the reduction of caliber from the 7.62 M14 to the 5.56 M16A1 or the replacement of the M1911A1 by the Beretta M9, this transition is still in its infant stages of development and use. Some years of full procurement and understanding how to fully apply it tactically are currently in the making. This change has many, especially within the Marine Infantry community, bemoaning the loss of the venerable SAW to a fundamentally different weapon. As did many over the M9 and M16A1. Throughout its first deployments with 1/9 and 1/3 [however] it has served its users well.

## Future Trends

Jim Storr noted that the basis for procurement of any infantry weapon, but specifically light machine guns, should be on a common-sense approach: 'They should be procured on the basis of the effect they create. That is a combination of killing individuals (which happens only rarely) and suppressing targets. Suppression is a critical element of infantry combat, largely because of what it enables.' Hopefully the Next Generation Squad Automatic Weapons Automatic Rifle programme can deliver this.

A Chinese PLA Marine firing the issue 5.8 × 42mm Type 95 light support weapon fed from a 75-round drum. (*Chinese Navy, Wenxuan Zhuliang*)

NGSW-AR at the time of writing has five manufacturers in the running; FN America, General Dynamics, PCP Tactical, SIG Sauer and Textron. Textron was the principal contractor involved in the earlier LSAT programme and as such probably has a significant advantage, although less so if the eventual ammunition chosen is not CT.

The specifications for the NGSW-AR stated a 20 per cent ammunition weight reduction when compared to conventional brass-cased rounds, an effective sound suppressor and a reduction in muzzle flash over the M249 it will eventually replace.

PCP Tactical have developed polymer cased ammunition for the .50 and .300 for SOCOM and thus may deliver a similar 6.5mm round. General Dynamics are thought to be developing an M240 or Mk 48 based platform, likely firing a CT version of the .338 Norma Magnum, although this is largely conjecture. Fabrique Nationale may enter a version of their HAMR that featured in the earlier USMC IAR trials.

SOCOM and Joint Special Operations Command are still both working toward a '6.5mm Assault Machine Gun' (AMG) which would likely use the 6.5mm Creedmoor that is being adopted for their Mk 20 and M110A1 rifles. If the NGSW-AR is adopted with a CT round this would mean SOF using a traditional round in the AMG whilst the infantry use the CT, which seems to go against any effort to simplify the logistics chain. The new SOCOM weapon could simply be a rechambered Mk 48 which in itself is a 7.62 × 51mm version of the 5.56 × 45mm Minimi (also available in an SOF modified and lightened version- the Mk 46).

The arguments to and for a 5.56 × 45mm or 7.62 × 51mm light machine gun will continue, as they do with assault rifles. William F. Owen sees two possible futures:

> The iron bar solution is to get a new-form 7.62mm LMG, such as the Negev NG7 or the Minimi 7.62 and put it back into the section in one of the fire teams or revert to the Gun Group Rifle Group which worked so well. This is

The US 7.62 × 51mm Mk 48 Mod0, recognizable from the Mk 48 Mod1 due to its rigid plastic stock rather than collapsible M4-type. (*US Army*)

where platoon and section organisation start to impinge on small arms issues and very few people have studied or understood the relationships.

Doug Beattie agreed from a British Army perspective:

> Never a fan of the LMG or the LSW although it [the L86A2] has better accuracy. Again there are some pros and cons; working in small groups, the LMG was really useful for close level protection and gave the appearance of more firepower and enable the ability to create fire lines to enable movement but it really is inaccurate and unreliable. I would rather have two GPMGs per section or return to the days of gun group and rifle group for each section.

The author will leave the last word on the subject to seasoned former Australian infantry NCO and sniper, Nathan Vinson who succinctly sums up the cyclical nature of small arms thinking:

> I do think we in the West tend to go in circles with regards to the type of weapons we carry within the rifle section. This can be seen with comparisons going back to the Second World War. British infantry sections for fire support carried the Bren – accurate yes, but limited on the ability to supress the enemy as it did not have a beaten zone or cone of fire, plus limited carriage of ammunition. However, the German equivalent carried the MG42, which had a higher rate of fire and a beaten zone.
>
> The British then in the 50s or early 60s brought into service the GPMG, or as they were called the MAG58, and we brought in the M60. Both great weapons that allowed the infantry section to increase their ability to supress the enemy and win the firefight at greater ranges. Then, at some time in the mid to late 90s, someone thought it would be a great idea to replace the 7.62mm weapon platforms with 5.56mm. The Brits did the same and got rid of the belt feed MGs from infantry sections and replaced them with the heavy barrelled SA80 equivalent. Crazy.

## Breaking News

As this book was being completed, the US Army issued a new requirement for the NGSW programme, pertaining to both the NGSW-AR and the NGSW-R. It outlines that the new platforms need to utilize 'Government provided 6.8 millimeter projectiles'. The new round appears to be type classified the XM1186 but little more is known as details regarding the ammunition is still on close hold to contractors only – the only reference is to a '6.8MM GENERAL PURPOSE (GP)'.

What we can glean from the government documentation is interesting but frustratingly incomplete with no detail on size and weight requirements, let alone any detail on the 6.8mm round. Consider that an earlier NGSW requirements document noted: '5.56mm Cased Telescoping Ammunition', '6.5mm Cased Telescoping Ammunition' and '7.62mm Cased Telescoping Ammunition' and we now have a new calibre stipulation. Rumours seem to indicate a high velocity 125-grain projectile based on the M855A1.

In the meantime, at least we have something of a working definition of both the NGSW-AR and NGSW-R:

- 'NGSW-R' refers to a prototype 6.8 millimeter rifle with sling, flash hider, suppressor, cleaning kit, flash hider/suppressor removal tool, and quantities of magazines required to provide a minimum of 210 stowed rounds.
- 'NGSW-AR' refers to a prototype 6.8 millimeter automatic rifle with bi-pod, sling, flash hider, suppressor, cleaning kit, flash hider/suppressor removal tool, and quantities of magazines/drums/belts/other required to provide a minimum of 210 stowed rounds.

One other pertinent point is that the new NGSW-AR needs to be able to 'provide interchangeable magazines between both weapons if NGSW-AR utilizes a magazine'. Readers will be reminded of the poor showing of the use of STANAG M16 magazines in the M249. Use of rifle magazines in the SAW was hindered by stoppages and the procedure was only recommended for in-extremis use. Hopefully the NGSW-AR will iron out any such issues prior to adoption.

The Textron AAI LSAT LMG prototype firing 5.56 × 56 CT ammunition. (*US Army*)

# CHAPTER EIGHT

# SUPPORT WEAPONS

## Overview

Along with their personal weapons, infantry soldiers also have access to a range of support weapons systems ranging from medium and general-purpose machine guns (GPMGs) to light mortars and rockets. Within this volume, primarily for reasons of space, we will restrict ourselves to the discussion of those machine guns and touch upon the humble grenade launcher.

During the Second World War, medium machine guns (MMGs) were typically of the same calibre as the standard infantry rifle and/or light machine gun. The Vickers was a good example, although some would term it a heavy machine gun as it was tripod-mounted. The definition of medium versus heavy is normally, however, based on calibre. A .50BMG Browning M2 or 12.7mm DShK is a heavy machine gun. A 7.62 × 54mm MG3 is, by comparison, a medium machine gun.

After the war, with the advent of the light machine gun (drawing from the US automatic rifle concept around the BAR), medium machine guns were normally of a heavier calibre than the LMG carried by the infantry squads or sections.

Estonian soldiers firing the 7.62 × 51mm Rheinmetall MG3 during a NATO exercise. The MG3 and MAG58 serve as the Estonian issue medium machine guns. (*US Army, Sgt. 1st Class Joshua S. Brandenburg*)

A good example is in Russian infantry platoons with the 7.62 × 39mm RPK which was issued at squad level. Their heavier machine gun, the 7.62 × 54mm PK and later PKM, was held at the company weapons platoon and either grouped for a particular operation or parcelled out to the platoons, dependent on need.

Similar organisational thinking still applies in many armies, although after the Afghan and Iraq wars 7.62 × 51mm machine guns are finding their way into the infantry section either through up-gunned versions of LMGs like the Maximi, or being pushed down from the weapons platoon. In the latter case, it will require some organisational consideration to decide what happens to the role, and tactical capability, formerly held by these MMGs. Section level MMGs will likely rarely see training in indirect fire or the use of sustained fire tripods which are things the gunners in competent weapons excel at.

At the squad or section level, the MMG provides a similar capability to the LMG – to establish a base of fire to suppress an enemy allowing manoeuvre against him. It can, and is, also used to establish fire dominance during an ambush or meeting engagement due to its rate of fire that can rarely be matched by any other weapon. It also provides a significant morale boost. A serving British Army Afghan vet explained to the author: '*GPMG was awesome and a battle winner, the TB* [Taliban] *hated it, and would try and target the GPMG gunner. Very effective, even the sound of it would have an effect both on the TB and our own troops.*'

A US Army 7.62 × 51mm M240L in action on an M192 tripod. (*US Army, Staff Sgt. Pablo N. Piedra*)

The 5.56 × 45mm L85A2 mounting the 40mm L123A3 UGL or under-barrel grenade launcher and newly issue Specter optic and Wilcox Rapid Acquisition Aiming Module (RAAM) grenade fire control system. (*Open Government License v3.0, Steve Dock*)

The grenade launcher, either in standalone or underslung mode, provides a similar suppressive capability with the added bonus of indirect fire or is very useful against enemy in firing positions with no overhead cover. The same soldier noted: '*UGL* [Underbarrel grenade launcher] *was also a great system and was used to great effect on tree lines and bun lines* [a line of vegetation/scrub] *with thick undergrowth to target the TB.*' Every positive must come with a negative and the grenade launcher is still a high explosive weapon and as such some targets are off-limits, a fact the British Army recognised: '*UGL has also been effective in*

A US Army soldier armed with the issue 5.56 × 45mm M4A1 carbine with Trijicon ACOG and underslung 40mm M320A1 launcher. Note the extended grenade sights atop the forearm. (*US Army, Staff Sgt. Pablo N. Piedra*)

*heavy TiCs* [Troops in Contact]*, but due to collateral damage and accuracy limitations has not been used in the large numbers first envisaged.'*

The weapon actually has a fairly recent history. Although grenade launcher devices affixed to infantry rifles have been in use since the First World War, a reliable, dedicated grenade launcher that was infantry portable only came into being during the Vietnam War. The 40mm XM148 and later XM203 were developed into the M203 toward the latter stages of the war.

Since then the M203 has served in every fire team in the United States Army and Marines and within many armies around the world. The Russians developed a number of similar types including the 40mm BG-15 and BG-25 (the Russians even produced a silenced version – the 30mm BS-1). Multi-shot 40mm launchers

|  | Calibre | Magazine | Weight Unloaded | Length |
|---|---|---|---|---|
| MAG58 | 7.62 × 51mm | Belt | 11.8kg | 1,260mm |
| M240B | 7.62 × 51mm | Belt | 12.5kg | 1,231mm |
| M240L | 7.62 × 51mm | Belt | 10.1kg | 1,231mm |
| MG3 | 7.62 × 51mm | Belt | 11.0kg | 1,225mm |
| MG5 | 7.62 × 51mm | Belt | 12.3kg | 1,202/960mm |
| PKM | 7.62 × 54mm | Belt | 7.5kg | 1,192mm |
| PKP | 7.62 × 54mm | Belt | 8.2kg | 1,164mm |

The venerable 40mm M79 which dates from the Vietnam War. The M79 was replaced by the M203 which was itself replaced by the M320 and M320A1. Many soldiers still consider the M79 a more accurate platform for launching grenades. (*USMC, Cpl Justin T. Updegraff*)

A New Zealand Army soldier firing the Canadian 5.56 × 45mm C7A2 with underslung 40mm M203. *(USMC, Sgt. Sarah Dietz)*

The Danish 7.62 × 51mm M60E6 with Elcan M145 optic which replaced their MG3 based MG62. *(US Army, Spc. Hubert D. Delany III)*

are now far more common, with most based on an original South African Armscorp/Milkor design. The USMC for instance issues the M32A1 which operates from a 6-round rotary drum. The British Army are currently trialling a similar platform.

## Calibres and Ammunition

Medium and general-purpose machine guns are of only two calibres – the NATO standard 7.62 × 51mm and the Russian 7.62 × 54mm. The future of at least NATO-compatible machine guns is probably going to be based on the .338 Norma Magnum calibre. Its 300-grain round is reported to be effective to ranges of 1,700 meters, dwarfing the 7.62 × 51mm and overmatching the 7.62 × 54mm.

The only fly in the ointment is the NGSW which may announce a machine gun component based on a 6.8mm round. This is unlikely as publicly-available documentation only refers to a rifle, DMR and AR variants. Textron, one of the primary contractors on the NGSW, has completed extensive work on 7.62 × 51mm cased telescoped ammunition during the earlier LSAT programme. It progressed to the point of unveiling a prototype weapon which weighed in at an impressive 6.6 kilograms. The weapon was designed to be able to be easily rechambered for the 6.5mm CT under development.

In straightforward comparison, the 6.5mm CT outperforms the 7.62 × 51mm in all areas although crucially, like any new ammunition, we have no actual data on how it performs against human targets, but all indications are that it will outperform the 7.62 × 51mm in this regard too. In fact, it appears to maintain its velocity for longer than the 7.62 × 51mm at extended ranges, meaning that 6.5mm CT rounds should fragment more consistently; all of this in a cartridge a third lighter.

Contractors working for SOCOM are fine-tuning polymer .338 Norma Magnum rounds (and for the .50BMG) and have recently issued their own requirement for lightweight ammunition for its machine guns. The 2018 requirements call for a minimum 40 per cent reduction in weight and offerings are required in both 7.62 × 51mm and the .338 Norma Magnum, the clearest indication yet that SOCOM will be transitioning to a platform for the Norma cartridge in the near

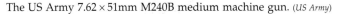

The US Army 7.62 × 51mm M240B medium machine gun. (*US Army*)

future. The SOCOM requirement calls for '*innovative belt link cartridge cases that are significantly lighter than brass cases and have increased internal volume, pressure ratings, corrosion resistance, long term storage, and structural integrity to withstand belt feed in machine guns and high rate of fire mini-guns*'.

The .338 Norma Magnum will likely be seen in the next generation M240L/ Mk 48 whilst the replacement for the Mk 46, as we have noted in the previous chapter, will likely fire the 6.5mm Creedmoor, if not the similar .260 Remington or .264 USA. The problem with the 6.5 Creedmoor as it stands today is that it causes far more wear and tear on barrels and working parts, requiring a new barrel to be fitted somewhere between 7,000 and 10,000 rounds, roughly half that of the life of a 7.62 × 51mm barrel in a M240 series weapon. This is not an issue with competing calibres like the .264 USA, but with SOCOM adopting the 6.5mm Creedmoor for its sniper support rifles, the likelihood as explained in the last chapter will be a 6.5mm Creedmoor for their Assault Machine Gun.

With regard to grenade launchers, 40mm and specifically the longer 40 × 51mm Medium Velocity, will increasingly be the most common type. The longer casing allows for greater ranges than the traditional 40 × 46mm Low Velocity – some designs can extend engagement ranges for a handheld or underbarrel launcher to 800 metres. The disadvantage with the newer MV rounds is their increased recoil which makes them more difficult to fire from lighter launchers like the M320 (they were also too long to fit into the breech of the older M203 design).

Reloading the side-opening 40mm M320A1 grenade launcher issued by the US Army and Marine Corps. This design allows for the use of a wider variety of grenade types and is easier to use than the M203. (*US Army, Sgt. 1st Class Teddy Wade*)

The 40mm M79's break-open design meant a simple process for reloading in comparison to the M203. (*USMC, Cpl Justin T. Updegraff*)

The German firm Rheinmetall has introduced a compromise in the form of the Low Velocity Extended Range (LVER) 40mm round designed specifically for the likes of the M320. Another way around the recoil issue with MV rounds is launcher designs like the Rheinmetall Cerberus which can reduce recoil by a fifth thanks to an innovative buffering system. Other designs are incorporating air burst fuses that can be dialled in to specific ranges to enable the grenade to detonate over an enemy firing point. Other new grenade designs include the MV HE/HEDP which is '*ideal for engaging and defeating lightly armored vehicles and other "soft skinned" targets at ranges of up to 700m'*.

The 25 × 40mm XM25 Punisher, developed from the OICW programme, was considered by many to be the next generation of infantry grenade launcher, but

The now cancelled 25mm XM-25 Punisher airburst grenade launcher. (*US Army*)

A Canadian soldier in Afghanistan launches an APAV40 F2 rifle grenade from a French 5.56 × 45mm FAMAS F1. *(Canadian Forces, MCpl Frieda Van Putten)*

its official demise in 2018 has left the field open for new entrants with many predicting the wider spread adoption of 40mm multi-shot launchers employing the LVER type round.

## Current Trends

Post Afghanistan, many of the world's armies are either procuring or maintaining 7.62 × 51mm platforms. Their value has again been demonstrated in increased penetrative power and increased range, despite the disadvantage of their extra weight versus their 5.56 × 45mm cousins. Interestingly, the medium and general-purpose machine gun has been largely absent from the discussion over precision or volume as the key component of suppression fire.

US Army infantry veteran Ron Dahlgren who served two tours in Afghanistan and one in Iraq:

> Suppressive fire [with the M240B] was taught as 100 percent volume. The idea being to keep the enemy pinned and scared to move while a maneuver element closed in to get them at close range. Furthermore, our weapons squad (one per platoon with 2 × 240B) would set up a support-by-fire position that was training to work in tandem so that the guns were 'talking' to provide near continuous firing at the objective.
>
> The weapon seemed to be treated as a way to increase the volume of fire for the squad. We didn't train much with a focus on accuracy and patience. Our training was more of the 'massing of fires' doctrine, where we just throw everything at the enemy to box them in while we close and kill.

The weight of current weapons systems is the principal downside to 7.62 × 51mm machine guns. As one British Afghan veteran related: '*GPMG is a proven weapon system and a real battle winner. It is just too heavy; add the weight of the ammo, your water etc then you do not last long on patrol.*' Another noted similarly: '*If it could be made lighter then great. I would never be without a GPMG on patrol, though heavy, where we could the ammo was distributed amongst the patrol to lower the weight for the gunner.*'

Canadian soldiers firing their 7.62 × 51mm MAG58 based C6 general purpose machine gun in sustained fire mode. (*US Army, Staff Sgt. Jason Hull*)

The titanium-based US Army 7.62 × 51mm M240L medium machine gun with shortened 20-inch barrel and collapsible stock. It is almost 2 kilograms lighter than the standard M240B. (*US Army*)

The M240L as we will detail in a moment, was a successful attempt to reduce the weight of the MAG58 design using lighter weight materials like titanium. Interestingly, the British Army's ITDU ran trials for a lighter weight GPMG for service in Afghanistan during the height of the Operation Herrick campaign. The then-new titanium-based design was frustratingly judged too expensive, although it met weight reduction targets.

The Russians have for decades had a much lighter design in the form of the superbly reliable 7.62 × 54mm PKM that weighs significantly less than its equivalents at around 7.5 kilograms. One wonders if Western militaries should have taken notes on the PKM design as well as the RPK when formulating doctrine around medium and light infantry machine guns.

One of the biggest recent initiatives is a US Army programme to introduce significantly lightened 7.62 × 51mm ammunition for the M240 series. Three options are currently on the table – one is moulded stainless steel, another is a hybrid of stainless steel and polymer and the third is a brass casing with polymer body. Intriguingly, the programme is being developed with input from the British Army as well as SOCOM.

A spokesperson unfortunately may have rather missed the point of lightening the soldier's load only to use that weight saving for more gear: '*We're currently working on drop-in replacement ammunition for the existing 7.62 family of weapons optimizing for the M240 family of machine guns. Ounces are pounds. So if we can take a pound out of a soldier's weight load, a soldier could be more effective by carrying other important things.*'

SOCOM and the USMC released a joint solicitation in 2017 for some 5,000 Lightweight Medium Machine Guns (LWMMG). In terms of requirements, the solicitation mentioned:

The LWMMG should fire the belted .338NM round of ammunition with a polymer case. The LWMMG should weigh less than 24 pounds unloaded with a barrel length of 24in. The LWMMG should have a rate of fire of between 500–600 rounds per minute. Weapon shall be compatible with current rail mounted aiming systems with the ability to incorporate more advanced fire control technology.

The system should include both a suppressed barrel and an unsuppressed barrel that can be rapidly changed. The LWMMG should include a tripod that is lightweight and provides the stability and accuracy required to engage targets at extreme ranges. The LWMMG should be able to mount in current machinegun mounts designed for the M240B/C. The weapon should have sufficient accuracy to engage area targets and vehicles at 2,000m.

Other nations have recognised the need for 7.62 × 51mm platforms. After replacing their ageing 7.62 × 51mm MG3s in 2005 with the 5.56 × 45mm Heckler and Koch MG4, German Army experiences in Afghanistan have led them to return to the larger chambering and are currently adopting the 7.62 × 51mm MG5 from Heckler and Koch to supplement the MG4.

Although the MG4 will officially remain in service (as at the time of writing): *'The MG5 will replace the machine gun MG3 as a medium machine gun. The fully automatic weapon allows short and longer bursts of fire with a range of up to 1,000 meters. The MG5 is used both dismounted with bipod and tripod as a support weapon. It has a rifle scope with four times magnification and red dot,'* according to the Bundeswehr's official statements.

Others are updating tried and true platforms. The Canadian Army has placed an order with Colt Canada to replace their ageing domestically-produced MAG58, the C6 GPMG, with the C6A1, itself a product improved variant of the excellent Belgian-designed weapon. Others have looked at the equally important question of ammunition carriage.

The Bundeswehr 7.62 × 51mm MG3 medium machine gun on the range in Afghanistan. *(US Army)*

Ukrainian troops have been seen with so-called *'Predator'*-style backpacks feeding belted link for their PKMs (named in reference to the 1980s sci-fi Schwarzenegger epic in which one American operator carries a minigun complete with backpack feed system and similar to the previously mentioned American *'Iron Man'* design). Russian SOF have used a similar system in Syria.

In terms of grenade launchers, standalone launchers, including the American M320 which can be equipped with a stock, are gaining in popularity. This is for two key reasons. One, standalone launchers are generally more accurate than the underbarrel version. Two, the weapon is far less cumbersome than a UGL combination and can be easily swapped out amongst members of an infantry squad. The US Marines for instance are considering issuing only standalone M320s as they make the M27 IAR very unbalanced.

The Bundeswehr conversely relied upon standalone handheld launchers like the Heckler and Koch 69A1 rather than adopt a UGL design until the AG36 was eventually adopted. The British too seem to be sticking to their L123A3 variant of the AG36. The Danish Army was a late adopter of UGLs, in fact there was no issue grenade launcher before 2013 and the LMT M203-2003 was adopted based on their Afghan experiences, mounted under their Diemaco C8 IUR assault rifles or as a standalone platform. Prior to this adoption, the Danes operating in Helmand alongside British were forced to rely upon a single Milkor Y2 that a Danish military police contingent had brought along to launch CS for crowd control. This was quickly loaded with 40mm HE grenades borrowed from the Brits and proved popular until Danish high command found out about it!

Multi-shot designs have proved popular such as the Milkor range which were adopted into American service as the M32 and M32A1. The Polish Army were intent on issuing their own domestically produced rotary 40mm design, the RGP-40, but for unspecified reasons the weapon did not meet issue standards and the contract was subsequently cancelled.

The 5.56 × 45mm M4A1 carbine mounting the 40mm M320 grenade launcher. (*US Army*)

The US Army's 40mm M320A1 which replaced the M203 in standalone mode.
(*US Army, Staff Sgt. Pablo N. Piedra*)

An Estonian Scout firing his 5.56 × 45mm Galil ARM fitted with 40mm Heckler and Koch AG-C grenade launcher. (*US Army, Sgt. Zeta Green*)

British Royal Marines in Lashkar Gah, Helmand Province, Afghanistan 2008. Note the L85A2 with 40mm L123A3 UGL. (*Open Government License v3.0, Sgt James Elmer*)

# Individual Weapon Summaries

## PKM Family

The Russian-designed PKM soldiers on around the world as the most common design after the Fabrique Nationale MAG58. It is relatively lightweight, exhibits impressive reliability and fires the potent 7.62 × 54mm round. In Russian infantry units however, the PKM has been replaced by the modernised PKP or Pecheneg variant. The PKP differs from the PKM in that its barrel is not designed to be replaced in the field, so it has been fitted with a heavier barrel (with a fixed carrying handle attached above it) that resists heat build-up and increases accuracy. The PKP has also appeared in insurgent hands in Syria, likely pilfered from a 2013 order to the Syrian Army.

A Chinese copy of the PKM, the 7.62 × 54mm Type 80, is retained by some PLA infantry squads who, like Western armies, appreciate the longer range of the larger cartridge. The Type 80 is like the PKM in most respects but can be easily switched from its normal bipod role to a sustained-fire tripod to an anti-aircraft mount, something many armies have eschewed since the Second World War, relying instead on .50 calibre designs in the AA role. The Type 88 however is the standard Chinese general purpose machine gun, firing the full power 5.8 × 42mm cartridge.

Another Chinese design, the Type 67 is a dedicated MMG but designed specifically for the light role. Visually it resembles an unholy partnership between the wartime Russian DP and the PKM; it was first adopted by the PLA in 1968

The Chinese PLA 5.8 × 42mm Type 88 (QJY-88) general purpose machine gun.
(*Commonwealth of Australia, Sgt. John Waddell*)

The Russian 7.62 × 54mm PKM general purpose machine gun being fired for familiarization during an exercise in the Ukraine. (*US Army, Sgt. Anthony Jones*)

although the latest variant, the Type 67-2, was type classified in 1982. It also appears to have fallen into the hands of insurgents in Afghanistan, Yemen and Syria.

The Polish Army uses the UKM-2000P which is based on the PKM (which it is replacing throughout the Polish Army) but has been significantly modernised and rechambered for the NATO 7.62 × 51mm round. Even bullpup variants of the PKM have been produced, including unofficial conversions constructed in Syrian insurgent workshops.

## MG3 Family

Although officially replaced by the MG5 from Heckler and Koch, the MG3 has served the German Army since 1959, making it one of the longest serving post-war designs, and will likely remain in service for a few more years as the MG5 filters down. A superbly constructed 'copy' of the MG42, the MG3 was appreciated for its utter reliability.

The MG62 was the Danish service name for the Beretta-produced MG3 known as the MG42/59 (and in service with Italian forces). The Danes carried the MG62 for a number of years on operations in Afghanistan. The MG62 was well-regarded, although soldiers acknowledged it was heavy and was getting to the end of its service life. It was replaced by an unlikely contender, the M60E6. The Austrian MG74 is an upgraded MG42/59 produced by Steyr Mannlicher, whilst the Spanish Army issue the MG42/MG3 which they refer to simply as the MG42.

The Italian Beretta produced MG3 version, the 7.62 × 51mm MG42/59. (*US Army, Spc. Shannon Westpfahl*)

## MAG58 Family

The most prolific MMG in the world is the MAG58. Used by nearly all Western armies, it has an outstanding reputation in terms of reliability. The Australian Army describe it thus: '*It is a fully automatic, belt-fed, air-cooled, gas-operated weapon, firing from the open bolt position, and is capable of a sustained high volume of fire. Stoppages can be easily and quickly remedied. The barrel is chromed internally to reduce wear.*'

Adopted by the British as the L7A2 GPMG, the Canadians as the C6 and now C6A1, the US Army as the M240B and the USMC as the M240G, the MAG58's dominance includes service in the armies of Argentina, Austria, Chile, Greece, Ireland, Israel, New Zealand, Sweden (who licence-produce the MAG58 as the Ksp 58, which has also been adopted by Estonia, Latvia and Lithuania), Uruguay and Venezuela, to name but a few.

As noted earlier, the weapon in its L7A2 and M240 guises were considered fight-winners by British and US troops respectively in Iraq and Afghanistan. The improved M240L, issued in limited numbers since 2009 (including a short barrel version that trimmed 4 inches from the 24-inch standard length), and supplemented by issue of the Mk 48 to infantry units in eastern Afghanistan, saw mobility being returned to squads equipped with the M240. The M240L reduced the weight by almost 2.5 kilograms, a significant saving when carrying a large lump of metal and plastic (and its ammunition) across Afghan mountains.

British Army machine gunner manning his 7.62 × 51mm L7A2 GPMG, affectionately known as the 'Gimpy' (pronounced with a 'j') or 'the General', Helmand Province, Afghanistan 2008. Note the Javelin crew on overwatch on the building roof. (*ISAF, Cpl John Rafoss*)

## Negev NG-7

As mentioned in the previous chapter, the Negev NG-7 is an up gunned version of the famous Israeli light machine gun officially adopted by the IDF in 2014 to replace the MAG58, although due to budgetary pressures the MAG is expected to still serve in infantry sections until at least 2020. The NG-7 comes equipped with an integral round-counting system which informs armourers when barrels need to be replaced. The NG-7 is available with both standard 20-inch barrel and a compact variant with 16.5-inch barrel. Unusually for an MMG, it also offers a semi-automatic firing mode and can be fired with its stock folded.

## AG36 Family

The 40mm AG36 from Heckler and Koch has been widely adopted by many armies. Originally designed as the grenade launcher attachment for the Bundeswehr's G36, versions have been adopted by the British, French (with the HK416) and Spanish (with their G36E). The largest user is the US military who have adopted the weapon in variants known as the M320 and M320A1.

The AG36 differs from older launchers like the M203 in that it features a side-opening breech allowing longer cased MV grenades to be employed. The USMC

A Lithuanian 5.56 × 45mm G36KA2 with 40mm Heckler and Koch AG36 launcher.
(*US Army, Staff Sgt. Megan Leuck*)

The 40mm Heckler and Koch AG36 grenade launcher. *(Heckler and Koch)*

are adopting the revised variant, the M320A1, in 2019 with one being issued to each fire team. Surprisingly they will not be under barrel mounted but standalone platforms.

## Milkor MGL Family

Best known for their 40mm M32 and M32A1 6-shot rotary grenade launchers in use with the USMC, Milkor also produce a range of launchers that are in widespread issue with the Brazilian, Georgian, Malaysian and Turkish armies. The weapon is also in use, naturally enough, with the South African National Defence Force.

Developed in the M32 variant from feedback from Marines fighting in Fallujah, it operates from the same principle as a revolver. Load the grenades into the rotary drum which slides open to the left, close the drum back into the weapon and start firing. It can accommodate all types of less than lethal and offensive grenades. The one drawback is its weight at 8.16 kilograms when loaded.

A Marine spokesperson explained the attraction of the weapon:

The M32A1 allows the individual to lay down a barrage of 40mm high explosive, dual purpose rounds as fast as [the shooter] can pull the trigger. This weapon becomes very important in the absence of MK19s [the 40mm automatic grenade launcher]. Moreover, a Marine can maneuver on foot

A US Marine firing the 40mm M32A1 grenade launcher, capable of emptying its 6-round drum in two seconds. The M32 and M32A1 are issued to Marines in the company weapons platoon and can be parcelled out to individual squads on a task by task basis. *(USMC, Cpl. Devon Tindle)*

with this weapon. It provides a high volume of firepower to fight out of an ambush. It can provide increased firepower at a higher rate at the small unit level in the attack or in the defense.

## Future Trends

Both medium and general-purpose machine guns will remain the mainstay of platoon and squad firepower, primarily because of their ability to deny enemy manoeuvre whether through suppressing an area target or establishing a beaten zone through which no enemy can safely pass. The future will see machine guns reduced in weight, with improved optics and sensors, and more than likely a change to 6.8mm and/or .338 Norma Magnum.

The weight of this ammunition will reduce with advances in CT and polymer casings and ranges will increase. The .338 Norma Magnum looks able to take over a number of roles traditionally held by the .50BMG. New projectiles will see increased armour-penetrating capabilities and the possibility of smart machine gun rounds looms just around the corner.

New methods of employment will see machine guns mounted on unmanned ground vehicles (UGV) and aerial drones controlled by the infantry platoon. The Russians even trialled a number of these UGVs in Syria although its Uran-9, equipped with a 30mm cannon and 7.62 × 54mm co-axial machine gun, had difficulty firing on the move and experienced '17 cases of short-term (up to one minute) and two cases of long-term (up to 1.5 hours) loss of Uran-9 control'.

Polish soldiers firing Fosforyt rifle grenades from their Beryl assault rifles, Afghanistan 2011. (*ISAF, Spc. David Zlotin*)

The newly-adopted Australian 5.56 × 45mm EF88 mounting the 40mm Steyr-Mannlicher SL40 grenade launcher. (*Commonwealth of Australia, LCpl MD Scheimer*)

As we noted earlier, the future of the grenade launcher will be in multi-shot designs that can accommodate the new generation of 40mm rounds, including smart projectiles and enhanced range rounds. One such newly introduced munition is the Raytheon Pike, a 17-inch long laser-guided round which according to its manufacturer is '... *the world's only hand-launched precision-guided munition. Fired from a rifle-mounted grenade launcher, the miniaturized weapon can travel one and a half miles and hit within 5 yards or less of a target, minimizing collateral damage'*.

## Breaking News

The Australian company DefendTex have developed a new 40mm munition, Drone-40, which allows the launch of a mini drone from any 40mm grenade launcher. The 40mm drone can be equipped with a camera and a small explosive charge, allowing it be used as an indirect fire weapon. Several armies including the US are showing much interest in the design.

# ABBREVIATIONS

| | |
|---|---|
| **ACOG** | Trijicon Advanced Combat Gunsight |
| **ADVAP** | US 7.62mm XM1158 Advanced Armor Piercing round |
| **AFAL** | USAF Armament Laboratory |
| **AH** | Attack Helicopter |
| **APC** | Armoured Personnel Carrier |
| **AUG** | Armee-Universal-Gewehr (Universal Army Rifle) |
| **CAWS** | Close Assault Weapon System |
| **COP** | Combat Outpost |
| **CQB** | Close Quarter Battle |
| **CSASS** | Compact Semi-Automatic Sniper System |
| **CZ** | Česká Zbrojovka |
| **DA** | Direct Action |
| **DARPA** | US Defense Advanced Research Projects Agency |
| **DMR** | Designated Marksman Rifle |
| **EOD** | Explosive Ordnance Disposal |
| **ESAPI** | Enhanced SAPI (Small Arms Protective Insert) |
| **FA** | Full Automatic |
| **FMJ** | Full Metal Jacket |
| **FOB** | Forward Operating Base |
| **GAO** | US General Accounting Office |
| **GMG** | Grenade Machine Gun |
| **GPMG** | General Purpose Machine Gun |
| **HEMI** | Human Electro-Muscular Incapacitation |
| **HMMWV** | High Mobility Multipurpose Wheeled Vehicle (Humvee) |
| **IDF** | Israeli Defence Force |
| **IED** | Improvised Explosive Device |
| **ISAF** | International Security Assistance Force (Afghanistan) |
| **IW** | Individual Weapon |
| **JGSDF** | Japanese Ground Self Defence Force |
| **JSOC** | Joint Special Operations Command |
| **JSSAP** | US Joint Service Small Arms Program |
| **JTAC** | Joint Terminal Attack/Air Controller |
| **LMG** | Light Machine Gun |
| **LSAT** | Lightweight Small Arms Technologies |
| **LSW** | Light Support Weapon |
| **MARSOC** | US Marine Special Operations Command |
| **MAUL** | Multi-shot Accessory Underbarrel Launcher |
| **MHS** | Modular Handgun System |

| **MRAP** | Mine Resistant Ambush Protected |
|---|---|
| **MRBF** | Mean Rounds Between Failures |
| **MRR** | Modular Rail Rifle |
| **NGSAR** | Next Generation Squad Automatic Rifle |
| **NGWS** | Next Generation Weapon System |
| **NZDF** | New Zealand Defence Force |
| **OICW** | Objective Individual Combat Weapon |
| **OP** | Observation Post |
| **OTM** | Open Tip Match |
| **PAiL** | Pistol Aiming Light |
| **PDW** | Personal Defence Weapon |
| **PID** | Positive Identification |
| **PIP** | Product Improvement Program |
| **PKM** | Pulemyot Kalashnikova |
| **PLA** | People's Liberation Army |
| **PMV** | Protected Mobility Vehicle |
| **RFI** | Request For Information |
| **RFID** | Radio Frequency Identification |
| **ROE** | Rules Of Engagement |
| **RPG** | Ruchnoy Protivotankovy Granatomyot |
| **RPK** | Ruchnoy Pulemyot Kalashnikova |
| **SASS** | Semi-Automatic Sniper System |
| **SASW** | Semi-Automatic Sniper Weapon |
| **SAW** | Squad Automatic Weapon |
| **SCW** | Sub Compact Weapon |
| **SDM** | Squad Designated Marksman |
| **SIPES** | Soldier Integrated Precision Effects Systems |
| **SMG** | Sub Machine Gun |
| **SOCOM** | US Special Operations Command |
| **SOF** | Special Operations Forces |
| **SOP** | Standard Operating Procedure |
| **SOPMOD** | Special Operations Peculiar Modification |
| **SPR** | Special Purpose Rifle |
| **SVD** | Snayperskaya Vintovka sistem'y Dragunova |
| **UAV** | Unmanned Aerial Vehicle |
| **UGL** | Under-barrel Grenade Launcher |
| **UOR** | Urgent Operational Request |
| **USMC** | United States Marine Corps |
| **UGV** | Unmanned Ground Vehicle |
| **WMIK** | Weapons Mounted Installation Kit |

# Index